Cavendish
Publishing
Limited

G000135056

'A' LEVEL LAW – PAPER I

TITLES IN THE SERIES

'A' Level Law - Paper I

'A' Level Law - Paper II

Administrative Law

Business Law

Child Law

Civil Liberties

Commercial Law

Company Law

Conflict of Laws

Constitutional & Administrative Law

Contract Law

Criminal Law

Criminal Litigation and Sentencing

Criminology

Employment Law

English Legal System

Equity & Trusts

European Community Law

Evidence

Family Law

Intellectual Property Law

International Trade Law

Jurisprudence

Land Law

Public International Law

Law of Tort

Revenue Law

Succession, Wills & Probate

Cavendish
Publishing
Limited

'A' LEVEL LAW – PAPER I

Paul Cappi, LLB, LLM, Dip in International Law
Senior Lecturer in Law, University of Plymouth

Mary Collins, LLB, LLM, Solicitor, PGCE
Senior Lecturer in Law, University of Plymouth

Edited by Peter Shears, BA, LLB, LLM
Director of Legal Studies, University of Plymouth

First published in Great Britain 1994 by Cavendish Publishing Limited, The Glass House, Wharton Street, London WC1X 9PX
Telephone: 0171-278 8000 Facsimile: 0171-278 8080

© Cappi, P and Collins, M 1994
First reprint 1995
Second reprint 1995

All rights reserved. No part of this publication may be reproduced, stored in a retrieval system, or transmitted in any form or by any means, electronic, mechanical, photocopying, recording or otherwise, without the prior permission of the publisher and copyright owner.

The right of the author of this work has been asserted in accordance with the Copyright, Designs and Patents Act 1988.

Any person who infringes the above in relation to this publication may be liable to criminal prosecution and civil claims for damages.

British Library Cataloguing in Publication Data

Shears, Peter
'A' Level Law – Paper I – (Lecture Notes Series)
I Shears, Peter II Series
344.2

ISBN 1-874241-74-0
Cover photograph by Jerome Yeats
Printed and bound in Great Britain

Preface

Studying law at any level can be a daunting process – at 'A' level it can be worse!

There are many 'A' level texts which are written to be broadening, deepening and inspiring books. Some of them achieve some of these goals.

These two texts – 'A' Level Law Paper 1 and 'A' Level Law Paper 2 – are different. They are written to cover the syllabuses of the key Examination Boards.

We have considered the published requirements of the JMB, the AEB and the University of London at 'A' and 'Advanced Supplementary' level and we have provided what we believe to be the material required by candidates for these examinations.

Of course, we have tried to be interesting, relevant and stimulating too, but the main aim is to tell students what we think you need to know to meet the expectations of the examiners. Each syllabus area has been covered by a subject specialist.

As to the techniques required in the examination room, we have also written a 'Questions and Answers' book to enable candidates to use the knowledge they acquire from these books to the best advantage when faced with the examination paper.

We have stated the law as we believe it to be in the early autumn of 1994.

All that remains is to wish you the very best of luck!

Peter Shears

Outline Table of Contents

PART FOUR
ASPECTS OF CONSTITUTIONAL LAW

Detailed Table of Contents

PART TWO
GENERAL PRINCIPLES OF ENGLISH LAW

PART FOUR
ASPECTS OF CONSTITUTIONAL LAW

Table of Cases

Table of Statutes

PART ONE
THE ENGLISH LEGAL SYSTEM

Chapter 1

Classification and Sources of Law

It is useful to be able to classify law for a variety of reasons including understanding the purposes served by law. Procedure and penalties may also differ according to whether one is considering criminal or civil law. Criminal law has, as one of its aims, the punishment of offenders who commit a crime against society. On the other hand, civil law (eg the law regulating the making of contracts), aims to compensate a party to a contract where the other party has broken his or her side of the bargain by an award of money damages.

1.1 Classification of law

Traditionally, classification of law has taken two forms. We have already mentioned the distinction between criminal law and civil law. Offences such as theft, robbery, burglary and murder are classified as criminal as these actions are sufficiently anti-social to warrant punishment by the State in the form of imprisonment of the offender or by imposition of a fine. Civil law, on the other hand, provides for the making of contracts, wills, ownership and transfer of property, regulates employment and consumer transactions and family matters. Apart from contracts where two or more parties have entered into a binding agreement which can then be enforced, the other main type of civil liability arises in tort. This covers acts or omissions where a person's interests have been adversely affected by the defendant such as physical injury, damage to property or the publication of defamatory statements.

1.1.1 Methods of classifying the law

Another way in which law can be classified is to distinguish between public international law which regulates the actions of states and the entering into of treaties between states on the one hand; and municipal law on the other. Municipal law can then be sub-divided into private law such as contract and tort which is simply an alternative term for civil law. Public law covers not only criminal law but also constitutional and administrative law. Private international law regulates conflict between the laws of different states in areas such as contract, tort and family matters.

Before leaving classification of law it is worth mentioning one other type of classification namely that between substantive and procedural law. Substantive law is the body of rules regulating the making of contracts or which regulates the commission of torts or crimes. This crosses the boundaries between civil and criminal and between public and private law and is concerned with defining an offence or a tort or the conditions which must be met for a contract to be legally binding. The substantive rules impose liability on a party proved to be in breach of the substantive rules and if this is a rule of criminal law a penalty may result or if this is a rule of civil law a remedy may be provided for the plaintiff.

Procedural rules regulate the conduct of court proceedings and aim to ensure fair play between the parties. Some examples include the disclosure of evidence to one's opponent; the meeting of deadlines for the service of documents; the need to prove the facts relied on by evidence such as documents or witnesses. The rules of evidence ensure that the court takes cognisance only of facts which are satisfactorily proved. The court will not as a general rule accept hearsay evidence as proof of alleged facts.

One of the underlying principles of criminal procedure is that the defendant is presumed innocent until proved guilty. The prosecution bears the burden of proving guilt beyond all reasonable doubt. Linked with this has been the principle that the defendant may choose to remain silent and need say nothing in his or her own defence. At the present time this right is under threat and it is likely that it will be replaced with the procedural rule that where a defendant remains silent adverse conclusions may be drawn. It might be useful here to cross-reference the material on this topic to Civil Liberties in Part 4 of Lecture Notes on 'A' Level Law – Paper 2 .

1.2   Sources of law

'Source' refers to the place where the law is found. Not only judges need to be aware of what the law is in order to apply it in reaching a solution to a dispute to be decided but also legal advisers – barristers, solicitors and other legal professionals – who, faced with a lay client with a legal problem, will need to offer advice on the basis of what the law is and may well have to predict the chances of success should a dispute go to court.

The need to find the law is not confined to the legal professional. The law student will also have the need to find the law so as to apply it in reaching a reasoned solution to problem questions.

1.2.1   Distinguishing between sources of law

A distinction is drawn between literary and historical sources of law. Literary sources are the official written sources of law such as law reports and the Queen's printer's copy of a statute. Historical sources emphasise the development of the law for example in the 13th century the rise of equity or in the 19th century the rise of statute.

At the present time the importance of European Community law is increasing in importance in relation to domestic law whereas customary law is no longer of any great importance.

Another way in which sources can be distinguished is that of principal and subsidiary sources. The former refers to legislation, delegated legislation, case law and European Community law that is the most important and authoritative sources of law. The latter refers to those sources which are of little importance and include custom, Roman law, ecclesiastical law and books of authority.

We will concentrate on the principal sources but so far as subsidiary sources are concerned custom will be briefly mentioned.

As a source of law custom is the oldest, originating from pre-Norman times, and which led to the development of the common law. In modern society there is little place for customary law in that it is unwritten and passed from one generation to the next by word of mouth. However on occasion a dispute comes before the court and one of the parties calls in aid, an alleged custom. It is for the court to decide the existence and extent of the alleged custom by applying various tests. In a county court judgment in 1990 an injunction was granted to New Forest Commoners against the National Trust over the size and depth of ditches dug by the Trust around the common land. The Commoners were able to prove the existence of their right to free access and use of the commons which had been interfered with by the ditches dug by the Trust.

A distinction is made between general and local customs but both must satisfy a number of tests and in addition local customs must be proved to have existed from 'time immemorial'. Most general customs have been incorporated into legislation or case law. Mercantile law is a good example where the law governing commercial transactions developed from the customs of merchants.

The tests used by the courts to establish the existence of custom include certainty, continuity, reasonableness, consistency and legality. As we have already mentioned a local custom must be proved to have existed since time immemorial (which in theory means 1189). The case of *Mercer v Denne* (1905) illustrates that, in practice, time immemorial is treated as having been proved where a local custom is shown to have existed within living memory of the oldest resident of the area: fishermen had used a beach for drying their nets and residents could recall such use as far back as 70 years. The landowner attempted to prevent the fishermen from using the beach but a presumption was raised in their favour which the landowner could not rebut.

In *Simpson v Wells* (1872) W alleged a customary right to obstruct a public footpath and called in aid an Act of 1361. This in itself rebutted any presumption that the alleged right had been established before 1361.

Books of authority are another subsidiary source. This possibly includes textbooks and a court may be referred to such books so as to assist it in deciding a case. Some famous and highly authoritative books include Coke's *Institutes of the Laws of England* (1628) and Blackstone's *Commentaries on the Laws of England* (1765).

The tradition which developed whereby the courts only made use of the works of deceased authors no longer applies and the works of writers still alive may now be referred to by counsel in arguing a case. An example is that of Archbold's *Pleading, Evidence and Practice in Criminal Cases*.

Taking the principal sources in turn we start with legislation.

1.2.2 Legislation	Legislation takes the form of an Act of Parliament or statute. A bill becomes law after a formal process in both Houses of Parliament and receipt of Royal Assent. The 'Queen in Parliament' is described as the supreme law maker and the doctrine of 'supremacy of Parliament' ensures that no other body can pass law in conflict with that of Parliament and that the courts cannot question the validity of Acts of Parliament. As we shall see later this doctrine is now subject to UK's membership of the European Community and that European law can take precedence over domestic law.

Public bills (initiated by government or private member) usually commence life in the House of Commons and some must do so, for example Money Bills.

Those starting in the House of Commons, once they have passed all stages, move on to the House of Lords where a similar procedure must be complied with before the bill receives the Royal Assent. By convention this is automatically granted and, since Queen Anne's reign, the Royal Assent has not been refused.

By the Parliament Acts 1911 and 1949 the powers of the House of Lords to delay or initiate bills is limited as this is seen as a threat to the supremacy of the elected chamber to make law.

A notable recent illustration of the workings of both Houses is provided by the passage of the bill to give effect to the Treaty of European Union (the Maastricht Treaty). The Bill took some 12 months to successfully pass all stages in the House of Commons and it was suggested that the government faced defeat in the House of Lords. In the result the Bill passed all stages in the Lords.

Other notable recent Acts include the Courts and Legal Services Act 1990; the Environmental Protection Act 1990; the Criminal Justice Acts 1991 and 1993.

A public bill which is presently before Parliament and which has given rise to much debate, both within and outside of Parliament, is the Sunday Trading Bill which will repeal the Shops Act 1950, if passed into law, following in the steps of some 30 failed bills. The Bill allowed for a choice to be made between three options for reform namely full deregulation, regulation and partial deregulation permitting limited opening between 10.00 am and 4.00 pm for large shops. The last option has been adopted following a free vote at the committee stage which was conducted by a Committee of the Whole House and not the more usual procedure of a Standing Committee. This demonstrated the strength of feeling that the policy, to effect change in this area, had to be settled once and for all.

The procedure for public bills is as follows:

1.2.3 The procedure for public bills

Assuming that the bill starts in the House of Commons it will start with a formal first reading to announce its title and its aims. This is followed by the second reading where its main principles are brought to the attention of the House and a debate follows. The bill then passes to a Standing Committee (or, if it is of fundamental constitutional or national importance, to a Committee of the Whole House as mentioned above) where its provisions are looked at in detail, often line by line. The committee reflects however the political balance of the House so that the government will ensure that the bill passes this stage without major amendment. Limitations may be placed on the amount of time to be devoted to particular provisions and some may not be discussed at all. The outcome of the Committee stage is then reported to the House and this is followed by the Third Reading at which no changes can be made to the principles of the Bill. On being passed the Bill goes to the House of Lords where it will go through a similar procedure. If amendments are made, and this is usual as was shown during the passage of the Criminal Justice and Public Order Bill for example, it will have to be reconsidered by the House of Commons. A compromise may be reached but if this is not possible the Commons has the final say. The powers of the House of Lords to introduce Bills and to delay government measures was curtailed by the Parliament Act 1911 and 1949.

Private bills are those promoted by individuals or groups for their own benefit or which relate to a locality or region.

Some recent examples illustrate the point: the Prices Patent Candle Company Ltd Act 1992 was passed to give wider powers to this trading company; the Cattewater Reclamation Act 1992 provides for the purchase and development of waste property in an area of Plymouth; the London Underground Act 1992; the Midland Metro Act 1992; the Avon Weir Act 1992 and the British Railways Act 1992. The procedure for private bills involves a first, second and third reading in both the House of Commons and Lords and also consideration of its provisions by a committee. Amendments may be made in either House but when agreement is reached the bill passes into law.

Private bills should not be confused with Private Members' Bills. The former concern a private, local or regional matter whereas the latter are of a public nature but which are promoted by a private member of Parliament. As the government controls the timetable of the House of Commons (and in practice this also applies in the House of Lords), private members have very little time at their disposal to promote bills. In addition they rarely have the benefit of Parliamentary drafters who are skilled in the preparation of government bills. Bills of a controversial nature may have to be left to the private member or be promoted first in the House of Lords particularly where the government has a small majority or a heavy legislative programme.

At the beginning of a new session of Parliament a ballot is held and the 20 private members who are successful may introduce a bill. Those with the first 10 places in the ballot may recover some of the expenses of promoting a bill from the government. There are usually many more members wishing to promote legislation than places available and those unsuccessful in the ballot may either make use of the 'Ten Minute Rule' under Standing Order 19 of the House, which permits a member to put down a motion at the start of public business on Tuesdays and Wednesdays for leave to introduce a bill or use the procedure by which government bills are promoted.

Some notable examples of Private Member Bills include the Abortion Act 1967 which was promoted by David Steel, as he then was, the Video Recordings Act 1984 and the Indecent Displays (Control) Act 1981.

A recent example of a Private Members' Bill which has not yet become law but which is likely to do so, is the Merchant Shipping (Salvage and Pollution) Bill promoted by David Harris MP, who came fifteenth in the 1993 ballot. This aims to improve the law of salvage by offering salvors an extra bounty if they prevent or reduce the risk of marine pollution when a ship is in danger and to speed up rescue operations and avoid a repetition of the Penlee lifeboat tragedy in 1981.

Michael Fabricant recently introduced a 'Ten Minute Rule' Bill designed to prohibit the practice of adding service charges to restaurant bills. It received little government support but illustrates that, although such bills rarely become law, a private member who feels strongly on a matter may raise public awareness and that in time the government may be persuaded to promote legislation. Alternatively the private member may gain sufficient support so as to promote a bill at a later date.

Legislation is one of the principal sources of law and an aspect of the doctrine of supremacy of Parliament concerns the role of the courts. The court is said to be merely the interpreter of legislation and cannot declare legislation to be invalid or unconstitutional. This, together with the other aspects of the doctrine, is subject now to EC law having precedence over domestic law following the decisions in *Factortame* (1990) and *Francovitch* (1992) (see para 1.2.11 below) where EC matters are in question.

Legislation is usually prospective in effect that is it applies in the future and will be given effect by the courts when called on to apply the law in resolving a dispute or when imposing criminal liability. A long established presumption is that, in the absence of express contrary provision, an Act is not to have retrospective effect.

An Act may take the form of an enabling or parent Act. This empowers others such as a government minister or local authority to make law by way of delegated legislation. In the case of a minister it will take the form of rules, regulations or orders. The composite term is statutory instruments. In the case of local authorities it is called bye-laws.

It became well recognised as long ago as the 19th century that Parliament had neither the time nor the expertise to legislate in minute detail in all areas then considered in need of reform. Parliament remains supreme in that it legislates on the general principles only leaving the fine detail to the delegate. In addition, Parliament asserts control over the passage of statutory instruments in some cases by way of a positive procedure whereby the rules, regulations or orders are placed before the House and a resolution in favour must be passed if the statutory instrument is to take effect.

The validity of an enabling Act cannot be challenged in the courts as we have already noted but the validity of delegated legislation can by means of the doctrine *ultra vires*. This doctrine assumes that Parliament may grant whatever power to make law that it chooses, but that the power granted to the delegate is thereby limited and must be complied with. If the delegate exceeds or abuses the power granted, the Queen's Bench Divisional Court of the High Court can declare an action of a delegate *ultra vires* and void.

A citizen aggrieved by the actions of a delegate (a local authority, public corporation or government minister) may seek redress by way of Order 53 of the Rules of the Supreme Court for judicial review or may attempt to use *ultra vires* as a defence to a civil claim or a prosecution for breach of the delegated legislation.

Another type of delegated legislation is an Order in Council. This refers to an order of the Privy Council, but the power to make such an order may originate from Parliament whereby a minister is authorised to make such an order or from the Royal Prerogative where the Queen (or a minister to whom she has delegated power) makes such an order.

A good illustration of the use of the prerogative is in the GCHQ case (*Council of Civil Service Unions v Minister for the Civil Service* (1985)), where the prerogative power was delegated to the Minister for the Civil Service who banned unions at the government communications head quarters without first consulting the employees. The House of Lords found on the facts that the ban was warranted on the grounds of national security and that no consultation was thereby required. The Law Lords however stated that the prerogative power would in suitable cases be subject to judicial review and that here, if national security had not demanded a ban, the employees would have had a legitimate expectation to be consulted before a decision was reached which adversely affected their terms of employment.

Delegated legislation has increased in use and is unlikely to decrease greatly. It has the advantages of speed, lower cost and use of the delegate's expertise in formulating detail leaving Parliament to address itself to policy and general principles. There are notable disadvantages, however, in particular the limitations on effective control by Parliament and especially the increasing use of a negative procedure whereby delegated legislation is approved in the absence of dissent.

The citizen is presumed to know the law but in reality this is impossible given the passing of hundreds of statutes and thousands of statutory instruments each year. The citizen may either resort to the courts to challenge an allegedly *ultra vires* exercise of power or attempt to defend proceedings for breach of delegated legislation but this will be both costly and time consuming.

We have already noted that the courts can challenge the validity of delegated legislation but not that of legislation itself on the basis of the sovereignty of Parliament doctrine. This is not to say however that the courts do not have an important function with regard to legislation.

The judge interprets the meaning to be placed on statutory provisions relied on when a case comes to court for settlement. Statutory provisions may be interpreted narrowly or widely and this gives a judge potentially great power in determining the future scope of the law. In interpreting statutory provisions the judges add to the body of case law and this may assist future courts in deciding disputes.

The judges have formulated rules of practice, which are to be found in case law, to assist them in giving meaning to statutory provisions when those provisions form the basis of a dispute to be decided. The traditional approach has been for the judge to look at the words of the statute to be interpreted and, from the words used by Parliament, gauge the meaning intended by Parliament.

A distinction was drawn between extrinsic and intrinsic aids to construction.

Little use was made of the former when interpreting domestic legislation for reliance was placed on finding the meaning of the words used from the words themselves. Notably records of debates in Parliament were not consulted as this was considered to be beyond the bounds of the court and could be argued to offend Article 9 of the Bill of Rights 1688 whereby proceedings in Parliament should not be questioned in any court or other place. In the case of *Pepper v Hart* (1993) the House of Lords held that reference may be made to Parliamentary debates recorded in the official journal of proceedings ('Hansard') when the court is asked to interpret a statutory provision which is ambiguous or obscure or leads to an absurdity providing the records consist of clear statements by a minister or another promoter of the Bill.

This appears a tall order to fulfil and is not such a radical innovation as at first thought and one which is unlikely to give rise to an 'opening of the floodgates'. Lord Mackay, the Lord Chancellor (dissenting in the case), referred to the policy issues of permitting access to Hansard including cost and delay in litigation.

It is likely that the *ratio decidendi* of *Pepper v Hart* will be restricted by later courts as a limited exception to the general rule. This will have the effect that Hansard will not be consulted by a court unless ambiguity or obscurity appears on the face of the legislation in question.

In the case of *Massmould v Payne* (1993) decided only days after *Pepper v Hart,* Vinelott J found that, as there was no ambiguity on the face of the legislation he was asked to interpret, he could not make reference to Hansard. This was also adopted in the case of *Sheppard v IRC* (1993) by Aldous J. The court was confined to the words used in the legislation where on their face they appeared clear. It was not for the court to compare such words with the meaning attributed to words used during the course of Parliamentary debate even though it appeared that Parliament had intended a different meaning to be attached to the words used in the legislation.

Thus if the court concluded that the legislative words could mean X or Y then Hansard could be consulted, but where the words only meant X then Hansard was not to be consulted even if during Parliamentary debate it was intended that the words mean Y. In *Van Dyck v Secretary of State for the Environment* (1993) which concerned the interpretation of a provision in the Town and Country Planning Act 1971 the Court of Appeal held that the provision was itself ambiguous but that Hansard was not sufficiently clear as to the meaning to be attributed to the words used and so was of no assistance to the court.

Any further development in the law to permit automatic access by the courts to Hansard could only be achieved by the House of Lords as the highest appeal court and in the exercise of its powers under the Practice Statement of 1966.

Another factor which has influenced the relaxation of the traditional or exclusionary approach to interpretation is that used in Continental jurisdictions and the European Court of Justice.

Judges in Continental jurisdictions view their role quite differently from that of the judge in a common law system. Case law does not develop by way of binding precedent, and legislative provisions are more concerned with general principle rather than precisely drafted provisions. The Continental approach is known as the purposive approach where the judge is not confined by the words used in a statutory provision but can consult extrinsic materials to assist him or her in finding the meaning intended by the legislator. The judicial role has greater scope and the judge can afford to be more dynamic in attaching meaning to statutory provisions.

Use of this approach by the English courts has been limited in that the judge is still governed in the first instance by the words used. If these are clear and unambiguous they must be applied. Greater reliance on the purposive approach may well have two results namely that judges in future may make greater use of extrinsic aids to construction and the style of drafting statutory provisions may become more like that used in Continental systems. The courts have had to change their approach when interpreting provisions emanating from, what is now, the European Union which are drafted in much more general terms. Here the courts have the assistance of the European Court of Justice to whom preliminary reference under Article 177 of the Treaty of Rome may be made in specified situations.

Lord Scarman in *Shah v Barnet LBC* (1983) stated that an Act should be read as a whole in conjunction with any permitted documents so as to find the purpose or policy intended by Parliament. The court could not however interpret an Act so as to give effect to its own views as to policy or purpose.

In *R v Registrar General ex p Smith* (1990) the court held that an applicant who wished to obtain a copy of his birth certificate under the Adoption Act 1976 was not entitled to information which would have enabled him to obtain a certificate and thereby discover the identity of his mother on the grounds that the absolute duty to supply such information was subject to a principle of public policy where there was a real risk of the commission of a serious crime by the applicant in the future against his mother. The court adopted a purposive approach in the face of clear and unambiguous legislative language as it was felt that if the legislator had been confronted with such a situation it would have been obvious that no information should be revealed. Public policy demanded that all statutes no matter when passed be subject to this principle and not merely those passed after declaration of the principle by the court.

Given that use of extrinsic aids to construction and the purposive approach are limited, the traditional approach will be for the courts, when interpreting legislation having effect within the UK, to make use of intrinsic aids to construction. These include referring to an interpretation section within the Act, the long title of a public Act (or in old Acts a preamble as is still the case with private Acts which set out its objectives), the 'literal', 'golden', 'mischief' and ejusdem generis rules of interpretation and others. Also reference can be made to the Interpretation Act 1978 and presumptions, for example, that legislation is presumed to have prospective effect in the absence of express words to the contrary.

We will consider each of these in turn but before doing so it is worthwhile mentioning the case of *Fothergill v Monarch Airlines* (1980) in which the House of Lords was asked to interpret the word 'damage' and concluded that although its use in the Carriage by Air Act 1961 was ambiguous it was to be construed as including 'partial loss'. This Act was passed with the intention of giving effect to the Warsaw Convention 1929 as amended and the court held that *travaux preparatoires* including the minutes of meetings at which amendments to the treaty were negotiated could be used to assist the court in construing ambiguities. In the result the plaintiff was unable to claim for items lost from his suitcase when he failed to give the requisite notice although he had done so with regard to damage to his suitcase.

When considering domestic statutes which do not attempt to give effect to international treaties or obligations entered into by the Crown, the courts have a much more limited role and traditionally are confined to construing the meaning of statutory provisions from the words used or by way of other recognised canons of construction.

1.2.5   Rules and presumptions

The starting point for the judge will be to apply a literal or grammatical meaning to the words used. This is known as the 'literal' rule.

It may have unexpected results as illustrated in *Whitely v Chappell* (1868) where an Act made it a criminal offence to personate 'any person entitled to vote at an election'. The defendant attempted to vote in the name of a deceased person but it was held that no offence had been committed as a deceased person was not a 'person' in a literal sense. Clearly the intention of the legislature was to prevent abuses of the electoral system and to rectify this shortcoming amending legislation was passed.

It might be questioned whether the court could or should have addressed itself to the question of what Parliament would have done if it had considered the problem. In *Ex p Smith* as we have seen, the court referred to public policy to justify it making an absolute rule subject to the principle of public policy. In *Whitely* the court made no attempt to 'second guess' Parliament and 'fill in the gaps' in the face of express words. In its view to have done so would have usurped the sovereignty of Parliament and have had the result of creating uncertainty in the law.

In some situations however the court will not apply the literal rule where, in the time honoured phrase, to do so would result in 'absurdity, repugnancy or inconsistency'. This exception to the literal rule is known as the 'golden' rule and is well illustrated by *Re Sigsworth* (1935), where a son who had murdered his mother was prevented from inheriting her property as her sole next-of-kin under the Administration of

Estates Act 1925 on the grounds that it would be repugnant to allow him to do so. On first impression it may be difficult to distinguish the reasoning in this case from that applied in *Ex p Smith*, but it must be remembered that in *Ex p Smith* the court was concerned not with past criminality, as in *Re Sigsworth*, but the possibility of future criminality and that the principle that a person should not profit from his or her own wrong was well recognised. It is therefore a question of degree and in *Ex p Smith* the court was willing to depart from the express words of the statute to a greater extent.

Should use of the golden rule not produce a reasonable result a court may make use of the 'mischief' rule where appropriate. This was defined in *Heydon's Case* (1584) and involves the court posing four questions when attempting to interpret a statutory provision:

- What was the common law before the Act was passed?

- What defect or mischief did the common law fail to remedy?

- What remedy does the Act attempt to provide?

- What is the reason for the remedy?

In *Gardiner v Sevenoaks RDC* (1950) a cave used to store films was held to be covered by an Act regulating safety measures in premises. The Act attempted to ensure the safety of places used for business purposes and as the cave was so used it was covered by the Act.

In *Gorris v Scott* (1874) a provision requiring the penning of sheep whilst on board ship, so as to prevent disease, was held not to apply to sheep washed overboard as a result of not being penned. This demonstrates the four questions above. The common law failed to prevent sheep becoming diseased when transported by ship. The mischief was the disease in such sheep. The statute provided that sheep were to be penned to prevent disease (but not their being washed overboard).

This rule involves the court in considering the purpose of the statutory provision which it is asked to interpret but this is not the same thing as the purposive approach. The latter has a broader scope than the mischief rule and at its widest may involve a court looking to the purpose of an Act even where the words used are not ambiguous. The purposive approach is still in a developmental stage in English law although no doubt *Pepper v Hart* (1992) could well assist its further development.

The other rules of statutory interpretation only apply in specific circumstances:

- *Ejusdem generis* ensures that general words which are preceded by particular words which form a class or 'genus' are interpreted in accordance with the class words. Thus in *Powell v Kempton Park Racecourse Co* (1899) Tattersalls open-air racecourse enclosure reserved for bookmakers was held not to be subject to a provision prohibiting the keeping of 'a house, office or other place for betting purposes' as this referred only to covered accommodation.

- The *noscitur a sociis* rule provides that the meaning of a word is to be gathered from its context. Thus in *IRC v Frere* (1964) the House of Lords held that 'interest' in the phrase 'interest, annuities or other interest' meant annual interest.

- *Expressio unius est exclusio alterius* roughly translated means that where something is expressed it must be taken to exclude something else. In *R v Inhabitants of Sedgley* (1831) rates were to be charged on 'lands, titles and coal mines'. This expressly excluded rates being charged on any other type of mine.

- The Interpretation Act 1978 or an interpretation section within the Act itself may offer the court some, albeit limited, assistance. The former provides, for example, that the masculine shall include the feminine unless a contrary intention appears and that the singular includes the plural and vice versa. Notable examples of the latter are s 118 of the Police and Criminal Evidence Act 1984 and s 119 of the Courts and Legal Services Act 1990.

- Presumptions, already mentioned above, may assist the court in interpreting a provision.

  We have mentioned the presumption that legislation will normally have prospective effect. Other examples are that criminal liability is not imposed without proof of fault in the absence of express statutory provision (*Sweet v Parsley* (1969)); the Crown is not bound by statute unless named and as stated in *Pyx Granite Co v Minister of Housing* (1960) it is presumed that the court's jurisdiction to try a case is not ousted unless expressly stated. In *Davis v Johnson* (1979) the House of Lords noted that reference could properly be made by the court to Law Commission reports and those of committees and commissions appointed by government or Parliament to assess the need for law reform. Usually such reports contain a detailed resumé of the law and the ways in which it might be reformed and this may well assist the court in attempting to interpret a provision.

- More recent cases which illustrate statutory interpretation include the following: in *Re Marr & Another* (1990) it was held *per curiam* ('in the opinion of the court') that where two sections of a statute conflict the court should apply the purposive approach so as to arrive at a sensible meaning rather than arbitrarily giving the later provision priority. The so-called 'rule of last resort' had become obsolete in respect not only of two sections of an Act but also with regard to two sub-sections within a section. In *Waltham Forest LBC v Thomas* (1992) the defendant who had resided with his brother prior to the brother's death was entitled to protection under s 87 of the Housing Act 1985 as having succeeded to the brother's secure tenancy albeit that they had only resided in that particular house some 10 days before the brother's death. By the terms of s 87 it was sufficient that the defendant had resided with his brother for 12 months before his death. It was not necessary that this was in the premises to which succession was claimed.

In *Knowles v Liverpool City Council* (1993) the House of Lords affirmed the decision of the Court of Appeal in holding that the word 'equipment' in the Employer's Liability (Defective Equipment) Act 1969 could refer to a flagstone. K, a flagger, sued his employers for injuries sustained from a faulty flagstone. The word 'equipment' in this provision had been earlier interpreted to include a ship in the case of *Coltman and Another v Bibby Tankers Ltd* (1987) which involved the loss of *The Derbyshire* a 90,000 ton cargo carrier.

It is by no means uncommon for the courts to be asked to interpret the meaning of one word as further illustrated in *A-G's Reference (No 1 of 1988)* where it was held that the recipient of inside information relating to a company's affairs who dealt in the company shares committed an offence of 'obtaining' such information under the Company Securities (Insider Dealing) Act 1985 not only where he had procured it on purpose but also where he had come by it without any positive action. The court was referred to the dictionary meaning of 'obtain' and to a White Paper which preceded the 1985 Act. In the light of the purpose of the Act the court concluded that the word 'obtain' meant no more than 'receive' and that an unsuspecting person who came by such information would only commit an offence if he or she then dealt in the shares of the company to which the information related.

In *Wychavon District Council v National Rivers Authority* (1993) the Council was accused of an offence under the Water Act 1989 s 107 of causing the discharge of sewage into a river. The question on an appeal by the Council was whether 'causing' included a failure to act promptly. It was held that 'causing' required a positive act whereas 'knowingly permitting' pollution would cover a failure to act promptly. The court was referred to the dictionary meaning of 'causing' and noted that in a penal section if a word is capable of bearing more than one meaning the one most favourable to the defendant must be adopted.

We will now move on to consider the other main source of law namely case law.

1.2.6   Case law

Case law is the other main source of law within the English legal system – a common law based system as opposed to a Roman law or codified system.

Common law in this context refers to the system of precedent or stare decisis and not simply to common law decisions. Thus it includes both the decisions of common law and equity.

Historically, precedent developed from common law decisions and from the 14th century were supplemented by the decisions of the Court of Chancery. Common law was uniform throughout the country and applied to all. It is said to have developed from local customs which applied at the time of the Norman Conquest. Judges travelled throughout the country 'on circuit' dispensing justice. On their return to Westminster, which traditionally was the central location of the English courts, the judges compared the customs which they had applied in resolving disputes.

Over the centuries a uniform law was moulded – established by means of the doctrine of *stare decisis* ('let the decision stand'). Judges were obliged to follow the decisions of superior courts and this ensured both a degree of certainty and fairness.

As a developed system of law the common law became rigid and unable to meet new demands on it in that it became over-reliant on fixed forms and failed to develop writs to meet new needs. Its very strengths became its weaknesses.

In the 14th century the Court of Chancery was founded by the Lord Chancellor. This dispensed 'equitable' remedies to those either denied a remedy at common law or who had been granted an unsatisfactory remedy.

Equity operated by way of 'maxims' and its remedies were discretionary. Some equitable maxims are as follows:

- 'equity is but a gloss on the common law';

- 'equity looks to the intent rather than the form';

- 'he who comes to equity must come with clean hands';

- 'equality is equity';

- 'delay defeats equity';

- 'equity acts *in personam*'.

The maxims illustrate the workings of equity and that it was not a complete system in its own right but attempted to fill in the gaps left by the common law. Equity was based on fairness and its remedies were awarded only at the discretion of the court which had to be satisfied as to the bona fides of the plaintiff.

Equity originated from the Lord Chancellor who was a cleric described as 'the Keeper of the King's Conscience', that is he acted as the King's confessor. One of the early criticisms of equity – 'equity varies with the length of the Chancellor's foot' – illustrates that in the early days equity reached decisions without reference to past cases and took a flexible approach in an attempt to achieve fairness and justice between parties to a dispute.

Increasingly equity remedied some of the defects of the common law, notably those of rigidity and over-reliance on the system of precedent. By the 15th century equity and common law were rivals and it was only in 1615 in the Earl of Oxford's Case that it was declared that where there was a conflict, equity would prevail.

It was not until the major reforms of 1873-75 in the Judicature Acts that this was put into statutory form and the administration of equity and common law were merged. Litigants could from this time seek both common law and equitable remedies in all courts although it was necessary to ask for an equitable remedy otherwise it would be assumed that common law damages would be sufficient.

In addition to equitable remedies such as rescission, injunction and specific performance, equity created concepts unknown at common law.

Two important examples are mortgages and trusts.

- Mortgages

  Equity looked to the substance of a transaction rather than merely the form it took and so, unlike the common law, equity would enquire into its purpose. In the case of a mortgage this allowed a lender to take security for the loan over an item of property owned by the borrower. It did not allow the lender any greater rights over the property than those which protected his security.

- Trusts

  Trusts allowed the ownership of property to be transferred to one person for the benefit of another. So, for example, where a parent wished his son to have the benefit of a piece of land but the son was under age, the parent could transfer ownership to a trusted person (or, in the case of land, at least two people) to hold in trust for the benefit of the son. On reaching full age it would then be usual for the trust to come to an end and the trustee to transfer the property to the beneficiary for his own use.

1.2.7   The doctrine of precedent

Having outlined the origins of common law and equity and mentioned that their administration was merged as a result of the Judicature Acts 1873-75 it is now necessary to say more about the workings of precedent.

Two factors are important in the development of precedent: the notion of a hierarchy of courts, and the accurate and efficient reporting of cases.

A court higher in the hierarchy has greater jurisdiction than a court lower in the hierarchy and its decisions will be more authoritative in the interpretation of the law and its application to the facts in a dispute.

It follows that the decision of a higher court and the reason or reasons for that decision will be binding on a later court lower in the hierarchy which is asked to decide a case on similar facts. On the other hand decisions of courts lower in the hierarchy can only be of persuasive authority for courts higher in the hierarchy. A decision of the Court of Appeal does not bind the House of Lords but the latter may take notice of a decision of the Court of Appeal concerned with similar facts. A similar rule applies to decisions of Scottish and foreign courts which are only of persuasive authority in English courts. Increasingly the English courts are being referred to decisions of Commonwealth and American courts as a means of providing guidance in the resolution of disputes.

No mention of persuasive authority would be complete without reference to *obiter dicta* (things said by the way). Where in the course of giving judgment a judge makes comments not directly relevant to the dispute in question such comments are described as *obiter dicta*. No matter what the place in the hierarchy of the court in which such statements are made or of the court to which such statements are referred such statements can only ever be persuasive authority.

In addition to hierarchy the other element in the development of precedent is the system of reporting cases that is recording decisions so that they can be referred to by counsel in a later case concerned with similar facts. There are many examples of law reports, some specialised, for example Lloyds Reports concerned with insurance and shipping matters, others general in nature such as the All England Law Reports, the Weekly Law Reports and the most authoritative, the Law Reports produced by the Incorporated Council of Law Reporting.

In addition to traditional law reports lawyers are increasingly resorting to data bases for retrieval of case decisions. The most well known of these is LEXIS which allows an authorised user access to the data base containing case reports from the UK, the European Community, Commonwealth, US and other jurisdictions.

It does not follow that a decision which is not reported is not a precedent. There have been instances where a decision is not reported for some time and then only when its full significance is appreciated. Thus counsel may well cite a case to a court which has not been reported and the court will take notice of it by way of oral evidence by counsel who appeared in the case. Lord Diplock in *Roberts Petroleum v B Kenny* (1983) and Lord Donaldson, the then Master of the Rolls, in *Stanley v International Harvester* (1983) attempted to discourage counsel from citing unreported cases from LEXIS, in particular those which demonstrated no great novelty or authority.

Only about a tenth of the decisions of the higher courts are reported and in any event there may well be a time lag in a court reaching a decision and its being reported in full. Various law reports offer only a summary of the decision reached (eg The Times Law Reports). The advantage of this lies in its speed from the date of decision to the date on which it is reported.

Previous reported decisions may assist the lawyer asked to advise his client or the judge having to reach a solution in a dispute. When consulting a law report there are several essential elements that must be present. Not only the facts of the earlier case must be reported together with the decision reached by the court but also the *ratio decidendi* (that is the reason or the reasons for the decision).

The court in reaching its decision may attempt to state the law by making a *per curiam* statement. However it may not always be so clear for a later court asked to apply a previous decision. Its interpretation of the *ratio decidendi* of the earlier court permits a later court either to develop the law or restrict its scope. A later court will have to assess the degree of similarity and dissimilarity between the facts of the case it is asked to decide and those of the earlier case. If the judge in the later case finds no significant dissimilarities and is bound by the earlier decision then the earlier decision will be applied. If the earlier decision is only persuasive authority the judge can use his discretion whether or not to apply the earlier decision. However where the earlier decision is a binding precedent the judge may be able or willing to 'distinguish' the facts of the earlier case from those of the case he is asked to decide. The advantage of distinguishing is that the law can develop to meet changing needs. Its disadvantage lies in over-use and the drawing of minute differences leading to uncertainty in the law.

1.2.8   The doctrine of precedent: as between the courts

The House of Lords is, as a general rule, bound by its previous decisions. This ensures a degree of certainty on which legal advisers stand a better chance of predicting the likely outcome of cases. The House of Lords has on many occasions stated that if it wrongly interprets the law it is Parliament's place to amend the law by way of legislation.

By the 1966 Practice Statement the House of Lords stated that it would depart from its previous decisions 'where it appears right to do so'. This has been used rarely but the case of *R v Shivpuri* (1986) illustrates that the House of Lords may decide that one of its earlier decisions had been wrongly decided. *Shivpuri* overruled the case of *Anderton v Ryan* (1985) where it was held that it was not an offence to attempt the legally impossible. In *Shivpuri* the defendant was convicted of an attempt at dealing in and harbouring a prohibited drug. In fact the substance was harmless although the defendant thought that he had in his possession a drug. As he had intended to commit the offence and had done an act more than merely preparatory to the commission of the offence liability was proved.

Other examples where this power has been used include *R v Secretary of State for the Home Department ex p Khawaja* (1983) which overruled *Ex p Zamir* (1980); *R v Hancock & Shankland* (1986) overruling *R v Maloney* (1985); and *Murphy v Brentwood DC* (1990) overruling *Anns v Merton LBC* (1978).

The House of Lords is not bound by a decision reached *per incuriam* (that is through carelessness in overlooking a relevant statutory provision or earlier decision).

Decisions of the House of Lords bind all lower courts providing statute has not overruled the decision and in the case of a decision reached on the grounds of public policy providing it remains socially appropriate.

The Court of Appeal (Civil Division) binds all inferior courts and as a general rule is bound by its own decisions. Three exceptions were noted in *Young v Bristol Aeroplane Co* (1944):

• the Court of Appeal can choose between two conflicting decisions of its own;

- the Court of Appeal is bound to follow a later House of Lords decision which conflicts with an earlier Court of Appeal decision but which does not expressly overrule it;

- the Court of Appeal is not bound by one of its own previous decisions which was taken *per incuriam* (failure to take account of a statutory provision or of a relevant case).

The position of the Court of Appeal has not always been so settled, as illustrated in the case of *Davis v Johnson* (1979) where Lord Denning (then Master of the Rolls) expressed the view that the Court of Appeal should be free to overrule one of its previous decisions where it was seen to be wrong. On appeal the House of Lords reprimanded the Court of Appeal for this view and suggested that only the exceptions in *Young v Bristol Aeroplane* were available.

This brings into question why we have two appeal courts. On the one hand, in theory at least, litigants are free to look to the House of Lords for an authoritative statement of the law. On the other, if the Court of Appeal is free to overrule its earlier decisions (although this may lead to uncertainty) it provides litigants with a shorter and cheaper route to settlement.

The Court of Appeal (Criminal Division) applies the rules of precedent less strictly than the civil division on the basis that each case is to be treated on its merits. In *R v Gould* (1968) it was stated that the court is bound by its previous decisions subject to the 'interests of justice'. The court will follow an earlier decision, even if thought to be wrong, if it results in the liberty of the defendant.

The High Court is bound by decisions of the House of Lords, the Court of Appeal and the Divisional Courts, but not by its own decisions. The Crown Court, county court and the magistrates' courts are also bound by the decisions of the higher courts but not by their own decisions.

In the case of the Divisional Courts where the supervisory jurisdiction is exercised in civil or criminal matters the court is not bound by its own earlier decisions but in appeals 'by way of case stated' in criminal matters as a general rule it is bound, unless the liberty of the defendant is at stake.

In so far as the decisions of higher courts are concerned the Divisional Courts are bound by the decisions of the House of Lords and Court of Appeal except the Divisional Court of the Queen's Bench Division where appeal lies direct to the House of Lords.

Strict application of the rules of binding precedent can lead to rigidity in the law. Several devices exist which allow the law to be developed and a judge who is otherwise bound by an earlier decision may avoid applying it. One such device is that of 'distinguishing' the facts of the present case from that of an earlier decision which would otherwise be binding. Caution is needed however, otherwise artificial differences might be used to justify not following decisions of a higher court.

Distinguishing permits the law to be developed to cover new situations but at the same time it may create uncertainty as to future developments.

Another device is to declare that an earlier decision was made *per incuriam* and that the law as stated in the earlier decision is incorrect. In *Rakhit v Carty* (1990) this was taken a step further when the Court of Appeal (Civil Division) held that it was not bound to follow a previous decision which was itself based on the authority of an earlier decision which had been made *per incuriam* in that it had failed to take account of a relevant statutory provision. Russell LJ referred to the rule in *Young v Bristol Aeroplane Co Ltd* (1944) and the limited exceptions to that rule referred to in *Young's* case and *Morelle Ltd v Wakeling* (1955) and *Williams v Fawcett* (1985) where the Court of Appeal is permitted to depart from one of its earlier decisions if that decision was made *per incuriam* or 'in rare and exceptional cases' which involve 'a manifest slip or error'.

The Court of Appeal was not declaring that a precedent binding on it was *per incuriam*, but that the precedent which appeared to be binding on it had followed a decision which was itself *per incuriam*. The Court of Appeal felt free to rectify the position some eight years after the first decision had been made. It is unlikely that this will be used often.

The law may also develop where on an appeal previous authority binding on the lower courts is overruled. The rule or principle will be restated by the higher court correcting the error fallen into by a lower court. This may result in the appeal being successful in which case the decision of the lower court is reversed.

The common law also develops as a result of later courts interpreting the scope and effect of binding precedent. It will not always be clear what the *ratio decidendi* of a case is, particularly in decisions of the House of Lords, where although there may be agreement as to the decision itself, their Lordships may differ as to the reasons for the decision. A later court may find that what was considered to be the *ratio* of an earlier decision is too wide, with the result that that will be only of persuasive authority.

Where a later court is faced with several conflicting decisions of the same level it will have to choose between them. In other cases what would otherwise be a binding precedent is found to be wrong or obscure or has been overruled by statute with the effect that the court asked to apply the precedent is not bound to do so.

Apart from such devices, judges have generally considered that they have a limited role to play in making law. They are the interpreters of the law and should not usurp the role of Parliament. The legislature is empowered to enact policy as the elected representative of the people. The role of the judge is limited to making law piecemeal as and when cases come before the courts for solution.

Judges are not elected but appointed and should not concern themselves with deciding between competing interests other than where the law (either in the form of statute or case law) already establishes where the line is to be drawn. We consider more fully the role of the judge in the development of case law in a later chapter.

It now remains to consider the impact on domestic law of membership of the European Community (which, with effect from September 1993, became the European Union following ratification of the Treaty of European Union which was given domestic effect by the European Communities (Amendment) Act 1993.

The other source of law to be considered is that emanating from what is now the European Union. The UK joined the European Economic Community, the European Coal and Steel Community and Euratom in 1973 undertaking to establish a common market with the existing members to approximate economic policies by abolishing customs duties and trade barriers and ensuring free movement of persons, services and capital within and between Member States.	1.2.9 European Community law

The Treaty of Accession was signed in 1972 and was brought into effect by the European Communities Act 1972. Similarly the Single European Act 1986 was given domestic effect in the UK by the European Communities (Amendment) Act 1986, and 1993 saw the ratification of the Treaty of European Union (the Maastricht Treaty) which has been given effect by the European Communities (Amendment) Act 1993 following some 19 months' discussion in Parliament.

Constitutional theory demands that an international treaty entered into by the Crown has no effect in domestic law unless and until it is given effect by legislation. Authority for this is to be found in the case of *Mortensen v Peters* (1906). This is an aspect of the doctrine of Parliamentary sovereignty and in legal theory these Acts may be repealed by a later Parliament with the result that the UK can be in breach of international law. The political reality is quite different and any attempt to repeal this legislation would result not only in political crisis but call in question the position of the courts and whether the judges would comply strictly with the doctrine of Parliamentary sovereignty or attempt to comply with law of the European Union. At the present time, with the doctrine still in place in so far as it gives effect to European Union law, developments have shown the courts of the UK willing to give European law priority where there is a conflict with domestic law.

1.2.10	The institutions of the European Union

There are five main institutions of the European Union namely:

- The Council of Ministers

  The Council of Ministers is made up of one representative from each of the 12 Member States, usually the foreign minister, by the appropriate minister for the business to be discussed. For example, when agriculture is being dealt with, Britain would be represented by the Minister for Agriculture, Fisheries and Food. The Council is the principal decision-making body and can conclude agreements on behalf of the Union. The presidency is rotated between each Member State on a six month basis. Decisions are reached in one of three ways: by simple majority, qualified majority or unanimously. Larger states have proportionately more votes.

- The Commission

  The Commission is the executive body likened to a 'civil service'. There are at present 16 members drawn from Member States but not equally. Commissioners swear an oath of allegiance to the Union and each takes responsibility for a subject. Its main function is the preparation of proposals for new legislation and the formulation of policy.

- The Parliament

  The Parliament, formerly called the European Assembly, has 567 members directly elected by Member States for a five year term. Members sit in party groupings, not according to state. The involvement of the Assembly in law-making was increased under the provisions of the Single European Act.

  This known as the 'co-operation procedure'. The Assembly can accept, reject or amend proposed legislative changes and it has a power of veto over the Commission's budget proposals. It can also dismiss the Commission on a two-thirds vote but these powers have not yet been used.

- The European Court of Justice in Luxembourg

  The European Court of Justice interprets Union law and its application to Member States and other bodies. The court follows the Roman law tradition in that no reliance is placed on precedent (although decisions of the court bind the courts of Member States). An inquisitorial approach is followed and no dissenting opinions are given. Counsel make written submissions and the court reaches a preliminary decision through its Advocate-General. A president is appointed by fellow judges and each Member State sends one judge to the court.

  Reference may be made (and in the case of Member States' final appeal courts, reference *must* be made) under Article 177 of the Treaty of Rome 1957 for a preliminary ruling as to the meaning or effect of Union law.

  The case of *Bulmer v Bollinger* (1974), in which Lord Denning MR laid down four guidelines as to whether a reference was necessary and six guidelines for the exercise of the discretion by other than a final appeal court, remains instructive as to the use of Article 177 although refined by later cases.

  In 1989 the Court of First Instance was inaugurated with the aim of easing the burden of the European Court of Justice and to speed up the hearing of cases.

  Use of Article 177 necessitates adjournment of a case in the domestic court pending the interpretation of Union law by the European Court. The delay may be several years and this of course increases costs for litigants.

- The European Council

  The European Council was established in 1974 and given formal recognition under the Single European Act 1986. This consists of heads of government and foreign ministers and who meet in 'summit' three times a year.

So far as application of European Union law within Member States is concerned, the view of the European Court of Justice and the views of domestic courts have not always been identical.

1.2.11   The application of European Union law

The UK courts are bound by the doctrine of sovereignty of Parliament and whilst the UK is a member of the Union, European law is given effect under the European Communities Act 1972 and subsequent legislation. The European Court has on many occasions stated that European law takes precedence over domestic law. Authority for this is to be found in *Costa v ENEL Case 6/64,* the *Internationale Case 11/70* and the *Van Gend en Loos Case 26/63.*

On 19 June 1990 the European Court again ruled that European law was to take precedence over domestic law in what has become known as the Spanish Fishermen case which involved the provisions of the Merchant Shipping Act 1988. In *R v Secretary of State for Transport ex p Factortame Ltd & Others (No 2) (1990)* the House of Lords granted interim relief to the applicants suspending the provisions of the 1988 Act.

A distinction has been drawn between *directly applicable* and *directly effective* provisions although this distinction is not always made clear in the judgments of the European Court. Regulations are directly applicable and bestow rights on individuals under Article 189 of the Treaty of Rome. No further measures need be taken by Member States to bring Regulations into effect. On the other hand Directives are binding only as to the result to be achieved and Member States are free to choose the form of implementation, subject only to a specified timetable.

To be directly effective a Directive must meet three conditions:

- firstly, the provision must be clear and precise in its scope and application;

- secondly, it must not be conditional;

- thirdly, there must be no room for a Member State to exercise its discretion in implementing the Directive.

If a Directive meets these conditions but otherwise is inadequately implemented by a Member State an individual can still rely on its terms in the domestic courts. This is known as 'vertical direct effect' in that an individual can look to his or her government for a remedy.

Authority is to be found in *Marshall v Southampton & SW Hants AHA* (1984) which concerned the compulsory retirement age of 65 for men and 60 for women. It was held that the Equal Treatment Directive had been broken and that this could be relied on as the employer was an organ of the State. An issue then arose as to whether direct effect could apply for the benefit of individuals who wished to bring claims not against the state, but another individual or private body. This became known as 'horizontal direct effect'. The cases of *Von Colson* (1983) and *Marleasing SA v La Commercial Int etc* (1989) show that the European Court called in aid Article 5 of the Treaty of Rome to get round the difficulty with the result that states (including domestic courts) must take 'all appropriate measures' to fulfil European obligations.

A further breakthrough was made in *Francovitch v Italian Government* (1992) when the European Court held that Francovitch should be awarded damages against the Italian government despite the Directive in question having been found to be insufficiently precise to be directly effective.

In *Van Gend en Loos* (1963) Article 12 of the Treaty of Rome was held to have vertical direct effect and this ruling was soon applied to other treaty provisions which satisfied the conditions above. Horizontal direct effect of treaty provisions was recognised in *De Frenne v Sabena* (1975).

So far as decisions, recommendations and opinions are concerned only, decisions are binding and may have direct effect.

When considering the attitude of the English courts to the application of European law two points are worthy of note. Firstly the use of Article 177 of the Treaty of Rome for the making of a preliminary reference for the interpretation of a European provision. As we have already noted the landmark case was that of *Bulmer v Bollinger* (1974), in which Lord Denning MR laid down guidelines to assist the court in deciding whether or not to make a reference. In his judgment the House of Lords as the final appeal court was under a duty to make a reference where one or both parties wished, providing it was necessary to do so on the basis of four guidelines. All other courts had a discretion and Lord Denning MR laid down six guidelines to assist a court with this question.

Later cases have refined Lord Denning's statements and it may be that a court other than the House of Lords may be the final appeal court in which case it will be under a duty to make an Article 177 reference.

The other point concerns the sovereignty of Parliament and how the English courts would deal with a clash between European law and domestic law. As we have already mentioned European law is given effect by way of the European Communities Act 1972 s 2(1) to (4) as subsequently amended. In strict legal theory this legislation could be repealed and a conflict created with European law. Even whilst remaining members of the European Union a clash between European and domestic law might arise. *R v Secretary of State for Transport ex p Factortame & Others (No 2)* (1990) illustrates the closest the UK has come to such a clash with the result that the Merchant Shipping Act 1988 s 14 was suspended pending final determination of the issues.

The question has often been posed as to how UK judges should react and four possibilities have been put forward:

- they could follow the traditional doctrine of implied repeal and give effect to the later legislation;

- they could ignore such later legislation unless it expressly repudiated European law;

- the judges could apply a rule of construction and interpret UK law consistently with European law;

- they could take a radical approach and apply European law.

In the light of the *Factortame* case and the ratification of the Treaty of European Union in 1993 there is every likelihood that the eventuality of a clash between European and domestic law whilst remaining members will be slight and should it arise be remedied not by the courts but amending legislation. Should legislation be passed in the future which repeals the European Communities Act 1972 as amended this raises much more fundamental issues and the reaction of the judges would depend on their view not only of their role within the constitution but of the constitution itself.

Classification and Sources of Law

Two traditional classifications of law are between criminal and civil law and public international law and municipal law.

Public international law regulates the relationships of States whereas municipal law is domestic law which can be sub-divided into civil (or private) law, public law (which includes criminal law) and private international law.

Methods of classifying the law

If law is to be applied in reaching solutions to problems knowledge of its source, or where to find the law, is essential.

Literary and historical sources are distinguished as are principal and subsidiary sources.

Principal sources (legislation; delegated legislation; case law and European Community law) are concentrated upon, whereas the subsidiary sources (custom, Roman law, ecclesiastical law and books of authority) are mentioned briefly.

Distinguishing between 'sources' of law

Public bills (initiated by the government or private members) and private bills are noted together with the procedure whereby bills become law.

Private Bills (which promote the interests of an individual or group) should not be confused with Private Members' Bills which are public bills promoted by an MP. Limited time and resources are available to the private member and he or she will have to compete for time to promote a bill in the Ballot or under the 'Ten Minute Rule'. Examples are the Abortion Act 1967, Video Recordings Act 1984 and Indecent Displays (Control) Act 1981.

The doctrine of Supremacy of Parliament is noted as are enabling Acts under which delegated legislation takes effect. The validity of delegated legislation may be challenged under Order 53 of the Rules of the Supreme Court on the ground that it is *ultra vires* the enabling Act. The advantages and disadvantages of delegated legislation are noted.

Legislation

Although the courts have no general right to challenge the validity of legislation (except where it conflicts with European Union provisions) their ability to decide the meaning of statutory provisions when trying cases gives them potentially wide scope for developing the law.

Statutory interpretation

Traditionally, the judges have tended towards a narrow approach confining themselves to the words of the statutory provision. In other words use has been made of intrinsic aids to construction (such as the long title or an interpretation section) in preference to extrinsic aids.

Two factors suggest this is changing: first the House of Lords' decision in *Pepper v Hart* (1993) later applied in *Massmould v Payne* (1993); *Sheppard v IRC* (1993) and *Van Dyck v Secretary of State for the Environment* (1993); and second the 'purposive' approach used in continental jurisdictions and the European Court of Justice applied in *Shah v Barnet LBC* (1983) and *R v Registrar-General ex p Smith* (1990).

The use of extrinsic aids to construction has long been recognised when a domestic court is interpreting a treaty provision given effect to by legislation (*Fothergill v Monarch Airlines* (1980)).

- The literal rule

  When interpreting a statutory provision the judge starts with the literal or grammatical meaning of the word(s) (*Whitely v Chappell* (1868)).

- The golden rule

  Where the literal rule would result in 'absurdity, repugnancy or inconsistency' the judge may attempt to extend the meaning of the words used to reach a reasonable result (*Re Sigsworth* (1935); *Ex p Smith* (1990)).

- The mischief rule

  Heydon's Case (1584) defines this rule. Four questions must be answered for it to apply, as illustrated in *Gardiner v Sevenoaks RDC* (1950) and *Gorris v Scott* (1874).

  The other rules apply only in specific circumstances:

- *ejusdem generis* (*Powell v Kempton Park Racecourse Co* (1899));

- *noscitur a sociiis* (*IRC v Frere* (1964));

- *expressio unius est exclusio alterius* (*R v Inhabitants of Sedgley* (1831));

- Interpretation Act 1978.

  Presumptions, such as legislation, are considered to have only prospective effect; criminal liability not to be imposed without proof of fault in the absence of express provision (*Sweet v Parsley* (1969)); the Crown is not bound by statute unless named.

  The following cases illustrate the rules of statutory interpretation:

- *Re Marr and Another* (1990)
- *Waltham Forest LBC v Thomas* (1992)
- *Knowles v Liverpool City Council* (1993)
- *Coltman and Another v Bibby Tankers Ltd* (1987)
- *A-G's Reference (No 1 of 1988)* (1988)
- *Wychavon District Council v National Rivers Authority* (1993)

Case law

Case law is the other main source of law, also known as 'precedent' or *stare decisis*. The historical development of common law and equity is given and the different meanings of common law mentioned. The development and use of equitable maxims and concepts such as mortgages and trusts. The merger of the administration of common law and Equity by the *Earl of Oxford's Case* (1615) and the Judicature Acts 1873-75.

The doctrine of precedent

Precedent develops as a result of the hierarchy of the courts and accurate and efficient law reporting. Binding and persuasive precedent is explained and examples of law reports are given including the All England Law Reports, specialist reports and data bases such as LEXIS.

The elements of a reported case, the facts, decision and *ratio decidendi* are noted and the process by which the law develops through case law.

The doctrine of precedent: as between the courts – each court is taken in turn from the House of Lords, the Court of Appeal (Criminal and Civil Divisions), the High Court and divisional courts through to the Crown Court, county court and magistrates' court.

- Practice Statement 1966 of the House of Lords
- *R v Shivpuri* (1986)
- *Anderton v Ryan* (1985)
- *R v Secretary of State for the Home Department ex p Khawaja* (1983)
- *R v Hancock & Shankland* (1986)
- *Murphy v Brentwood DC* (1990)
- *Young v Bristol Aeroplane Co* (1944)
- *Davis v Johnson* (1979)

Several devices exist to ensure development of the law to meet changing needs. One is distinguishing the facts of the case to be decided from an earlier decision which would otherwise be binding. These are illustrated in case law (*Rakhit v Carty* (1990); *Morelle v Wakeling* (1955); *Williams v Fawcett* (1985)).

- European Community law

  UK membership of the European Community: European Communities Act 1972; the European Communities (Amendment) Acts 1986 and 1993. Implications of membership on the doctrine of supremacy of Parliament (*Mortensen v Peters* (1906)).

The institutions of the European Union

The main five institutions are noted: the Council of Ministers; the Commission; the Parliament; the European Court of Justice and the European Council. Each is briefly described and in particular the role of the European Court of Justice in Luxembourg in interpreting European law. The Court of First Instance was set up in 1989 to ease the burden on the Court.

- Article 177 Treaty of Rome

- *Bulmer v Bollinger* (1974)

The application of European Union law

The European Court of Justice has always treated European law as having precedence over domestic law (*Costa v ENEL*, the *Internationale* case and *Van Gend en Loos*. Of particular note is *R v Secretary of State for Transport ex p Factortame Ltd & Others (No 2)* (1990) where the House of Lords (following applications to the European Court of Justice) granted interim relief to suspend the provisions of the Merchant Shipping Act 1988.

The attitude of the English courts has been shaped by the supremacy of Parliament doctrine but following *Factortame* and the European Communities (Amendment) Act 1993 it is likely that precedence will in future be accorded by the UK courts to European law.

Regulations are directly applicable: Article 189 Treaty of Rome. Directives may be directly effective and a distinction is drawn between 'vertical direct effect' and 'horizontal direct effect'.

Marshall v Southampton & SW Hants AHA (1984); *Von Colson* (1983); *Marleasing SA v La Commercial Int* (1989); *Francovitch v Italian Republic* (1992) allowed a claim even though the directive was insufficiently precise to be directly effective.

Treaty provisions, like directives, may be directly effective (both vertically and horizontally) (*Van Gend en Loos* (1963) and *De Frenne v Sabena* (1975)).

Of decisions, recommendations and opinions only decisions are binding and so may have direct effect.

Chapter 2

The Court System

Although we often talk of 'the courts' as if to imply a uniform and precise group this is not always the case. The courts comprise a hierarchy within which each court has a separate jurisdiction regulating its powers, type of business and personnel.

The hierarchy of the courts is best explained by way of a diagram.

Figure 1 sets out the structure of the civil and criminal courts with the avenues of appeal.

2.1   Classifying the courts

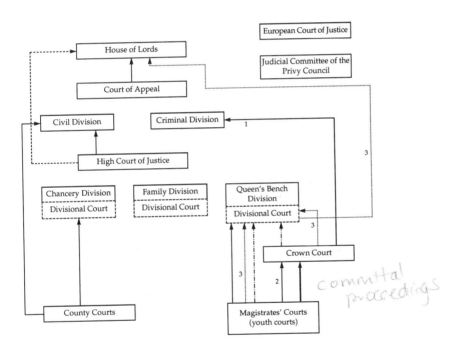

Key

——▶ Main avenues of appeal

------▶ Leapfrog appeal (Administration of Justice Act 1969 Part II)

···········▶ Appeals by way of case stated (Administration of Justice Act 1960 s 1)

——▶ Committals

–·–·–▶ Application for judicial review

1   Appeals against jury decisions only (Criminal Appeal Act 1968)

2   Defendant can appeal against conviction and/or sentence if pleaded not guilty. If pleaded guilty, can only appeal against sentence

3   Application by way of case stated, by prosecution or defence

Figure 2 illustrates the types of business dealt with.

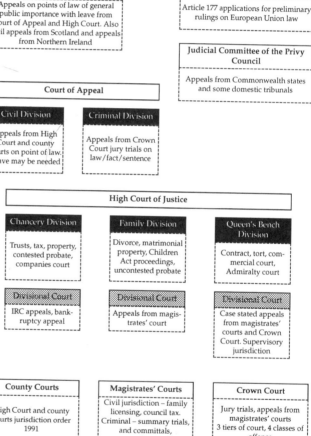

Figure 3 sets out the personnel of each court and is considered in the next chapter.

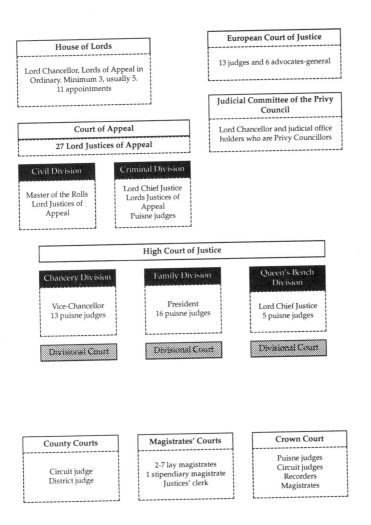

It is usual to classify the courts into those exercising criminal jurisdiction and those exercising civil jurisdiction. In the main this is useful but some courts exercise both criminal and civil functions. For example, the magistrates' courts and the Queen's Bench Division of the High Court. The latter is primarily a civil court but which has an important supervisory jurisdiction in criminal matters by way of judicial review or case stated.

Courts can be classified according to whether they exercise appellate functions, or are first instance or trial courts. However, in the case of the High Court and the Crown Court, both functions are exercised, for example the Crown Court may have appeals from magistrates' courts referred to it and try indictable (the most serious) offences.

Courts can also be classified into superior and inferior courts. The former include the Crown Court, the High Court, the Court of Appeal and the House of Lords which have unlimited jurisdiction. The latter include the magistrates' courts and the county court which have limited jurisdiction, in criminal matters according to the seriousness of the offence, and in civil matters according to the value of the claim. The High Court exercises a supervisory jurisdiction over inferior courts and tribunals and, for this purpose, the Crown Court when exercising its appellate jurisdiction is also subject to supervision by the High Court.

When considering the composition and structure of the courts it is also useful to note the role of the European Court of Justice in interpreting European law and hearing preliminary references made to it by domestic courts under Article 177 of the Treaty of Rome.

The part played in the administration of justice by tribunals is also worthy of note, as is the role of specialist courts such as Coroners' Courts, the Judicial Committee of the Privy Council, the Court of Protection and the Restrictive Practices Court. We will now take each court in turn and consider its role in the hierarchy.

2.2   House of Lords

The House of Lords developed from the Curia Regis (King's Council) and dates from Norman times. It is the highest appeal court in the UK – appeals come from Northern Ireland, England and Wales and Scotland – although, in the case of Scotland, only in civil matters.

The Appellate Jurisdiction Act 1876 provided for the appointment of salaried life peers to hear appeals. These are known as the Law Lords but their full title is that of Lords of Appeal in Ordinary. Their number has gradually been increased to the present maximum of 11. Lay peers may not participate in the judicial sittings of the House and, by convention, when the Law Lords participate in debates concerned with controversial non-legal matters, they do so in a personal capacity.

So far as appeals from England and Wales are concerned, the House of Lords in its judicial capacity hears appeals from the Court of Appeal (Civil Division) on points of law of general public importance, but leave is required from the Court of Appeal or the House of Lords' Appeals Committee. By the Administration of Justice Act 1969 a 'leapfrog' procedure is provided allowing an appeal from the High Court, in its capacity as a trial court, directly to the House of Lords. The trial judge has a discretion to certify a point of law of general public importance concerning the construction of legislation or the effect of a binding precedent. Leave of the House of Lords is also required. Appeal also lies from the Court of Appeal (Criminal Division) on points of law of general public importance under the Criminal Appeal Act 1968. Leave of the Court of Appeal or House of Lords is required.

Decisions of the House of Lords are binding on all other courts and until the Practice Statement of 1966 the House of Lords considered itself bound by its own previous decisions. It now departs from such a decision where it sees fit to do so, for example, where a past decision is found to be *per incuriam* although this power is exercised with caution so as ensure a measure of certainty in the law.

The House of Lords is no longer the supreme legal authority in European Union matters. A reference under Article 177 of the Treaty of Rome to the European Court of Justice will determine the application of European law and this was clearly demonstrated in *R v Secretary of State ex p Factortame* (1990).

The Criminal Appeal Act 1968 abolished the Court of Criminal Appeal and provided for the establishment of civil and Criminal Divisions. The former hears appeals on questions of law from the High Court and on law and fact from the county court. If an appeal is successful the court may reverse the lower court's decision, amend it, or order a re-trial.	**2.3** **The Court of Appeal**

Section 16 of the Supreme Court Act 1981, as amended by the Courts and Legal Services Act 1990, governs appeals from the High Court. The County Courts Act 1984, as amended by the 1990 Act, governs appeals from county courts. In both cases leave may now be needed.

The Criminal Division hears appeals from decisions of the Crown Court in its capacity as a trial court. It has no part to play in appeals from magistrates' courts or Crown Court appellate decisions. An appeal from the Crown Court may be against conviction or sentence and concern law or fact.

By s 17 of the Criminal Appeals Act 1968 the Home Secretary may make a reference to the Court of Appeal following a conviction on indictment or on a finding of not guilty on indictment by reason of insanity.

Section 36 of the Criminal Justice Act 1972 provides for an Attorney-General's reference on a point of law to the Court of Appeal following an acquittal of a defendant for an opinion on the point of law in question. The acquittal will not be disturbed but the point of law can be clarified. Leave is not required.

Sections 35 and 36 of the Criminal Justice Act 1988 provide for a reference by the Attorney-General to the Court of Appeal for a review where he considers that an unduly lenient sentence was passed. This is only available for indictable offences or an either way offence specified by an Order of the Home Secretary (of which there has been none made to date). Leave of the Court of Appeal is required. The Court of Appeal may quash the sentence and replace it with any appropriate sentence up to the maximum available in the Crown Court and a further reference is possible to the House of Lords. The Home Secretary has recently proposed an extension in the scope of ss 35 and 36 by way of statutory instrument.

Decisions of the Court of Appeal bind all lower courts. In civil matters the Court of Appeal is bound by the House of Lords and its own previous decisions, unless one of the exceptions in *Young v Bristol Aeroplane Co Ltd* (1944) applies.

In criminal matters the court will depart from its earlier decisions when it considers it is in the interests of justice to do so as stated in *R v Gould* (1968).

2.4 Divisional courts of the High Court

Divisional courts exercise the appellate function of the High Court. Each division of the High Court has a divisional court. Thus the Queen's Bench Division Divisional Court hears appeals from the magistrates' court and the Crown Court by way of case stated and judicial review.

The Magistrates' Court Act 1980 s 111 provides for an appeal by way of case stated where an error of law or an excess of jurisdiction is alleged. If prosecution or defence allege some illegality in the trial or appeal process application is made for judicial review under Order 53 of the Rules of the Supreme Court.

Some tribunals including the Solicitors' Disciplinary Tribunal may also have a right of appeal. An appeal by way of case stated involves the magistrates' court or Crown Court setting out their findings of fact and prosecution or defence, applying to the Queen's Bench Division Divisional Court for a determination of a question of law in dispute.

The Family Division Divisional Court hears appeals from the magistrates' courts on matrimonial matters and the Chancery Division Divisional Court appeals from the county court in bankruptcy and tax matters.

Appeals are heard by two or three judges of the appropriate division. Decisions act as precedents for future cases except in magistrates' courts where an appeal against acquittal by the prosecution by way of case stated ensures the setting of clear legal precedent and the avoidance of backlogs.

In civil matters the divisional courts are bound by their own decisions and the decisions of the higher courts. In turn their decisions bind the High Court in the appropriate division and all lower courts.

An appeal by way of case stated lies to the House of Lords under the Administration of Justice Act 1960 s 1(1)(a), providing leave is obtained and a point of law of general public importance is in question. By s 18(1) of the Supreme Court Act 1981, criminal matters are not to be dealt with on appeal to the Court of Appeal, but directly by the House of Lords under s 1 of the 1960 Act.

2.5   The High Court

The High Court together with the Court of Appeal and the Crown Court comprise the Supreme Court of Judicature. As we have noted the High Court is made up of the Queen's Bench, the Chancery and the Family Divisions.

The Queen's Bench Division is the busiest, trying large numbers of cases in contract and tort particularly personal injury claims. It has a residual jurisdiction over all cases which are not dealt with by the other divisions.

The Commercial Court was established by the Administration of Justice Act 1970 as a separate court. Within this division, the judges are empowered to act as arbitrators. In addition there is an Admiralty Court.

As we have noted before, this division exercises a supervisory jurisdiction over inferior courts and tribunals and regulates the actions of public bodies by way of judicial review. The prerogative writ of *habeas corpus* and the orders of *certiorari, prohibition* and *mandamus* may be granted in appropriate circumstances.

The Chancery Division deals with contested probate matters, trusts, mortgages, bankruptcy, company and partnership, sales of property and taxation matters. In addition there is a separate Patents Court and a Companies Court.

The Family Division has jurisdiction over matrimonial matters including dissolution of marriage, wardship, adoption and guardianship of minors. It also deals with uncontested probate matters.

The High Court is based in the Strand in London but in addition sits in some 15 regional centres and the judges of the High Court travel on circuit to the regions.

2.6   The Crown Court

The Courts Act 1971 abolished Quarter Sessions and Assizes and replaced them with the Crown Court which tries indictable offences (following committal proceedings in the magistrates' court, see para 2.8 below) and triable either way offences where the defendant elects jury trial rather than summary trial in the magistrates' court. There may be a tactical advantage for a defendant electing trial by jury in the Crown Court, this is most often used in cases of theft where the defendant, or his or her defence counsel, may feel more confident of an acquittal before a jury compared with a case-hardened magistrate.

By the Criminal Justice Act 1988 the right in the defence to make challenges of potential jury members (known as the right to a peremptory challenge) was removed with the result that the defence can now only make challenges by showing good reason.

The Runciman Commission recommended in 1993 that the right of the defendant to elect jury trial should be limited but this has not been included in the Criminal Justice Bill presently before Parliament. The Supreme Court Act 1981 regulates its work. Crown Courts also have limited civil jurisdiction mainly in licensing matters.

The Crown Court also hears appeals from magistrates' courts and have the power to sentence defendants tried summarily for offences triable either way where the sentencing powers of the magistrates' courts are insufficient. This is governed by s 38 of the Magistrates' Court Act 1980 as amended by s 25 of the Criminal Justice Act 1990. It applies to defendants aged 18 or over where the magistrates are of the opinion that the offence or combination of offences associated with it, was so serious as to warrant a greater punishment than is within their power, or that a term of imprisonment longer than the court can impose is necessary to protect the public from serious harm where a violent or sexual offence has been committed by a defendant aged 21 or over.

County courts are governed by the County Courts Act 1984 as amended and are presided over by a Circuit Judge, who normally sits alone. Some 300 county courts exist in England and Wales administered by District Judges. The Courts and Legal Services Act 1991 s 74 removed the office of Registrar and this was replaced by that of District Judge with effect from 1 January 1991.

The county court is a local court which traditionally had a limited jurisdiction determined by way of geographical area and the value of the claim. The High Court and County Courts Jurisdiction Order 1991 made under ss 1 and 120 of the Courts and Legal Services Act 1990 by the Lord Chancellor with effect from 1 July 1991 abolishes many of the financial limits on county court jurisdiction, and stipulates higher limits in some cases and lays down criteria for determining where proceedings are to be commenced, tried and enforced.

In essence most claims below £25,000 are to be tried in the county court as are equity and probate matters up to £30,000 and personal injury claims up to £50,000. Claims of between £25,000 and £50,000 which do not involve complex law or fact can be tried in the county court and also straightforward claims over £50,000 which had been started in the High Court can be transferred to the county court.

The small claims procedure is to be used for claims up to £1,000 in value and for claims in excess of this value where both parties agree and complex matters are not involved. This provides an informal arbitration procedure where a party appears in person or assisted by a lay person. Usually it will not be necessary to have legal representation and in any event costs for legal representation are not awarded. It is an alternative to the formal and often expensive county court trial. Most small claims involve sale or supply of goods and services, debt or accident claims.

The Courts and Legal Services Act 1990 s 11 provides a framework for the removal of restrictions on lay representation in county court claims. By s 11(1) the Lord Chancellor is empowered to make orders removing any such restrictions on representation by lay persons sometimes referred to as 'McKenzie Friends' (from the case of *McKenzie v McKenzie* (1971)).

2.7   The county court

Magistrates' courts hear some 98% of all criminal cases and, in addition, have limited civil jurisdiction in matrimonial and licensing matters. By s 10 of the Courts and Legal Services Act 1990 provision is made for civil jurisdiction in family proceedings under the Children Act 1989.

2.8   The magistrates' court

Some 560 magistrates' courts exist throughout England and Wales staffed by lay or stipendiary magistrates, or as they are traditionally called Justices of the Peace. In larger towns and cities stipendiary magistrates sit alone to decide cases whereas lay magistrates usually form a bench of three, but any number between two and seven may sit. They are advised by a Clerk to the Justices but he or she can only offer advice as to the law and not assist the magistrates in reaching their decisions. In 1992 some 29,000 lay magistrates and 76 stipendiary magistrates had been appointed.

As we have already seen, offences fall into one of three categories:

- indictable;

- triable either way; or

- summary offences.

The magistrates' court can try summary offences and those which are triable either way where the defendant does not elect trial by jury in the Crown Court. The Magistrates' Courts Act 1980 ss 31, 32 and 133 set out the magistrates' sentencing powers. The maximum sentence which can be imposed for a triable either way offence listed in Schedule 1 of the Magistrates' Courts Act 1980 and which is tried summarily is generally £5,000 and/or six months' imprisonment for any one offence. Triable either way offences not listed in Schedule 1 are subject to a sentence of imprisonment of six months or the maximum period provided for in the Act creating the offence whichever is *less*. Whereas the maximum fine that can be imposed is the *greater* of £5,000 and the amount provided in the Act creating the offence.

For summary offences s 37 of the Criminal Justice Act 1982 as amended by s 17 of the Criminal Justice Act 1991 imposes a standard scale of fines ranging from £200 to £5,000.

As already noted s 38 of the Magistrates' Court Act as amended provides for committal for sentence to the Crown Court.

In the case of indictable offences the magistrates hold committal proceedings to examine the evidence against the defendant and establish whether a *prima facie* case has been made out by the prosecution warranting jury trial in the Crown Court.

There are two types of committal proceedings, the so-called 'old style' or 'full' committal, where the court hears the evidence for both sides, and a 'new style' or 'paper' committal, where the court does not hear witnesses, but relies on written evidence alone. Suggestions have been made for the abolition of old style committals which are now rarely used.

Appeals from magistrates' courts lie to the Crown Court against sentence only where the defendant pleaded guilty and against both conviction and sentence where he or she pleaded not guilty (s 108 Magistrates' Courts Act 1980). Appeals also lie to the Queen's Bench Division divisional court by the prosecution or the defence for judicial review or by way of case stated.

Magistrates also try cases in youth courts, formerly juvenile courts (renamed by the Criminal Justice Act 1991 s 70), against those aged under 18 years of age (s 68). By s 24(1) of the Magistrates' Court Act 1980 a juvenile must be tried summarily except in the case of homicide where he or she is jointly charged with an adult who is to be tried on indictment and the magistrates consider it is in the interests of justice to commit them both for trial; or the juvenile is 14 and is charged with an offence punishable with 14 years' imprisonment or more. The presumption is that juveniles are to be tried summarily in the youth court but in limited circumstances a juvenile may be tried in an adult's magistrates' court, for example, he is jointly charged with an adult or proceedings started on the basis that he was an adult.

There are several important differences between a youth court and an adult magistrates' court. The former should sit at a different time and place from the ordinary court; the general public should be excluded; the bench must have three magistrates one of whom should be a woman; reporting restrictions apply to details of the case and those involved; and the conduct of the proceedings is less formal.

At the outset we mentioned some specialist courts including the Judicial Committee of the Privy Council, Coroners' Courts, the Court of Protection and the Restrictive Practices Court. We will briefly consider each of these in turn.

2.9   Other courts

The Judicial Committee of the Privy Council consists of all Privy Councillors who hold (or have held) high judicial office including the Lord Chancellor and former occupants of this office, the Law Lords and Commonwealth judges.

2.9.2   The Judicial Committee of the Privy Council

Usually five members sit to hear appeals from those few Commonwealth countries which have retained a right of appeal. It also hears appeals from Ecclesiastical Courts and domestic tribunals including the General Medical Council. Its decisions are not binding either on itself or other UK courts but are of great persuasive authority.

2.9.2	Coroners' Courts	

Coroners investigate by way of inquest the cause of death and (most usually) where that death has been sudden, violent or unnatural. The death of prisoners, those in police custody and mental patients will also be investigated and a reason established for the cause of death.

The coroner, who must be a barrister, solicitor or medical doctor of at least five years' standing, may be assisted by a jury. Where it is suspected that death resulted from, for example, murder or manslaughter, poisoning or road accident, a jury must be summoned.

The identity of the deceased is then established and also the place and time of death. Various verdicts may be returned including death by natural causes, misadventure, suicide or unlawful killing. Coroners are not able to return a verdict implicating any person in the murder or manslaughter of a deceased. A case in point is the recent verdict of unlawful killing returned in connection with a serious road accident at Sourby Bridge in Yorkshire when several people were killed by a lorry that went out of control. This verdict can be used as evidence in any criminal prosecution that is brought by the Crown Prosecution Service and in civil proceedings by relatives in the tort of negligence.

Coroners also inquire into the ownership of property which is found and appears to have no owner. Gold, silver, coins, bullion and plate which have been hidden by someone unknown with the likely intention of returning to collect the horde is known as 'treasure trove'. This, by default, passes into the ownership of the Crown. An inquest determines whether such items are treasure trove or were abandoned or lost in which case the finder or the owner of the land or property on which they are found may have some claim to them.

2.9.3   The Court of Protection

The Court of Protection aims to protect and administer the property of those who are incapable of managing their affairs due to mental illness. The Mental Health Act 1983 provides for the appointment of judges of the Chancery Division to oversee the workings of the court. It is usual for close relatives of the patient to be appointed receiver of the property which is then managed for the benefit of the patient.

2.9.4   The Restrictive Practices Court

The Restrictive Practices Court investigates restrictive trading agreements between manufacturers of goods and those who provide services. The court is a superior court of record and its personnel are 'puisne' judges of the High Court appointed by the Lord Chancellor, one judge from Scotland and one from Northern Ireland. They are assisted by up to 10 lay assessors appointed by the Queen on the Lord Chancellor's recommendation having special knowledge or experience in industry.

One judge and two lay assessors sit to decide cases. Matters of law are decided by the judge. The lay assessors assist with questions of fact. The legislation with which the court is concerned includes the Restrictive Trade Practices Act 1976 and the Resale Prices Act 1976 as well as Articles 85 and 86 of the Treaty of Rome.

The Court System

Diagrams illustrate the structure of the courts, types of business dealt with and the personnel of each court. The courts can be classified into those exercising criminal or civil jurisdiction; appellate or first instance courts and superior or inferior courts.

- Appellate Jurisdiction Act 1876

- Administration of Justice Act 1969 - 'leapfrog' appeal

- Criminal Appeals Act 1968

- Practice Statement 1966

- Article 177 Treaty of Rome and Factortame case

Section 16 Supreme Court Act 1981 (as amended) – appeals from the High Court.

County Courts Act 1984 (as amended) – appeals from county courts.

Criminal Appeals Act 1968 – established a civil and a Criminal Division and provided for appeals from the Crown Court acting as a trial court in criminal matters. Section 17 provides for a reference by the Home Secretary to the Criminal Division in certain circumstances.

Section 36 Criminal Justice Act 1972 and ss 35 and 36 Criminal Justice Act 1988 provide for references by the Attorney-General to the Criminal Division.

Each division of the High Court has a divisional court which exercises appellate jurisdiction. The divisional court of the Queen's Bench hears appeals by way of case stated and applications for judicial review.

- Magistrates' Courts Act 1980 s 111

- Administration of Justice Act 1960 s 1(1)(a)

The High Court, Court of Appeal and the Crown Court comprise the Supreme Court of Judicature. The business of each of the three divisions (Queen's Bench, Chancery and Family) are considered as are specialist courts such as the Commercial Court.

The Crown Court

The Crown Court tries indictable and those triable either way offences where the defendant elects jury trial. Business is regulated by the Supreme Court Act 1981.

The Crown Court also has an appellate jurisdiction and the power to sentence defendants tried summarily for offences triable either way (s 38 Magistrates' Court Act 1980 (as amended by s 25 Criminal Justice Act 1990)).

The county court

The business of the court is described, including the small claims procedure. Changes in jurisdiction and replacement of Registrars with the title 'District Judge' brought about by the Courts and Legal Services Act 1990 are mentioned.

The High Court and County Courts Jurisdiction Order 1991.

The magistrates' court

The jurisdiction of the court in criminal matters is described including trial of summary offences and those triable either way where the defendant does not elect jury trial. Committal proceedings are also noted as are committals to the Crown Court for sentencing. The sentencing powers of magistrates under ss 31, 32 and 133 of the Magistrates' Courts Act 1980 and s 37 of the Criminal Justice Act 1982 (as amended by s 17 of the Criminal Justice Act 1991) are noted. Appeals to Crown Court and Queen's Bench Divisional Court are mentioned as is the role of magistrates in the youth court (formerly the juvenile court).

Other courts

The jurisdiction and functions of the following specialist courts are briefly considered:

- The Judicial Committee of the Privy Council
- Coroners Courts
- The Court of protection
- The Restrictive Practices Court

Chapter 3

The Personnel of the Courts

We have already mentioned in passing some of the personnel of the courts, but here we will treat each in greater detail and consider some of their roles. It will become clear that reference to 'the judges' is not to a homogeneous group but rather a disparate collection of individuals who work at different levels.

Two issues are of particular importance:

- the question of the selection and appointment of judges and their suitability for the roles performed; and

- the role of the judge in making decisions and in developing the law to meet changing needs.

As we have seen, magistrates are either unpaid voluntary appointees who form a bench of between two to seven members or are stipendiary or paid magistrates who sit alone to decide cases in courts in London and other large cities.

The lay magistrate can claim expenses for travelling, loss of earnings and subsistence and is usually not qualified in the law. They are appointed by the Lord Chancellor under s 6 of the Justices of the Peace Act 1979 and various disqualifications apply, for example, undischarged bankrupts. In practice others will not be appointed including those over the age of 60 and those convicted of serious offences.

Two main criticisms are made of the appointment process:

- that it favours appointment of the socially better off; and

- that it fails to accommodate the ethnic minorities.

The Lord Chancellor attempts to maintain a political balance as well as balance between the sexes. The ratio of male to female is about 3:2. There is also the need to attract younger people to seek selection. Local advisory committees advise the Lord Chancellor and they are assisted by area subcommittees whose members' names remain secret.

Within one year of appointment the newly appointed magistrate must undertake a training course in sentencing aims and practice, criminal law and evidence and the role of the court clerk and others.

Magistrates are required to sit at least 26 times a year and in practice most sit more frequently and thereby acquire experience and training whilst performing their role.

3.1 Introduction

3.2 Magistrates

Section 6 of the 1979 Act also provides for the removal of magistrates by the Lord Chancellor where circumstances demand, for example, where they are convicted of a serious offence. By s 8 a magistrate's name may be placed on the supplemental list and as a result he or she will not be able to sit in court but will be entitled to retain the title of Justice of the Peace and carry out minor functions such as the witnessing of documents. This will be done if a magistrate becomes unfit to carry out judicial duties and on reaching the age of 70 (or, in the case of those who have held high judicial office, the age of 75).

Sections 13 and 31 formerly provided for stipendiary magistrates to be appointed by the Queen on the recommendation of the Lord Chancellor from barristers and solicitors of at least seven years standing. The Courts and Legal Services Act 1990 replaces eligibility by status with advocacy qualification. Retirement is at the age of 70, unless the Lord Chancellor permits an extension to the age of 72, and removal can be ordered for misbehaviour or incapacity.

Magistrates are appointed for a commission area and outside of London this is equivalent to a county. In London there are six commission areas. Magistrates must reside within 15 miles of their commission area unless the Lord Chancellor otherwise directs. Each commission area is divided into petty sessional divisions and each division has a court. A magistrate is assigned to a court by the Lord Chancellor and this is usually the division in which he or she resides or works. Section 19 of the 1979 Act provides for the appointment of a magistrates' courts Committee made up of magistrates from each division to oversee administrative matters and the appointment of magistrates' clerks under s 26.

Section 26 has been amended by the Courts and Legal Services Act 1990 to provide for advocacy qualifications as defined in s 71(3). Magistrates' clerks were appointed from barristers or solicitors of at least five years standing or who had at least five years experience as an assistant to a magistrates' clerk. The Justices' Clerk (Qualifications of Assistants) Rules 1979 provide that an assistant cannot act as a clerk in court unless qualified as a barrister or solicitor or has undergone specified training.

Section 117 of the Courts and Legal Services Act 1990 amends s 28 of the Justices of the Peace Act 1979 to enable rules to be made under s 144 of the Magistrates' Courts Act 1980 for the delegation of the duties and powers entrusted to a magistrates' clerk to his or her deputy or assistant.

The clerk performs two main roles namely court administration and advising the magistrates on the law. Clerks are not empowered to make decisions for or on behalf of magistrates but can only offer advice as to the relevant law or powers of sentencing. In *R v Uxbridge Justices ex p Smith* (1985) it was held that the clerk could offer advice to the magistrates after they had retired to consider their decision, but should not attempt to advise them on their decision. The Practice Direction (Justices: Clerk to the Court) 1981 sets out guidance as to the role of the magistrates' clerk.

District judges are appointed by the Lord Chancellor from solicitors of at least seven years' standing and were formerly known as county court registrars. Section 74 of the Courts and Legal Services Act 1990 created the new title of district judge with effect from 1 January 1991.

3.3   District judges

Eligibility for appointment is now governed by s 71 and Schedule 10 of the 1990 Act which provides for advocacy qualifications. His or her main function is to act as a clerk in charge of the administration of the county court and operates the small claims arbitration procedure. In addition he or she is empowered to decide other cases where the parties agree and where a point of law is not in question. Where the law is in dispute or the facts complex the claim it is decided by the county court judge.

These are appointed by the Crown on the advice of the Lord Chancellor and formerly were barristers of at least 10 years' standing or Recorders in post for at least five years. Section 16(3) of the Courts Act 1971 has been amended by the Courts and Legal Services Act 1990 s 71 and Schedule 10 and replaces eligibility by status with advocacy qualifications.

3.4   Circuit judges

Office-holders such as district judges and chairs of industrial tribunals are eligible for appointment having been in post full-time for at least three years. Circuit judges serve in the Crown Court and county court.

Recorders are part-time judges who sit in the Crown Court and who formerly were appointed by the Crown on the advice of the Lord Chancellor from barristers or solicitors of at least 10 years' standing. Provision is now made for appointment based on advocacy qualifications. On appointment a recorder is required by the Courts Act 1971 to sit for not less than one month each year.

3.5   Recorders

High Court judges are also known as 'puisne' judges or justices of the High Court and are appointed by the Queen on the Lord Chancellor's advice. Formerly barristers of at least 10

3.6   Judges of the High Court

years' standing were eligible but the Courts and Legal Services Act s 71 and Schedule 10 provide for appointment from those with a 10 year High Court qualification or from circuit judges in post for at least two years. There are at present some 83 High Court judges assigned throughout the three divisions and they hear the most serious offences in the Crown Court.

3.7	**Lord Justices of Appeal**	Lord Justices sit in both divisions of the Court of Appeal and are appointed by the Queen on the advice of the Prime Minister. At present there are some 27 in number. Formerly they were appointed from barristers of 15 years' standing or from High Court (puisne) judges but s 71 and Schedule 10 of the Courts and Legal Services Act 1990 provide for appointment from those with a 10 year High Court qualification or from judges of the High Court.

3.8   Lords of Appeal in Ordinary

Lords of Appeal in Ordinary are more usually referred to as the 'Law Lords' and, on appointment by the Queen on the Prime Minister's advice, become life peers.

Formerly barristers of at least 15 years' standing or 'puisne' judges in post for at least two years, or Lords Justice of Appeal were eligible for appointment but Schedule 10 of the 1990 Act amends s 6 of the Appellate Jurisdiction Act 1876 to take account of the advocacy qualification based on rights of audience.

It is usual for Lords Justice of Appeal to be appointed. They sit in the House of Lords and can perform both a judicial and a legislative function and are also members of the Judicial Committee of the Privy Council.

3.9   The Lord Chancellor

More is said of the Lord Chancellor's office in para 3.13 when we consider the judicial officers, but it is useful to note here that the Lord Chancellor, or to give him his full title, the Lord High Chancellor of Great Britain, ranks eighth in the order of precedence after the Queen and this denotes the status of his office as being the head of the English judiciary, President of the Chancery Division of the High Court and of the House of Lords in its judicial capacity.

He is appointed by the Queen on the Prime Minister's advice and performs functions in all three branches of government. In addition to being the head of the judiciary he is a member of the Cabinet and is Speaker of the House of Lords. He sits in the Judicial Committee of the Privy Council and as noted above he advises the Queen on the appointment of puisne, circuit judges and recorders and appoints magistrates.

The occupant of the Lord Chief Justice's office ranks next in importance to the Lord Chancellor and is appointed by the Queen on the advice of the Prime Minister and, on appointment, is made a life peer. He is head of the Queen's Bench Division of the High Court and the Criminal Division of the Court of Appeal.

3.10 The Lord Chief Justice of England and Wales

The Master of the Rolls is also appointed by the Queen on the advice of the Prime Minister and is head of the Civil Division of the Court of Appeal. He is responsible for the admission of solicitors to the Roll of the Supreme Court.

3.11 The Master of the Rolls

All those mentioned above except magistrates, district judges, circuit judges and recorders hold office 'during good behaviour' and may be removed from office by the Crown following an address to both Houses of Parliament.

Salaries are paid out of the Consolidated Fund and are fixed by statute. This ensures that judges of the superior courts are independent of the Executive. The Judicial Pensions and Retirement Act 1993 makes provision for the retirement of all judges at the age of 70, whereas previously retirement was at 75 for High Court judges and 72 for circuit judges (with the possibility of an extension for a further three years). This change is to be phased in and will not affect any judge presently in post.

3.12 Terms of employment

Having discussed the structure of the courts, their functions and the personnel of the courts, we should consider the issues arising from the appointment and selection of the judges and the effectiveness of the judge in developing the law to meet changing needs.

3.13 Selection and effectiveness

So far as the selection and appointment of judges is concerned we have seen that 'the judges' is not a homogenous concept, and a distinction can be made between judges of the superior courts, appointed by the Queen on the advice of the Prime Minister, and those of the inferior courts appointed by the Lord Chancellor.

Some critics question why it is that the Prime Minister should have any involvement in appointments; there is an inherent danger that the judiciary may be manipulated by a strong Prime Minister and government to serve its political goals. Furthermore appointment by the Lord Chancellor is not without its critics and it has on many occasions been proposed that the office of Lord Chancellor be replaced by a Ministry of Justice.

3.13.1 Selection and appointment

The present Lord Chancellor, Lord Mackay of Clashfern, has shown the potential, if not actual, conflicts in interest between legislative, executive and judicial functions which he performs. His zeal for reforming the courts, legal services and the provision of legal aid and advice has brought him into conflict with the Law Society, the General Council of the Bar and others concerned with the legal system.

On the question of the independence of the judiciary the means by which members of the judiciary can be removed from office is also important. As we have noted superior court judges hold office 'during good behaviour' and can only be removed by a joint resolution of both Houses of Parliament.

Even where independence is prized (albeit not guaranteed by a written constitution) this will not ensure that the decisions made are impartial. There is usually no question of blatant bias in the sense of bribery or corruption but rather the suggestion that the composition of the judiciary is such that judges are drawn from a narrow section of society and give effect to the morals and values of that group. Judges are seen as 'establishment' figures who are remote from, and who have little understanding of, the pressures and motives of the general population.

The counter-argument suggests that the very fact that members of the judiciary are remote and have undergone training and gained experience means that wise and well considered decisions can be made. It is inevitable that some mistakes are made but these should be quickly remedied by way of an appeals system and ultimately by means of a review body independent of the judiciary.

The debate continues with suggestions that there should be greater opportunities for appointment from the ethnic minorities and from women. To speed up the process some would like to see positive discrimination in favour of these two groups but to date this has been rejected in favour of appointment on merit and the dismantling of many of the barriers to entry to the judiciary.

Helena Kennedy QC in *Eve Was Framed* describes the average British judge as white, male, conservative, Oxbridge and public school educated, and between the ages of 60 and 65. She quotes statistics prepared by the Lord Chancellor's Department for March 1991 to the effect that 'only one judge out of 550 was black' and only 'one Lord Justice, two High Court judges and 19 circuit judges were female'. She highlights the often subtle prejudice and stereotyping that abound in the judiciary and that those who suffer in consequence of this are not only women and those from the ethnic minorities but also those who do not fit into traditionally accepted social groups such as homosexuals, gypsies, the unemployed and vagrants.

Traditionally members of the judiciary have been drawn from the ranks of barristers with very few exceptions. Judges have been appointed following secret deliberations between the higher ranks of the judiciary, the Lord Chancellor and the Prime Minister. Reasons are not given for non-appointment as is the case with the appointment of barristers to Queen's Counsel. However this is set to change following the Courts and Legal Services Act 1990 Part III ss 71 to 76 which permit those with an advocacy qualification based on rights of audience (as defined in s 71(3)(a)-(f)) granted by an authorised body to seek appointment.

In June 1993 the first solicitor, Michael Sachs, was appointed the first High Court judge from outside the Bar under these provisions. Sections 27 to 33 of the Act, which permit solicitors rights of audience in the higher courts having obtained advocacy certificates, will no doubt increase the numbers of solicitors who in future seek appointment to the judiciary.

The Bar Conference in 1993 highlighted the secrecy and non-accountability of the appointments system and speakers suggested that this leads to allegations of discrimination and loss of confidence. Calls were made for published selection criteria and for set targets for the appointment of women and those from the ethnic minorities.

Positive discrimination was rejected and full confidence in the present selection process, managed by the Lord Chancellor's Department, was expressed by Sir Thomas Legg, permanent secretary at the Department. He attempted to justify the wide but confidential consultation process in that it ensured those who were consulted would make valuable contributions. It was noted that the Lord Chancellor had made proposals for reform in July 1993, including progressive introduction of the use of open advertisement for judicial vacancies, better forecasting and planning of numbers and expertise of judges, more specific job descriptions and the qualities looked for, further encouragement to women and ethnic minority applicants, the involvement of suitable lay people in the selection process and progression towards competition for posts at the lower levels.

In 1992 'Justice', the all-party, independent law reform body, published a report of a committee chaired by Robert Stevens which recommended the creation of a judicial commission to oversee judicial appointments, training and the maintenance of high standards.

The Lord Chief Justice, Lord Taylor, rejected such proposals suggesting that the present system is satisfactory and that any such change would undermine the independence of the judiciary. Following publication of the Royal Commission Report on Criminal Justice he agreed that judges should become more interventionist so as to ensure advocates gave shorter speeches during trials thereby reducing costs and delay.

In 1978 the Judicial Studies Board was established following the publication of Lord Bridge's working party report with overall responsibility for judges' training. On appointment, one week's formal training takes place and visits are arranged to a prison and a young offender's institution, an interview with a probation officer and one week shadowing an experienced judge. Refresher courses are offered on a voluntary basis to assist judges in keeping abreast of changes in the law.

Comparisons can be drawn between our system and that in European states and America. Not only is the training more rigorous but the notion of a career judge pervades most other jurisdictions. This is unlike our system which has traditionally seen the appointment of judges only from the ranks of barristers. In France, for example, judges are appointed and trained 'on the job' and training lasts from four to six years. In America many of the judges are elected, so selection is conducted in public, with public participation, where the criteria for appointment are clearly stated.

It may be too much to suggest that we should move from an appointment to an elected system but proponents for reform suggest that the appointment system must become more open and accountable if the judiciary is to become more representative of society. Objective criteria open to public scrutiny can ensure that the most able candidates for appointment not only present themselves but become appointed. Many critics of the present system would welcome assurances that change will evolve but do not wish to see revolutionary changes. Given the involvement of judges in crucial areas of everyday life, both in the criminal law and in areas such as judicial review, it is vital that the appointment of members of the judiciary, training and discipline be seen to be more open and subject to scrutiny.

Professor Griffiths in *The Politics of the Judiciary* analysed the social class origins of the judges from 1820 to 1968 and concluded that the overwhelming majority of members were drawn from the upper and middle classes and were invariably male, middle-aged and public school and Oxbridge educated.

His study is no doubt dated but more recent studies, for example, in a survey conducted by the *Solicitors Journal* in

March 1992 of the general public in six major towns, some 65% considered that judges are out of touch with everyday life. Some 79% considered that there should be more women judges and 69% that judges should be appointed to reflect ethnic mix. Some 47% thought that judges should retire at 65 and 23% at the age of 60.

Tony Gifford, a barrister, published research in 1986 which confirmed the narrow social background of the judges and studies by the Lord Chancellor's Department confirm the minority representation of women and ethnic minorities. In addition in a study commissioned by the Bar Council and the Lord Chancellor's department in 1992 sexual discrimination at the Bar was shown in obtaining pupillage, conduct of interviews and the types of cases handled.

Recent cases suggest that some judges are out of touch with general feeling. Thus Judge Prosser sentenced a schoolboy rapist in Gwent to a three year supervision order and ordered compensation of £500 to his victim for 'a good holiday to help her get over the trauma'. This was subsequently overturned on appeal. Ian Starforth Hill QC referred in one case to the eight year old victim of a sexual attack as 'no angel' and in another case imposed a conditional discharge on two men who had unlawful intercourse with a 13-year-old girl.

Judge Raymond Dean was reported in the press as having told a jury trying an allegation of rape at an Old Bailey trial that 'when a woman says no she doesn't always mean it'.

In the face of these and many more instances reported in the press a radical overhaul of the appointments system was called for. 'Justice' as long ago as 1972 proposed the creation of an appointments committee to advise the Lord Chancellor.

At present the Lord Chancellor exercises an almost absolute discretion based on such factors as professional ability, experience, standing and integrity, sound temperament and physical health regardless of sexual or ethnic origin, political affiliation or religion. He obtains evidence of these qualities confidentially from members of the judiciary and outside observers. Critics suggest that this is inward looking and favours those candidates who fit the preconceptions and stereotypes of those already in post. Furthermore the system is not open to scrutiny and is subjective in nature.

Two other points are worthy of mention:

- The changing practice of judges being permitted to speak on public occasions: this has been exemplified by the Lord Chief Justice openly disagreeing with the Lord Chancellor and airing his views following the Report of the Royal Commission on Criminal Justice, his opposition to the Asylum Bill and proposed cuts in legal aid provision. In the past a convention had developed that judges, other than the Lord Chancellor, would not make political or otherwise controversial statements in public. Lord Chancellors adopted what became known as the 'Kilmuir Rules' whereby judges were advised not to participate in radio or television programmes;

- The need to appoint more High Court judges led to a confrontation between the Lord Chief Justice and the Lord Chancellor early in 1993 when the former was interviewed by *The Sunday Times* and was quoted as saying that 83 High Court judges were insufficient resulting in an over-stretched system.

3.13.2 The effectiveness of the judge as law-maker

We will now move on to consider the role of the judge in making decisions and developing the law.

The declaratory theory of law states that judges do not make but merely declare what the law is and as a consequence the social characteristics and values of the judge is of no importance. The judge makes decisions founded on the statement of the law to be found in precedent or statute and has no power to make law or inconsistent decisions.

Both Bentham and John Austin concluded that judges do in fact make law. Bentham described the common law as 'the product of Judge & Co' and Austin wrote that judges made law as a result of the implicit command of the sovereign. Both Bentham and Austin were 19th century positivists who were concerned with the law as it is rather than with how it ought to be. Neither attempted to deny that the law might have faults and in the case of Bentham he described the common law as 'dog's law' in that it was only after a wrong had been committed that a penalty would be imposed. However, the positivist school suggests a limited judicial role in making law in that the judge should not attempt to usurp the role of Parliament and concern himself with policy issues. On the one hand, the declaratory theory suggests that the judge does not at any time or in any way make law, whereas at the other extreme, it is suggested that judges are a product of the society in which they live and work and as a result make value-laden choices when making decisions. This is not to deny their independence and impartiality but rather to recognise that their backgrounds and past experiences will have some bearing on their decisions. It must be noted however that this takes no account of their training and experience which instils objectivity and acts as a counterweight to personal influences.

It is surely a question of degree, rather than saying that judges do not at any time or in any way make law (the declaratory theory), or at the other extreme that judges are law-makers in the sense of legislators concerned with ensuring its development in a particular way to meet certain goals. It is suggested that the better approach is to recognise that where there is no clear relevant rule in precedent or statute governing the question in dispute, the judge will develop the law by reference to principle or logical consistency and in so doing may resort to extra-legal matters such as morality, justice, expediency or social policy to justify his decision.

Judges are most often concerned with piecemeal development of the law rather than wholesale changes to effect their vision of how the law should respond to or shape major questions. Social policy in our age is left to Parliament as the representative of the people and to whom those concerned with or about reform in the law can lobby and make known their views. This is not to deny that judges have views on the purposes of law in general and particular laws and of their own role in society, but these views should not have free rein as judges are not elected and only deal with disputes as and when they arise.

The recent House of Lords decision in *Cambridge Water Company v Eastern Counties Leather plc* (1993) illustrates the relationship of judge and Parliament. Lord Goff, delivering the main speech, said that:

> '... it did not follow from those developments [legislation imposing liability for environmental pollution on the basis of the polluter pays principle} that a common law principle such as the rule in *Rylands v Fletcher* should be developed or rendered more strict to provide for liability in respect of such pollution.'

In the result it was considered appropriate that strict liability in *Rylands v Fletcher* should only arise on proof of foreseeability of damage.

The outcome might well have been different had not Parliament enacted the Environmental Protection Act 1990 and other legislation to give effect to European obligations or if the decision had been made several years ago. The tort of negligence is largely regulated by the common law and continues to develop, albeit within bounds, for example, in the area of nervous shock claims.

This is illustrated in the House of Lords case of *Alcock v Chief Constable of South Yorkshire Police* (1992) involving claims arising out of the Hillsborough Stadium disaster where *dicta* of Lord Wilberforce in *McLoughlin v O'Brian* (1983) were applied so that liability for nervous shock would only arise where such injury was reasonably foreseeable and other conditions were satisfied including proximity of the relationship between the plaintiff and the defendant; ties of love and affection; proximity of time and space of the plaintiff to the accident; or its immediate aftermath. Lord Oliver warned against extending the law in a direction for which there was no pressing policy need and no logical stopping point as this was the province of Parliament following public debate and representation as to where the line ought to be drawn. He considered the position of a mother who sees her son negligently walk in front of a car and who, as a result, suffers nervous shock. Proximity and foreseeability could be proved but the policy of the law might prohibit a claim on the basis that the son had not acted tortiously towards his mother. He suggested even greater complexity might arise where the son had been 75% to blame and the car driver 25% to blame and that such policy considerations should be tackled by Parliament as is the case in Australia.

In past times, courts may well have had the primary role in deciding the future course of the law but in recent years judges have deferred to Parliament in many areas and emphasised the need for logical consistency and to decide similar cases alike. This rather begs the question what is meant by similar cases and inevitably the judge has to make choices. However, the judge is not alone in his task. He is assisted in the adversarial system by the advocate who presents a dispassionate view of the law and helps the judge in reaching a reasoned decision after weighing the available options.

By reasoning from well established rules or principles the integrity and independence of the judiciary is preserved. Binding precedent ensures continuity and certainty in the law although it may lead to rigidity. The *ratio decidendi* depends on principle but a later court may widen or narrow its application.

Other means by which the law may develop include the use of distinguishing previous cases on their facts, overruling and disapproving and holding that an otherwise binding precedent was decided *per incuriam*. The common law may need to be flexible where Parliament is slow to act. In areas involving moral issues the judges may extend the law by prohibiting actions which they consider to be wrong. Should their view of what is right or wrong conflict with popular opinion Parliament may well be called on to pass amending legislation. The recent House of Lords case of *R v Brown* (1993), involving prosecutions under ss 20 and 47 of the Offences

Against the Person Act 1861 for sado-masochistic actions, illustrate the two opposing views that where legislation should prohibit socially undesirable behaviour the courts should apply it, and it is for Parliament to rectify any error. The alternative view taken by those who dissented was that the benefit of the doubt should lie in favour of the defendants and if this was unsatisfactory it was for Parliament to make such actions unlawful.

The policy issues involving questions of life and death were considered in *Airedale NHS Trust v Bland* (1993) when the House of Lords decided that treatment of a patient in a persistent vegetative state could lawfully be ended where it was shown that there was no hope of recovery. The court emphasised that euthanasia was prohibited by law and that, in cases such as this one, safeguards be provided by the court and that all the issues should soon be considered by Parliament.

Professor Dworkin in his writings on law and the legal system disagreed with Professor Hart that law was merely a system of rules. Dworkin distinguished between rules, principles and policies which he called 'rules' and 'non-rule standards'. He rejected the idea that judges should, or do make law stating that they look for the soundest theory to assist them in deciding hard cases. The judge is concerned with the formulation of principle whereas Parliament is concerned with policy. Principles must be weighed and may conflict but they provide reasons for deciding a case in a certain way. Policy is a standard which sets out a social goal to be achieved. It is not the province of the courts. Dworkin referred to the New York case of *Riggs v Palmer* (1889) to illustrate the principle that 'no man should profit from his own wrongdoing', which was applied to reach a solution where a murderer claimed to be entitled under his victim's will. The rule allowing inheritance created uncertainty and it was held that it was overridden by the fundamental principle.

Principles may lead to the development of a rule or alternatively a rule may lead to the formulation of a principle. We have referred to the cases of *R v Registrar-General ex p Smith* (1990) and *Re Sigsworth* (1935) when considering statutory interpretation (Chapter 1 para 1.2.5) and these illustrated the dilemma facing a court where a clear rule conflicted with a fundamental principle. The court in each case looked to the issue of policy and decided each on the basis of the principle. Should the courts overstep the limits of law-making it will be for Parliament to redefine the boundaries as to the future scope and effect of the law.

Professor Dworkin talked of the role of the judge in deciding 'hard' cases where no rule applied by which the judge was bound. As *Ex p Smith* and *Re Sigsworth* demonstrate, this may be interpreted by the court to include a case where although a rule applies, the judge prefers not to apply it on the grounds of unfairness or public policy. In this sense the judge does make law and justifies his or her doing so by reference to principle or fairness. The result may be short-lived, for if Parliament passes amending legislation in specific terms the course of the law may be changed.

3.14   Judicial officers

In this section we shall consider the roles of the Lord Chancellor, the Attorney-General, the Solicitor-General and the Director of Public Prosecutions.

3.14.1   The Lord Chancellor

As we have already noted (at para 3.8), the Lord Chancellor carries out roles in all three branches of government. He is head of the judiciary and is President of the Supreme Court. He is a member of the Cabinet and is the Speaker of the House of Lords.

The constitutional position of the office of Lord Chancellor has recently come into question, given the political controversy over cuts in legal aid provision and reform of the courts and the legal profession. The Lord Chancellor has faced challenges by way of judicial review on the question of legal aid provision and, although these were not successful, the court held that the Law Society had a sufficient interest in bringing the claim and a legitimate expectation to be consulted before changes were brought about.

Such challenges illustrate the potential conflict which can arise between the political and judicial functions performed and warned against in the doctrine of separation of the legislative, judicial and executive powers. In recent years calls have been made for a Ministry of Justice to replace the office of Lord Chancellor which has existed for centuries in an attempt to ensure a more equal separation of powers.

3.14.2   The Attorney-General

The Attorney-General is a political appointment like that of his deputy, the Solicitor-General. Traditionally, he has been appointed by the Queen from the ranks of barristers but this may change in the future since the passing of the Courts and Legal Services Act 1990.

He represents the Crown in civil cases and as prosecutor in important criminal cases such as serious breaches of the Official Secrets Acts. Some prosecutions cannot commence without his consent and others, for example a private prosecution, may be terminated by his entering a *nolle prosequi* (an order not to proceed). He is head of the English Bar and supervises the work of the Director of Public Prosecutions. He is also principal legal adviser to the government, particularly on issues of international and constitutional laws.

The Attorney-General represents the public interest for example in cases where a public nuisance is alleged. The case of *Airedale NHS Trust v Bland* (1993) is instructive in that the Attorney-General was represented as *amicus curiae* (friend of the court) and submitted that it would be in the best interests of the patient for treatment to cease.

The present occupant of the office, Sir Nicholas Lyell, has recently been called to give evidence before the judicial inquiry into 'the arms to Iraq affair' chaired by Scott LJ. The advice dispensed to government ministers in connection with their signature of public interest immunity certificates issued under s 28 of the Crown Proceedings Act 1947 has been questioned and members of the Opposition have called for his resignation.

As already noted, the Solicitor-General assists the Attorney-General in the carrying out of his functions and acts as his deputy in his absence or when a vacancy occurs. Like the Attorney this is a political appointment and despite the title, the Solicitor-General has traditionally been appointed from the ranks of barristers.

3.14.3 The Solicitor-General

The Prosecution of Offences Act 1985 radically altered the system of prosecutions in England and Wales by establishing the Crown Prosecution Service (CPS) and in redefining the powers of the Director of Public Prosecutions (DPP). It is the responsibility of the DPP, the present occupant of the office being Barbara Mills, to co-ordinate prosecution policy and oversee the running of the independent prosecution service. Since the passing of the 1985 Act it is the DPP who decides which cases are to be prosecuted.

3.14.4 The Director of Public Prosecutions

The police are charged with the investigation of crime and, on completion of their investigations, the file must be handed to the CPS for a decision to be made as to whether a prosecution is to be brought.

The CPS is established in regional centres each with a Chief Crown Prosecutor who is assisted by Crown Prosecutors. Much criticism has been made of the lack of efficiency of the CPS and of the many decisions not to proceed with a prosecution or where a prosecution has commenced but no evidence is offered at the hearing with the result that the case fails.

With the coming into force of ss 27 to 33 of the Courts and Legal Services Act 1990 giving solicitors rights of audience in the higher courts, no decision has yet been reached as to whether solicitors employed by the CPS (and elsewhere) should be given extended rights of audience.

3.15   The legal profession

Traditionally, we have had a divided legal profession in England and Wales. Legal practitioners have trained and practised either as solicitors or barristers. The barrister has been seen by some to be the senior member of the profession advising and representing the client in court only on the recommendation of a solicitor. The solicitor is often described as the general practitioner of the profession advising the client direct, preparing documents on the client's behalf, such as wills and contracts, and representing the client only in the lower courts. Solicitors are the 'office' lawyers to be found in any high street or business quarter of towns and cities and who since 1985 have been able to advertise the types of services offered.

Legal executives are a body of legal professionals in their own right who work in solicitors' offices. Traditionally they were referred to as solicitors' 'managing clerks' but in recent times they have had much more responsibility for their own work usually in the areas of matrimonial, conveyancing and probate matters. They have their own governing body, the Institute of Legal Executives.

The relationship between barrister and solicitor and that of the client is governed by rules of etiquette many of which have been, and no doubt will be, further relaxed following the reforms under the Courts and Legal Services Act 1990. One of the purposes of the rules was to maintain the division and the monopolies of both sides of the profession, for example, the barrister maintained a monopoly over rights of audience, that is the right to represent clients, in all courts.

Thus the primary function of most barristers was to act as advocates and this craft was learnt largely 'on the job' during one year spent in pupillage (under the supervision of an experienced barrister) and following Call to the Bar by appearing in magistrates' and county courts. During the first six months of pupillage the pupil expects to be closely supervised by the pupil master and assists the latter by reading instructions from solicitors, drafting documents and accompanying the pupil master to court. In the latter six months the pupil might be permitted to take cases on his own behalf and work with much less supervision.

Not all barristers spend the majority of their time in court or preparing for trial. Those at the Chancery Bar for example spend much of their time receiving instructions from solicitors to offer advice on points of law concerning disputed wills or rights on intestacy, transfers of property or rights under trusts and settlements. However, the result is a detachment from direct contact with the client and the needs of running a business.

Barristers operate as sole practitioners, unlike solicitors who usually form partnerships, in what are known as 'sets of chambers'. Traditionally these are offices where the barrister takes a tenancy of a room and pays for the privilege of having the services of a clerk to chambers. Most are located in London near the Inns of Court and the law courts. The four Inns of Court (Gray's Inn, Lincoln's Inn, Inner and Middle Temples) are the only surviving Inns (there were many others dating back to the 14th century).

For some years the provincial Bar has been developing with barristers setting up chambers in modern offices outside London and no doubt this will continue apace with the changes brought about by the Courts and Legal Services Act 1990.

Barristers are now able to advertise their services and to come increasingly into direct touch with clients, in particular professional and corporate clients. Following the academic stage of training a student seeking Call to the Bar is required to join an Inn and dine in hall on 18 occasions. Each Inn is governed by senior members known as Benchers, who are often judges, who regulate conduct and discipline. Traditionally the Inn was not only a place of work but where barristers lived and this is thought to be one reason for the continuation of dining to ensure the perpetuation of the customs and traditions of this side of the profession.

The academic stage involves a law graduate or student (who has passed the Common Professional Examination or a Diploma in Law, offered at a recognised institution), taking a full-time one year course at the Council of Legal Education in London leading to the Bar Final examinations. Having completed the examinations and dining the student applies for Call to the Bar by his or her Inn of Court.

Barristers can be of two ranks, the senior known as 'Queen's Counsel' and the less senior known as 'Juniors' (although this has nothing to do with age). Those who have been in practice and who consider the time is right may apply to the Lord Chancellor's department for the change in title and status. Application is made each year and not all will be successful at the first or later attempts. No reasons are given for refusal and deliberations are conducted in secret. An applicant who is successful is entitled to have 'QC' after his or her name, may be assisted in court by junior counsel and is entitled to wear a strip of silk on his or her gown whilst in court. This has given rise to the reference to 'taking silk' by a barrister appointed as a QC. The other consequence of appointment is that the QC is more able to choose the cases he or she wishes to take and is not so strictly bound by the 'cab-rank' rule, which provides that a barrister should be ready and willing to take any case of a type with which he is familiar passed to him or her by the clerk to chambers.

The barrister has for some two centuries been extremely visible when appearing in court due to the robe, wig, wing collars and black attire required as standard dress. This is only one area which demonstrates that the legal profession is steeped in history and tradition and that the pace of change is often slow.

However, a debate was generated in 1992 as to whether wigs and robes should be disbanded and although this was settled in October 1993 in favour of retention of wigs and gowns the question has re-emerged following the ending of the barristers' monopoly over rights of audience in December 1993. In October 1993 a joint statement by the Lord Chancellor and Lord Taylor, the Lord Chief Justice, confirmed that judges and members of the legal profession should retain wigs and gowns.

A consultation paper in 1992 received responses from 520 organisations and individuals, 67% of which were in favour of retaining daily court dress. Only 15% favoured total abolition of all formal dress. It was thought that the authority and status of the court, the law and the profession were assured by maintenance of formal dress. The question has now been posed as to whether solicitors who obtain advocacy certificates under ss 27-33 of the Courts and Legal Services Act 1990 should wear wigs and black gowns or retain their traditional court dress of grey gown. It appears that representatives of the Bar will oppose adoption by solicitors of dress traditionally worn only by barristers although some still wish to see all formality removed.

The barrister receives written instructions known as a 'brief' from instructing solicitors which may involve any one or a combination of three things:

- it may require simply advice as to the appropriate law to be applied to the facts outlined in the brief;

- it may require the drafting of a document; or

- it may require representation by the barrister in court.

The barrister has traditionally had an honorarium arrangement with instructing solicitors. It has been binding in honour only with the result that a barrister has been unable to sue for his fees and in some cases solicitors or their firms have been blacklisted for consistent failure to pay fees promptly. This will now change whereby s 61 of the 1990 Act permits barristers to enter into legally binding contracts for the provision of their services.

By s 62 immunity from suit in the tort of negligence and breach of contract is extended to all those with advocacy rights, that is, covering the conduct of cases in court and the immediate preparation for trial. Thus the immunity also applies to those who become authorised litigators under ss 27 and 28 of the Act and to those authorised by the Lord Chancellor under s 11 to exercise rights of audience and to conduct litigation.

The common law established the immunity of barristers and the cases of *Rondel v Worsley* (1967) and *Saif Ali v Mitchell & Co* (1978) demonstrate that both barristers and solicitors, when acting as advocates, had immunity against claims in negligence. This rule has now been enacted under the above provisions. Not only is there immunity from civil claims but the Legal Services Ombudsman is not empowered to investigate allegations of misconduct of proceedings or matters closely connected with this under s 22(7)(b) of the Act although in his first annual report in 1992 the first Ombudsman, Michael Barnes, who was appointed on 1 January 1991 (and re-appointed in 1994), criticised this immunity and stated that he wished to challenge the limits of his jurisdiction.

The liability of a solicitor for negligent advice is clearly shown in *Ross v Caunters* (1979) which is mentioned in more detail in para 3.14.1. In *Kelly v ITE* (1982) the Court of Appeal held that an opposing client could sue a barrister for breach of duty, for negligent conduct of proceedings or preparation for trial. This will now apply to all who are authorised to conduct litigation or exercise rights of audience.

As we have seen, the traditional role of the solicitor has been that of the businessman offering legal services to lay and professional clients on a wide variety of legal, financial and other matters. Like the barrister with a monopoly over advocacy, the solicitor had various monopolies including land transactions (conveyancing), probate (the preparation of wills and the handling of estates on a person's death) and the right to conduct litigation.

The Administration of Justice Act 1985 abolished the conveyancing monopoly and established 'licensed conveyancers' able to compete with solicitors in the conduct of the purchase and sale of property. Sections 34 and 35 of the 1990 Act establish the Authorised Conveyancing Practitioners Board to develop competition and supervise authorised conveyancing practitioners. Section 53 permits the Council for Licensed Conveyancers to become an authorised body for the purposes of granting advocacy rights and rights to conduct litigation.

Conveyancing had been the 'bread and butter' work of the majority of small-to middle-size firms of solicitors and with its loss came calls for the abolition of the barristers' monopoly over rights of audience. The monopoly over probate matters has been removed by ss 54-55 of the 1990 Act and the right to conduct litigation by s 28 of the Act.

So as to avoid confusion it is worth noting the distinction between rights of audience (advocacy) and the right to conduct litigation. The interpretation section of the 1990 Act, s 119, offers assistance. The right to conduct litigation is the right to commence proceedings in any court and to have the conduct of matters which are ancillary to proceedings such as entering an appearance on behalf of a client. Rights of audience permit one person to represent another in court. Usually this will be for a fee but under s 11 of the Act a person may be assisted by a friend or lay adviser commonly referred to as a 'McKenzie Friend' from the case of *McKenzie v McKenzie* (1971).

In December 1993 it was announced that the Lord Chancellor and four senior judges had approved the application by the solicitors' governing body, the Law Society, for solicitors in private practice to be granted rights of audience in both civil and criminal proceedings in the House of Lords, the Court of Appeal, the High Court and the Crown Court. This was effected under ss 27-33 of the 1990 Act and alters the traditional divide between solicitors and barristers. Barristers will now have to compete with solicitors. This was much welcomed by the Law Society although it is uncertain how many of the 50,000 solicitors in private practice will undergo the necessary training to obtain advocacy certificates. Those in criminal practices reliant on legal aid funding will be the most likely to do so and also those engaged in commercial and financial work in London.

The General Council of the Bar, the governing body for barristers, stated that it was not adverse to fair competition but that solicitors should ensure that clients are advised of their right to be represented by a barrister. Two points should be mentioned here:

- solicitors have always had rights of audience in the lower courts, that is the county and magistrates' courts; and

- in limited cases solicitors have had a right to appear in the Crown Court for example on an appeal from the magistrates' and in certain Crown Courts designated by the Lord Chancellor such as Truro in Cornwall where in the past the cost and delay of having counsel travel from London or the provincial Bar could be prohibitive.

This is preserved by s 67 of the 1990 Act which substitutes a new s 83 of the Supreme Court Act 1981. Solicitors also had limited rights to appear in the High Court but usually only in chambers (the private rooms of the judge concerning matters which were not to be dealt with in open court, such as applications concerning children). In the case of *Abse & Others v Smith* (1986), a libel action involving the MP Cyril Smith, it was stated that a solicitor would be permitted to appear before the High Court to read out a prepared statement but was not entitled to present arguments to the court. It was the role of the barrister to present contentious issues to the court.

As we have noted, the governing body of solicitors is the Law Society which performs two roles. (Not all solicitors are members of the Society but those in practice are under an obligation to obtain and renew a practising certificate and contribute to the indemnity fund to cover claims brought by clients for malpractice.) The Society not only provides social facilities for its members but by regulations made under the Solicitors Act 1974 as amended, provides for the education and training of students, the discipline of all solicitors and the fees and scales of remuneration of solicitors.

Training to become a solicitor involves completion of the academic stage by way of law degree or non-law degree and Common Professional Examination or Diploma in Law, completion of the professional stage by way of a full-time Legal Practice Course at a recognised institution and the apprenticeship stage formerly referred to as 'articles of clerkship' but which is now referred to as the 'trainee solicitor' stage where practical experience is gained under the supervision of an experienced solicitor for two years.

Following qualification the trainee is admitted to the Roll of Solicitors maintained by the Law Society and supervised by the Master of the Rolls. Non-graduates who have qualified as legal executives may enter the profession once they have become Fellows of the Institute of Legal Executives and have completed the Legal Practice Course. Where continuous legal employment is shown the Law Society may waive the requirement that he or she undertakes traineeship.

Not all solicitors enter private practice; some take up appointments in the civil service, local government, the court service, for example, as magistrates' court clerks and with the Crown Prosecution Service. As noted above those who are not in private practice have not yet been granted rights of audience in the higher courts. Solicitors in the Crown Prosecution Service have made representations to the Lord Chancellor to have the rights of audience extended to them in the higher courts provided for under the 1990 Act.

Two other changes brought about by the 1990 Act permit the establishment of multi-disciplinary and multi-national practices (s 66) and arrangements for the charging of conditional fees (s 58). By s 66 all statutory and common law prohibitions on barristers and solicitors in England and Wales entering into partnerships with other professionals (such as accountants or taxation specialists) or foreign lawyers are removed, but the Law Society and Bar Council may make rules prohibiting or restricting their members from entering into such practices. By s 58 of the Act, those providing advocacy or litigation services are permitted to enter into a written contract for the fee to be payable 'only in specified circumstances' including where an action is successful. This section applies to barristers, solicitors and others offering services in personal injury claims, proceedings in the European Court of Human Rights or Commission and claims in insolvency. Such agreements have no effect where a client is legally aided and if entered into before the legal aid certificate is issued the agreement ceases to have effect on issue of a certificate.

The effect of such an agreement is that it provides for 'no win, no fee' but the fee will be the normal rate charged for that type of work uprated by a proposed maximum of 100% to cover the risk to the lawyer of having no fee if the case was lost.

Traditionally, solicitors in private practice have been restricted to operating as sole practitioners or in partnership with other solicitors. As we have seen, this has now changed in so far as those who can enter into partnership with solicitors. By s 90 of the Act, the Administration of Justice Act 1985 s 9 is amended to provide for contributions to the Compensation Fund (maintained by the Law Society to meet claims from clients who have suffered at the hands of a dishonest solicitor) from incorporated bodies with the effect that solicitors are now able to form limited companies.

3.15.1   Complaining about the
          legal profession

In the past much criticism has been made of the complaints procedures and in particular the lack of remedies available to a client aggrieved by the actions of a barrister. In December 1993 the Bar Council set up a 'standards review body' with lay membership to oversee the quality of service, fees and provide an overhaul of the complaints procedure. Shoddy standards and poor court performance are also to be tackled and it is likely that such conduct will result in warnings or disciplinary proceedings.

At the present time the Professional Conduct Committee of the Bar Council hears complaints against barristers and, in serious cases, these are referred to the Disciplinary Tribunal of the Inns of Court which has wide powers including suspending, fining up to £5,000 and striking off a barrister. No provision is made for the payment of compensation although the Tribunal may order that fees be repaid or forgone. A barrister may also be reprimanded or advised as to future conduct.

As we have noted, barristers have immunity from claims in the tort of negligence for their conduct in court, but as was shown in the case of *Saif Ali v Mitchell & Co* (1978) this does not apply to pre-trial advice.

Under ss 21-26 of the 1990 Act the Legal Services Ombudsman, appointed by the Lord Chancellor, replaces the office of the lay observer and oversees the handling of complaints against both solicitors and barristers. By s 21(7) of the Act the Ombudsman is prevented from investigating matters determined or being determined by a court, the Solicitors' Disciplinary Tribunal, the Disciplinary Tribunal of the Inns of Court, other tribunals specified by order of the Lord Chancellor and where immunity from suit applies.

So far as solicitors are concerned, an aggrieved client has several means at his or her disposal for obtaining redress although it may not be straightforward as is illustrated by the protracted litigation by Peggy Wood whose claim against several firms of solicitors and the Law Society itself has been ongoing for some 10 years. In recent years the number of complaints have soared.

In 1986 the Solicitors' Complaints Bureau was established and funded by, but acting independently of, the Law Society. Formerly all complaints were handled by the Law Society but little trust between the profession and the public was engendered given that the Law Society represents solicitors.

The Bureau has wide-ranging powers to effect a solution including conciliation, investigation and adjudication. If conciliation, which is voluntary and only appropriate where communication has not broken down, does not effect an amicable settlement, the more formal process of investigation may be resorted to. In serious cases the Bureau will refer the case to the Solicitors' Disciplinary Tribunal which has similar powers to the tribunal regulating barristers including the power to fine, strike off and suspend. Its findings are published and it has recently been announced that it will conduct its hearings in public. Appeal lies to the Queen's Bench Division Divisional Court of the High Court.

As we have noted, solicitors can be sued in the tort of negligence when not acting as advocates. The case of *Ross v Caunters* (1979) concerned the negligent preparation of a will and it was held that the solicitor was liable in tort to a third party who would have inherited under the will if it had been properly drafted. The Bureau has set up a panel of solicitors who offer private clients who allege negligence on the part of their solicitor, an initial free interview followed by an investigation leading to civil action in appropriate cases.

All solicitors (whether in private practice or paid employment involving the provision of legal services) must hold a practising certificate. This has been made clear by s 85 of the 1990 Act amending s 1 of the Solicitors' Act 1974 which left the matter in doubt. Those in private practice are also required to contribute to the Compensation Fund and hold indemnity insurance to meet successful claims made against them for malpractice. The former provides a safeguard for clients whose monies have been misappropriated by dishonest solicitors (or their staff) and where the loss cannot be recovered by any other means. The Law Society has complete discretion in making awards of compensation from this fund. As we have noted the Legal Services Ombudsman oversees the handling of complaints, but a time limit of three months applies. By s 22(2) the Ombudsman may investigate the matter to which a complaint relates (ie not only the complaint itself) but s 22(7) imposes restraints on the types of complaint investigated.

Many complaints arise out of questions over fees. The Solicitors' Practice Rules 1991 attempt to ensure that full information is given to the client about who is handling his or her case, progress, likely cost and what he or she should do if not satisfied with the standard of service. Solicitors' charges are usually costed according to time and complexity of the subject matter and will be subject to VAT and include expenses (called 'disbursements') which the solicitor has incurred, for example, stamp duty or land registry fees.

A distinction is drawn between costs incurred on matters not involving litigation (called non-contentious matters) and costs incurred in litigation (contentious matters). In the former, disputes over the costs charged can be referred to the Law

Society whereas in the case of the latter the costs will be subject to the scrutiny of the court and a process called 'taxing' the costs, that is assessing whether the bill is a reasonable one. In non-contentious matters the client should first of all query the bill but, if this does not result in agreement he or she can request the solicitor to obtain a remuneration certificate from the Law Society, that is, a statement that the bill is a fair and reasonable one. If the client fails to pay the bill and does not request the solicitor to obtain a remuneration certificate the solicitor can only sue on the bill following service of a formal notice of the client's right to such a certificate and for the bill to be taxed by the court. On receipt of this notice the client has only 28 days within which to request the solicitor to obtain the certificate. This must be done at the solicitor's expense in all cases. The Law Society may confirm or reduce the bill and a client who remains dissatisfied may then resort to taxation by the court.

Having looked at the traditional roles of barristers and solicitors and some of the many changes made by the Courts and Legal Services Act 1990 it is time to make some concluding remarks about the legal profession and its future development. Given the important changes extending advocacy rights and rights to conduct litigation and that solicitors now have the right to appear in the higher courts, the question as to whether or not we should have a fused profession will no doubt re-emerge.

3.15.2   The legal profession: a conclusion

Suggestions have been made that the titles 'solicitor' and 'barrister' should be replaced by 'attorney' and 'advocate' respectively in order to identify more clearly the type of work performed by each. The attorney is the desk lawyer whereas the advocate appears in court. This would mark another step along the path to fusion where a lawyer would be competent to both advise and represent the client in court. The titles 'solicitor', 'attorney' and 'proctor' originally denoted non-advocates who conducted preparation of cases in the Chancery, common law courts and the Ecclesiastical and Admiralty Courts respectively.

Barristers were apprentices-at-law and those with rights of audience in the superior courts were known as serjeants-at-law. Reforms were made by the Judicature Acts 1873-75 resulting in the division between barristers and solicitors. The Law Society had been incorporated in 1831 and received its Royal Charter in 1845. Given that the legal profession of today has evolved, the changes brought about by the 1990 Act and regulations made under it are likely to be accepted in time. It is still too early to gauge the full implications of the changes but s 17 of the Act sets out two objectives:

- the development of legal services by providing new and better ways and wider choice of provider whilst maintaining proper and efficient administration of justice; and

- the second is described as the general principle and applies only to rights of audience and rights to conduct litigation. Such rights should be granted where the criteria provided in s 17(3) are met. These include appropriate education and training; membership of a recognised professional body; in the case of advocacy rights, that advocacy services will not be withheld on the grounds that a case is objectionable; the conduct, opinions or belief of the client are unacceptable to the advocate or any section of the public; or on any ground relating to the source of finance such as legal aid.

This has been described as the principle of 'non-discrimination' and applies to all advocates and those with rights to conduct litigation. Section 17(5) expressly permits rules of conduct to be made by authorised bodies permitting their members to withhold their services where it would be reasonable in all the circumstances to do so (eg where a proper fee is not offered).

The authorised bodies referred to are at present the Law Society and the General Council of the Bar in relation to advocacy rights and the Law Society in relation to rights to conduct litigation. Section 29 of the Act sets out the procedures for application to the Lord Chancellor by other bodies for the grant of such rights.

We have noted when looking at the appointment of judges that by the provisions of s 71 of the Act solicitors and members of other authorised bodies with advocacy qualifications based on rights of audience will be entitled to seek appointment to the judiciary and this will no doubt have implications as to its future composition.

The progress of reform has been much slower and at times very controversial than certainly the Law Society would have liked, with allegations that the Lord Chancellor was driven by political motives to cut costs particularly in respect of the funding of legal services.

On the other hand it might be argued that we have come a long way along the path to fusion since the Benson Report of 1979, the Marre Report of 1988, the three Green Papers of 1989, the White Paper and the Courts and Legal Services Bill and then the Act of 1990 subsequently followed by regulations made by the Lord Chancellor giving effect to the provisions of the Act.

The Personnel of the Courts

Two issues are considered, namely the selection and appointment of judges and their effectiveness in performing their roles.

Judges

The appointment and functions of each of the following are considered in turn: magistrates, district judges, circuit judges, recorders, High Court Judges, Lord Justices of Appeal, Lords of Appeal in Ordinary.

Also mentioned are the offices of Lord Chancellor; Lord Chief Justice and Master of the Rolls.

- Terms of employment

Courts and Legal Services Act 1990

High Court Judges and those ranked above them hold office 'during good behaviour' and may only be removed by the Crown following an address to both Houses of Parliament.

Judicial Pensions and Retirement Act 1993

- Selection and effectiveness

(a) Selection and appointment

Superior court judges are appointed by the Queen on the advice of the Prime Minister whereas judges of the inferior courts are appointed by the Lord Chancellor.

Critics of the present system question the involvement of the Prime Minister; the potential conflict of interest of the Lord Chancellor; the threat to judicial independence and impartiality; the under-representation of ethnic minorities and women; the 'establishment' bias of judges drawn from a narrow section of society and the secrecy of the system. Proposals for reform are considered, as are ss 71 to 76 of the Courts and Legal Services Act 1990.

June 1993 saw the appointment of the first solicitor to the ranks of High Court Judge under ss 27 to 33 of the 1990 Act. The greater freedom of judges to speak publicly is also noted. Studies into the background of judges are considered as are recent instances quoted in the press suggesting that judges are out of touch with modern society.

(b) The effectiveness of the judge as law-maker

The declaratory theory states that judges do not make law but this has lost favour and it is recognised that judges contribute to the development of law. Mention is made of the positivist views of Bentham and Austin and some recent case law illustrations including:

Cambridge Water Company v Eastern Counties Leather plc (1994)

Alcock v Chief Constable of South Yorkshire Police (1992)

R v Brown (1993)

Airedale NHS Trust v Bland (1993)

R v Registrar-General ex p Smith (1990)

Judicial officers

In this section the roles of the Lord Chancellor, the Attorney-General and the Director of Public Prosecutions are considered.

The legal profession

The traditional divide is between barristers and solicitors. The barrister was often considered the senior member of the profession performing the function of specialist adviser to the solicitor and as advocate. The solicitor was the general practitioner offering advice and other legal services to the lay client. The governing bodies of solicitors and barristers are mentioned as is the role of lawyers in industry, local and central government and the court service. The training and functions of each are considered together with the historical development, the traditional terminology and the changes brought about by the Courts and Legal Services Act 1990, Part I.

In particular:

- ss 27 to 33 – advocacy certificates;
- s 61 legally binding agreement for barristers' services;
- s 62 immunity from suit in the tort of negligence and breach of contract (*Rondel v Worsley* (1967), *Saif Ali v Mitchell & Co* (1978), *Ross v Caunters* (1979) and *Kelly v ITE* (1982));
- s 67 preserves the right of solicitors to appear in designated Crown Courts;
- s 66 permits multi-disciplinary and multi-national practices;
- s 58 provides for the charging of conditional fees.

Complaining about the legal profession

The methods by which complaints are handled against solicitors and barristers are dealt with, together with proposals for reform including the 'standards review body' of the Bar Council.

Sections 21 to 26 of the Courts and Legal Services Act 1990 establish the Legal Services Ombudsman (which replaces the Lay Observer) who oversees complaints against both sides of the profession. Disciplinary procedures are regulated by the governing bodies – the Bar Council and Inns of Court for barristers and the Law Society for solicitors. In addition, the Solicitors' Complaints Bureau was set up in 1986 replacing the handling of complaints by the Law Society. Section 85 of the 1990 Act requires that all solicitors acting as such must hold a practising certificate and contribute to the Compensation Fund and hold indemnity insurance.

Actions in negligence may be brought against those not acting as advocates. Many complaints relate to fees and the Solicitors' Practice Rules 1991 lay down procedures for dealing with such complaints.

The question of fusion of the legal profession is discussed including the suggestion to rename solicitor 'attorney' and barrister 'advocate' to reflect their traditional functions and the changes under the 1990 Act.

The legal profession: a conclusion

Chapter 4

Legal Aid and Advice Schemes

4.1   Background

The first State-aided scheme to assist those unable to afford legal services was provided by the Legal Aid Act 1949 which set up the Legal Aid Fund from which those who satisfied a means test could qualify for financial help to bring or defend civil and criminal claims. This Act was later amended by Acts in 1974, 1979 and 1982.

A major overhaul was made with effect from 1 April 1989 by the Legal Aid Act 1988 which introduced a new framework which was intended to supersede all previous legislation. Before 1988, administration of the Civil Legal Aid scheme and the Legal Advice scheme were vested in the Law Society but as a result of the 1988 Act administration passed to the Legal Aid Board. Administration of the Criminal Legal Aid scheme remains in the hands of the magistrates' courts and Crown Courts with overall responsibility vested in the Lord Chancellor. Suggestions to transfer responsibility to the Legal Aid Board have not met with approval.

The Legal Aid Board therefore administers the Legal Advice and Assistance scheme including Advice by way of Representation (ABWOR) and the Civil Legal Aid schemes under the supervision of the Lord Chancellor who, each year, issues regulations under powers conferred on him by the 1988 Act.

In 1993, the following regulations were the subject of judicial review proceedings brought by the Law Society who contended that they were *ultra vires* since they failed to promote the purposes of the 1988 Act: the Civil Legal Aid (General) (Amendment) Regulations; the Civil Legal Aid (Assessment of Resources) (Amendment) Regulations; the Legal Aid in Criminal and Care Proceedings (General) (Amendment) Regulations; and the Legal Advice and Assistance (Amendment) Regulations.

The challenge by the Law Society was unsuccessful and the regulations took effect imposing drastic cuts in eligibility for legal aid and advice. The figures below are taken from the 1993 regulations but further amendments have been made with effect from 11 April 1994 and these are shown in brackets.

England and Wales is divided into 13 areas each with a Legal Aid Office and an Area Committee made up of practising solicitors and barristers. The Area Office decides whether or not to grant assistance by applying a 'merits' test and deals with the Legal Advice scheme. The Area Committee deals with appeals against the refusal of assistance. Means tests are conducted by the Legal Aid Assessment Office of the Benefits Agency of the DSS.

We will now consider each of the three types of State assistance taking first the Legal Advice and Assistance scheme (commonly referred to as the 'Green Form' scheme after the colour of the form completed on the client's behalf by the solicitor).

4.2   Legal advice and assistance (the Green Form scheme)

This scheme is regulated by Part III of the Legal Aid Act 1988 and regulations made thereunder each year by the Lord Chancellor. Preliminary advice, letter writing and applying for legal aid are covered. This scheme has been severely limited in scope with the result that assistance with probate and succession matters, will drafting, conveyancing and undefended divorces and advice and assistance in court is available only in special cases.

An applicant who satisfies a means test administered by the solicitor to determine financial eligibility will be entitled to two hours free advice (three hours in undefended divorce proceedings) on matters of English law. Financial eligibility depends on disposable capital and income calculated as follows with effect from 12 April 1993 (amendments for 1994 are shown in brackets):

Capital Limits

No dependents	£1,000
1 dependant	£1,335
2 dependents	£1,535
Each additional dependant	£100

Income Limits

Weekly income limit	£61 (£70)
Weekly dependents' allowances:	
Partner	£25.00 (£26.00)
Dependents under 11	£15.05 (£ 15.65)
11-15	£22.15 (£23.00)
16-17	£26.45 (£27.50)
18 and over	£34.80 (£36.15)

On 12 April 1993 the contributions system was abolished, and, as a result, a person is ineligible if income or capital exceeds

the above limits. Reference to disposable capital and income indicates that certain expenses and allowances can be deducted from gross capital or income to arrive at the eligibility limits. In the case of income the above allowances can be deducted together with sums covering rent, mortgage payments, fuel and living expenses. In the case of capital (such as savings, a house or a car) certain types of property are exempt, such as the main or only home, household furniture and tools of trade. Those in receipt of income support, family credit or disability working allowance automatically qualify on income but may be ineligible if disposable capital exceeds the above limits.

Under the Green Form scheme assistance will only be free in very few cases. Where the actual cost of the work performed by the solicitor exceeds the contributions made, if any, the shortfall can be claimed by the solicitor from money or property recovered or defended for the client. This is what is known as a 'statutory charge' which is imposed to ensure payment of legal fees. Some property is exempt including the first £2,500 in matrimonial proceedings, maintenance payments, welfare benefits, the main or only home, furniture, tools of trade and one-half of a redundancy payment. Only where exempt property is recovered or defended or where no property is involved in the claim will the shortfall be met by the Legal Aid Board.

By the Legal Aid Act 1979 the Green Form scheme was extended to cover advice by way of representation (ABWOR). This permits the solicitor to prepare a case and represent the client in most non-criminal cases in the magistrates' courts, in county courts where authorised, before Mental Health Tribunals, and where prisoners face disciplinary charges. In addition, applications under the Children Act 1989 are covered as are some criminal matters. The Legal Aid Area Office exercises its discretion as to whether to make an award and a right of appeal lies to the Area Committee. In cases of urgency the magistrates' or county court may grant assistance. Under this scheme not only must financial eligibility be shown but also that reasonable grounds exist for bringing or defending a claim. This is known as a merits test which also applies in awards of Civil Legal Aid.

The financial limits for ABWOR for 1993 (amendments for 1994 in brackets) are as follows:

Capital Limits:

No dependents   £3,000

1 dependant   £3,335

2 dependents	£3,535
Each additional dependant	£100

Income Limits:

Lower weekly income limit	£61.00 (£63.00)
Upper weekly income limit	£147.00 (£153.00)

Weekly dependents' allowances are the same as under the Green Form scheme.

Those on income support automatically qualify on capital and those on income support, family credit or disability working allowance qualify on income. Where disposable income exceeds £61.00 per week (£63.00 for 1994) but does not exceed £147.00 per week (£153.00 for 1994) contributions are payable of a third of the excess of income over £61.00 (£63.00) throughout the proceedings. No contributions are payable if weekly disposable income does not exceed £61.00 (£63.00). Where a change in circumstances result, ABWOR may be withdrawn as is the case where a claim is ill-founded.

4.3   Civil legal aid scheme

This is regulated under Part IV of the 1988 Act (as amended) and provides assistance for claims in the High Court and county court, the Lands Tribunal, the Commons Commissioners and the Employment Appeal Tribunal. Important exceptions are inquests, arbitration, tribunals and defamation claims. An applicant's eligibility is decided on two grounds – a merits test and a financial means test – by the Legal Aid Board Area Office and an Assessment Office of the DSS Benefits Agency respectively. As a general rule, both tests must be met if assistance is to be awarded. In proceedings under the Children Act 1989, however, the general rule is that neither test need be met.

4.3.1   Merits test

An applicant must show that he or she has reasonable grounds for bringing or defending the claim and that it is reasonable in all the circumstances to grant legal aid. In the event of doubt a limited legal aid certificate may be granted requiring authorisation by the Legal Aid Board of further work to be done. The criteria applied include whether the claim involves a question of law or fact, whether alternatives exist such as resort to arbitration, the applicant's motive in wishing to bring or defend the claim and whether or not he or she can meet any claim made against him or her and whether some benefit would result from the claim.

4.3.2   Financial eligibility

This is based on disposable yearly income and disposable capital. Disposable income is that which is left after appropriate allowances and living expenses such as rent, mortgage payments and fuel are taken out of gross income. Disposable capital includes savings and other assets excluding the main or only home, furniture and tools of trade. In calculating disposable capital and income the value of property which is 'the subject-matter of the proceedings' is excluded. This will depend on whether it is in jeopardy as a result of the proceedings. If so, its value is excluded. Maintenance payments are taken into account in calculating eligibility.

Capital Limits:

Lower capital limit	£3,000
Upper capital limit	£6,750 (personal injury claims £8,650)

Special rules apply to pensioners permitting some capital to be disregarded. Co-habitees and spouses are assessed on their joint income and capital except where they live apart or have contrary interests.

Income Limits:

Lower income limit yearly	£ 2,294 (£2,382)
Upper income limit yearly	£6,800/personal injury claims £7,500 (£7,060/£7780)

Dependents' Allowances per year:

Partner	£1,304 (£1,356)
Dependant under 11	£785 (£816)
11-15	£1,155 (£1,199)
16-17	£1,379 (£1,434)
18 and over	£1,815 (£1,885)

Contributions are payable where disposable capital exceeds £3,000 and monthly contributions from income are payable where disposable income exceeds £2,294 (£2,382) in the amount of 1/36th of the excess throughout the case. Those on income support receive free assistance.

When both tests are met an offer of legal aid is made which the applicant is free to accept or reject. An offer may be made subject to contributions and no right of appeal lies to the Area Office against contributions ordered. On acceptance by the applicant of an offer, a legal aid certificate is issued. If the case later proves hopeless the applicant's solicitor must report this to the Area Office which has a discretion to withdraw the certificate. Duties are owed to the Legal Aid Board by both the applicant and his or her solicitor to inform the Area office of changes in circumstances, address, to co-operate fully and to pay contributions when due.

As we have noted above in respect of the Green Form scheme, legal assistance is often not free and a statutory charge may be imposed to pay for legal fees. When considering Civil Legal Aid it is necessary to distinguish between the situation where the winner is legally aided and that where the loser is legally aided.

- Winner legally aided

  The general rule about payment of litigation costs is that 'costs follow the event'. This means that the loser will have to meet not only his or her legal costs but also those of the winner. If the winner is legally aided the judge will probably order the loser to pay all costs and, in theory, this will ensure that the winner will not have to meet any of the costs of the action. However, in practice this is not always the case either because the loser fails to pay or no order is made by the court, or the loser disappears or becomes bankrupt. In any event the loser will submit the question of costs to the court for 'taxation'. This is a process whereby the costs are scrutinised by the court to see if they are of a reasonable amount. Only in rare cases will the loser have to meet the full amount of costs leaving a small shortfall to be met from the winner's contributions, if any, or by way of the statutory charge over damages or property recovered. The result may be that the winner ends up with little or nothing even where at the outset free legal aid was granted. Spouses should never litigate over family assets in excess of £2,500 which is the only exempt property under this scheme.

- Loser legally aided

  At the court's discretion the loser may be ordered to pay 'a reasonable amount' towards the costs of the winner. Usually this amounts to two contributions by the loser but any shortfall has to be met by the winner by way of statutory charge. Any shortfall of the loser's costs is paid by the Legal Aid Board. The statutory charge cannot be waived and only in exceptional circumstances can it be postponed.

  In cases of emergency, for example, that of battered wives, cases involving children or eviction from property, an emergency legal aid certificate may be granted following a telephone application. A full application is made later and if the applicant turns out not to be eligible he or she will be liable for all costs.

4.4 Criminal legal aid

Criminal legal aid is regulated by Part V of the 1988 Act and provides assistance to those accused of criminal offences. Private prosecutions are not covered so an individual who wishes to bring a private prosecution, for example, where they or a member of their family has been the subject of an offence and where the Crown Prosecution Service decides not to prosecute, will be responsible for funding the case. In the event that the case is successful an order for costs may be made out of public funds but any shortfall will have to be met by the individual.

As with Civil Legal Aid the applicant must satisfy both a merits and a means test but the provisions of each are different.

4.4.1 Merits test

It must be shown that the application is 'desirable in the interests of justice'. The criteria were set out in the Widgery Criteria of 1966 and are now enacted in s 22 of the Legal Aid Act 1988. These include the complexity of the issues involved; the ability of the defendant to understand the proceedings due to inadequate knowledge of English; mental illness or disability; the need to trace or interview witnesses by the defendant or the need to cross-examine prosecution witnesses; the desirability of legal representation of the defendant so as to protect the interests of another, for example, a child when sexual abuse is alleged and the defendant would wish to cross-examine the child; conviction likely to result in imprisonment or loss of livelihood.

Some 97% of Crown Court defendants are granted legal aid but defendants in the magistrates' courts are only granted legal aid in 'serious' cases and this includes defendants committed for trial to the Crown Court.

4.4.2 Financial eligibility

The capital limit is £3,000 and the weekly income limit is £45.00 (for 1994 £47.00). The weekly dependents' allowances are the same as for the Green Form scheme. Those on income support, family credit or disability working allowance receive free legal aid. For those with disposable capital in excess of £3,000 contributions from capital are payable and for those with a weekly disposable income in excess of £44.00 (£46.00) a weekly contribution from income of £1 for every £3 or part in excess is payable. Those aged 16 or over apply on their own behalf whereas parents or guardians apply for those under 16.

The court has a discretion at the end of a case to order the defendant to pay additional costs but the court must take into account the sentence imposed. No appeal lies against such an order and even if the defendant is acquitted he or she may be ordered to pay additional costs.

4.5	**Duty solicitor scheme**

This is regulated by Part III of the 1988 Act and the Legal Aid Board Duty Solicitor Arrangements 1990. This scheme offers free legal advice to those questioned by the police at a police station or elsewhere whether or not arrested. No means test or financial eligibility applies and a suspect may choose either his or her own solicitor or the 24 hour duty solicitor or one whose name appears on a list retained by the police. This scheme also covers attendance at the magistrates' court and by s 58 of the Police and Criminal Evidence Act 1984 and the Codes of Practice suspects must be informed of their right to a solicitor under this scheme.

Having now described the main provisions of the State schemes we need to consider the alternatives available, the main defects of the State schemes and proposals for reform.

4.6	**Alternatives**

Several private schemes have been set up over the years the most well known being the '£5 scheme' operated by solicitors on a voluntary basis who offer 30 minutes of advice for £5 (or other stipulated sum). No limitations apply as to the number of solicitors consulted on a matter but only advice can be obtained. In 1987 the Law Society established the ALAS-scheme where volunteer solicitors offer free initial interviews to accident victims.

Another means by which legal services are provided free is through law centres. These are funded by local authorities in the main although central government may provide some funding. Law centres are located in London and other large cities and employ solicitors on a full-time basis and the client receives free legal advice and representation. Law centres have seen severe financial pressures in recent years and although popular with those in need of legal assistance they have not always been popular with government since their role has involved questioning social policy on matters such as housing, State benefits, family matters and employment rights.

Advice on legal matters and other problems may be sought from legal advice centres and the Citizens' Advice Bureaux. The former offer advice mainly on consumer or housing matters and act as a referral agency, often in conjunction with the latter. The Citizens' Advice Bureaux form a national scheme offering free and independent advice on legal and other social matters. Most towns throughout the country have a Bureau staffed by volunteers who undertake training courses to enable them to offer specific advice on social benefits, housing, family and employment matters. Since the recession one of their main areas of work is in debt counselling. Solicitors offer their services on a voluntary basis in some bureaux on a rota basis.

In the chapter on Arbitration and Tribunals we consider alternatives to litigation. in recent years a concept imported from America has received attention, namely ADR or 'alternative dispute resolution'. It is a fundamental notion of a civilised State that an individual with a grievance, either against the State or another individual, should be able to obtain justice. Traditionally, this has been through the courts of law or by way of a tribunal. Given the adversarial nature of litigation and its high costs in both money and time and in recent times the financial stringency applied to State funding the need for alternatives such as mediation, conciliation and arbitration to arrive at solutions by agreement and reconciliation have increased. It is unlikely that such alternatives will replace traditional means of resolution but certainly they are likely to be used increasingly where their effectiveness surpasses adjudication by the courts.

A traditional assumption has been that with adjudication in a court of law comes the need for professional representation. As we have seen in the chapter on the legal profession this no longer simply refers to representation by barristers but under the reforms given effect to by the Courts and Legal Services Act 1990 rights of audience are extended to solicitors (and in future will be extended to those who are not barristers or solicitors but who satisfy the requirements of 'authorised bodies' and demonstrate fitness to practise as advocates).

Section 11 of the Act provides that the Lord Chancellor may, by order, remove restrictions on those with rights of audience or rights to conduct litigation in specified county court proceedings. This extends the use of what became known as a 'McKenzie Friend' that is a person able to sit in court and offer advice and support to a litigant in person. The recent case involving a 77-year-old widow, Peggy Wood, who sued the Law Society in the tort of negligence, illustrates the use of an adviser for those who wish to represent themselves in court.

Other voluntary initiatives include the Hoxton Legal Advice Service (LAS) which offers free legal advice to members of the public by part-time volunteers some of whom are qualified lawyers and some law students. This was referred to in an article in the *Solicitors' Gazette* (1993) and advice is offered on housing and employment matters, debt, taxation and consumer affairs and State benefits. Advisers refer those likely to be eligible for legal aid to local law firms and for others the LAS offers advice and, at the court's discretion, represents clients in court.

Given the rising cost of legal services and the cost-cutting exercise in the provision of State-funded legal aid and advice schemes together with an ever increasing 'unmet need for legal services' some or all of the above may relieve the pressure on the State system. However, it might be argued that much more far-reaching reform is needed.

Some suggestions for reform include contingency legal aid whereby litigants who are successful subsidise the costs of the scheme. Another proposal is for a safety-net scheme and provides that those above the legal aid limit are required to spend their capital down to a set limit (the safety net) and then apply for legal aid. This was put forward by the Lord Chancellor but leaves some important questions unanswered including what would happen if legal aid was refused and what about an applicant who gave up before reaching the safety-net?

Another proposal was for a sliding scale of eligibility depending on the type of case. Thus, in personal injury claims the eligibility levels could be increased to take account of the increased complexities.

Another proposal, which has subsequently been enacted in s 58 of the Courts and Legal Services Act 1990, is for payment of legal fees on a contingency basis. The lawyer (both barristers and solicitors are covered) is paid only for winning a case. By s 58 lawyers will be paid on a 'no win, no fee' basis but, unlike the American system, not by way of a percentage of the damages awarded but on the normal hourly rate or fixed sum fee uprated by a proposed maximum of 100% to compensate for the risk of receiving no fee should the case be lost. Those able to provide litigation and advocacy services may enter into a binding written agreement for a conditional fee. It is intended that lay representatives and others with litigation rights and rights of audience will be covered by the provisions. However, s 58 only applies to personal injury claims, insolvency matters and proceedings concerning the European Convention on Human Rights before the Commission or Court.

Such agreements and the grant of legal aid are mutually exclusive so that once legal aid is granted the agreement ceases to have effect. The provisions have yet to be finalised and in any event it will take some time to appraise their effectiveness. However, their use will provide the client with a wider choice when deciding whether to proceed with a claim.

Having considered the position of the client and the shortcomings of State provision it is also necessary to consider the position of the provider of legal services. Fundamental change has been taking place as to the eligibility of those able to provide legal aid and advice under the State schemes. The Lord Chancellor put forward proposals to franchise the provision of legal services in 1992 and in 1993 suggested that its future lay in competitive tendering for franchises. This met with some dissension from the Legal Aid Board and has yet to be worked out.

However, by November 1993 the first franchises had been applied for by firms of solicitors who had to satisfy criteria laid down by the Board. The first franchises were awarded in January 1994. Government policy aims to cut the cost of legal aid and this can be achieved by way of competitive tendering for legal aid franchises. Those satisfying the criteria of the Board and who offer the lowest bid to provide legal services will be successful. Other proposals for cutting costs include a pay freeze for legal aid practitioners (the rate of charges have always been lower for legal aid work), ending the practice of paying a solicitor to attend court with a barrister, removing the need for lawyers to attend unopposed adjournments in magistrates' courts, removing the need for a junior counsel to attend with a QC and imposing cost penalties on parties to divorce proceedings who fail to co-operate and thereby incur costs. We have already mentioned conditional fees and these should reduce the costs in personal injury claims.

Other cost-cutting measures which have been proposed will see an end to legal aid provision at sentencing hearings in the magistrates' courts where the defendant pleads guilty and is not at risk of a custodial sentence. Other proposals suggest amendments to the duty solicitor scheme and at the end of 1993 the Lord Chancellor put forward proposals in a Green Paper for greater use of mediation in matrimonial matters.

Some commentators have described the funding of legal services as in crisis and it is hard to accept cost-cutting on the one hand and on the other the drive towards encouraging the citizen to be more aware of his and her rights and to seek redress through the courts. As yet the implications of franchising remain to be seen and whether or not competitive tendering will be implemented. If it is and is limited only to franchised firms this will have far-reaching effects on the provision of legal services including the role of Advice Centres and Citizens' Advice Bureaux. One thing does remain clear and that is the ever increasing unmet need for legal services and a legal system which is overburdened.

In the recent Management Statement for the Legal Aid Board published by the HMSO in 1994 for the Lord Chancellor's Department, the main objective of the legal aid system, the courts and the justice system as a whole 'is to resolve disputes and to assist people in pursuing their rights and understanding their obligations'. This is no doubt a most laudable objective but it demonstrates a fundamental shift from the principles espoused in 1948 when the State assisted schemes for legal aid and advice were established. The original schemes were designed to ensure that those who were unable to afford to bring or defend a legal claim would receive State funded assistance. Furthermore, the emphasis then was on obtaining justice and fairness whereas now the movement is towards alternative dispute resolution which may well speed up the resolution of disputes and encourage compromise. However, a disadvantage is that those who are financially or emotionally weak may settle for much less than what a court adjudicating on a dispute would award. Further legal aid cuts are planned and it is too early to say how provision of legal services and the way in which they are funded will develop.

Summary of Chapter 4

Legal Aid and Advice Schemes

Background

The Legal Aid Act 1949 set up the first State system of assistance for those with a legal problem and who were unable to meet the cost of legal services. Changes were made in 1974, 1979, 1982 and the present Act is the Legal Aid Act 1988. Administration of the Green Form scheme (including ABWOR) and Civil Legal Aid is the responsibility of the Legal Aid Board supervised by the Lord Chancellor by way of regulation. Criminal Legal Aid is still administered by the courts.

Legal advice and assistance (the Green Form scheme)

The Legal Aid Act 1988 Part III and regulations are updated each year. It covers preliminary advice, letter writing and applying for legal aid. Financial eligibility must be proved and this depends on disposable capital and income as defined in the regulations. If met, two hours of free advice are permitted (three hours in undefended divorce proceedings). Contributions have been abolished but the statutory charge may apply to meet the costs of the advice. The ABWOR Scheme (Advice By Way of Representation) permits limited representation before the magistrates' courts in non-criminal matters; Mental Health Tribunals, some cases before the county court and prisoners' disciplinary hearings. Financial eligibility has to be shown by way of disposable capital and income but the limits are different from the Green Form scheme.

Civil Legal Aid scheme

The 1988 Act Part IV and regulations cover claims in the High Court, county court and some tribunals. Eligibility depends on a merits test and a financial means test. The merits test, administered by the Legal Aid Board Area Office, is explained, as is the calculation of disposable capital and income by the DSS. Contributions may be payable and the statutory charge will apply to meet the costs of the claim where property (other than 'exempt' property) is recovered. Special provisions will apply to the award of costs where either the winner or loser is legally aided.

Criminal Legal Aid scheme

The 1988 Act Part V and regulations cover assistance to those charged with a criminal offence. Both a merits test and a financial means test have to be satisfied but the provisions of each are different from Civil Legal Aid.

The Duty Solicitor scheme

The 1988 Act Part III and the Legal Aid Board Duty Solicitor Arrangements 1990 offer free legal advice to suspects being questioned by the police at a police station or elsewhere and covers attendance at the magistrates' court.

Alternatives

Private schemes include the £5 fixed fee interview offering 30 minutes advice for the stipulated sum and the ALAS scheme established by the Law Society in 1987 offering free advice to accident victims. Other alternatives include Law Centres, Legal Advice Centres, Citizen Advice Bureaux and Alternative Dispute Resolution (ADR) which includes mediation and conciliation. Extensions in rights of audience and the use of 'McKenzie Friends' are also noted, as are other voluntary schemes such as the Hoxton Legal Advice Service. The high costs of legal services and the cost-cutting carried out in 1993 (and challenged by way of judicial review by the Law Society) is noted together with proposals for reform.

The effects of s 58 Courts and Legal Services Act 1990 which provides for payment of legal fees on a contingency basis are discussed as are the award of legal aid franchises to providers of legal services.

Chapter 5

The Layperson and the Law

The magistrates' court deal with 98% of all criminal cases, at least initially. In 1992 some 566 magistrates' courts sat in England and Wales staffed by 29,450 lay magistrates (stipendiary magistrates numbered 76). In 1990 some 95% of all offenders were sentenced in the magistrates' courts. Two to seven lay magistrates sit at any one time (although usually there will be a bench of three). Special rules apply in youth courts (formerly called Juvenile Courts) whereby at least one of three magistrates must be female. The court is also required to sit on different days and in a different place and restrictions on reporting will be imposed.

The Lord Chancellor appoints magistrates on the recommendation of the Magistrates' Commission. Retirement is at the age of 70 years. In the chapter on the court system we considered the jurisdiction and powers of the magistrates and the role of the clerk. Here we will confine our comments to some of the criticisms that are made of lay magistrates.

Magistrates are often said to be 'case-hardened', and that a defendant might be advised to elect for jury trial at the Crown Court where he or she is accused of a 'triable either way' offence such as theft. Such a defendant, represented by a good counsel, may well be acquitted whereas the likelihood is that trial summarily in the magistrates' court would result in conviction.

Magistrates may also be seen to be too much under the control of the court clerk but, of course, this may only be as it seems and in any event a clerk is not permitted to make a decision for the magistrate, but only to offer advice as to the law.

Another criticism is that a bench of three magistrates will comprise two less senior magistrates and a more experienced magistrates who acts as chairman. The chairman will have the casting vote and the other two may defer to what they see as his or her better judgment. It is often pointed out that lay magistrates have relatively little knowledge of law, evidence and procedure and, in addition, little training. Over-reliance on the court clerk may result from the inability of justices to reach a decision taking into account complex provisions.

Magistrates are also drawn from a narrow social background and some have described them as 'do-gooders' who, for want of other things to fill their time, fulfil this public role. Allied with this is the criticism that magistrates are

5.1   Lay magistrates

'middle-aged, middle class and middle-minded', and that in all the system encourages the provision of justice 'on the cheap'.

On a more positive view, some of the advantages of encouraging people to come forward to serve as justices include the following: the system is cost-effective and if paid personnel were to be employed or the role of the magistrates' court was to be dispensed with the administration of criminal justice would at best become long and expensive and at worst would grind to a halt. The lay magistrate offers a different perspective from that of the professional judge and may well have a better appreciation of fact.

Magistrates are required to sit at least 26 times a year and average attendance is greater. At the same time a magistrate who regularly sits over several years will no doubt build up a vast amount of experience in the working of the court and the criminal justice system.

The magistrate is assisted by a trained professional, the clerk, and this ensures consistency and accuracy in decision-making. The Runciman Royal Commission (which reported in July 1993) recommended that in 'either way' offences where the defendant can at present elect for jury trial, the defendant should no longer have that right. If the Crown Prosecution Service and the defendant agree as to the mode of trial this would determine the question. If the defence does not agree with the view of the Crown Prosecution Service the matter should be referred to the magistrates to determine the mode of trial. Legislation should lay down the criteria to be considered by the magistrates when deciding this question.

A further recommendation of the Commission was the abolition of committal proceedings which would result in offences being classified only as summary (for trial in the magistrates' court) or indictable (for trial in the Crown Court by a jury).

The Police and Magistrates' Court Bill, presently before Parliament, contains the following provisions which, if enacted, will reform the workings of the magistrates' courts and the role of the court clerk: the Lord Chancellor will have power to merge or adjust the number of magistrates' courts Committee Areas with the aim of reducing the number by about a half in the 18 months following enactment of the provisions to between 50 and 60. Each new area will be headed by a Chief Justices' clerk who will be appointed on a five year fixed-term performance related contract. New appointments to Justices' clerks will also be on fixed-term contracts and the Lord Chancellor will have to approve the appointment of Chief Justices' clerks and chairpersons of Committee Areas.

The Lord Chancellor's Department, in promoting these changes, have stressed that in its view there is no threat to the independence of Justices' clerks but magistrates and their clerks have protested at the reforms which they say on the one hand will increase bureaucracy and cost and on the other compromise the independence of clerks and the trust which exists between magistrates and their clerks.

This year sees the marking of 800 years of tradition in the office of coroner.

5.2   Coroners

The office was established in 1194 and since that time the powers of the coroner have been successively narrowed until, today, their main functions are the holding of inquests into suspicious deaths within their area and into the status of property alleged to be a treasure trove.

Coroners can be assisted by a jury of between seven and 11 persons and a majority verdict is acceptable providing that no more than two jurors dissent.

Coroners are appointed by the local authority in whose area they serve and can only be dismissed by the Lord Chancellor for misbehaviour. On average some 180,000 deaths are referred to coroners in any one year and of these some 20,000 result in inquests. Coroners have an important role to play in recommending improvements in safety standards and their findings may give rise to criminal or civil proceedings.

The role of the coroner is mentioned more fully in the chapter on the personnel of the courts.

Lay assessors are employed in the wide range of tribunals which have been established by statute to supplement the work of the courts in adjudicating disputes involving an aggrieved citizen and an administrative agency of the State.

5.3   Lay assessors

Some examples include National Insurance Tribunals, Rent Tribunals, and Industrial Injuries Tribunals and these are more fully considered in the chapter on tribunals and alternative dispute resolution.

Lay assessors may assist in the deliberations of the Restrictive Practices Court which sits as a superior court of record comprised of a High Court Judge and two laypersons.

The Admiralty Court, within the Queen's Bench Division presided over by a High Court Judge, also relies on the assistance of two nautical assessors (members of Trinity House) who are competent to advise on technical maritime matters.

By s 14 of the Courts and Legal Services Act 1990, s 63 of the County Courts Act 1984 is amended so as to enable district judges and circuit judges to appoint expert assessors.

Section 14(2) provides that in any proceedings a judge may, on the application of a party to the proceedings, summon an expert assessor that is a person 'of skill and experience in the matter to which the proceedings relate' and who may be willing to sit with him and act as an assessor.

Power also exists for the judge to summon such a person in the absence of an application by either party in prescribed proceedings as defined by s 119(1) of the Act to be provided for by regulation. District Judges have similar powers but only in prescribed proceedings.

Another area where lay assessors may assist a judge in reaching a decision where complex matters arise is in criminal fraud trials. Suggestions have over the years been made that juries are unsuitable to decide issues of fact in such trials and also the need for judges to be assisted by those expert in financial matters was made clear in the 'Blue Arrow' and 'Guinness' fraud trials in 1992. The Roskill Committee on Fraud trials which reported in 1986 recommended the use of assessors in place of juries in complex criminal fraud trials.

5.4   The jury

In considering the issue of the role of the layperson in the administration of justice it is the use of the jury, particularly in criminal trials in the Crown Court, that fires the imagination and gives rise to much debate as to its effectiveness.

The jury has been described as 'a bastion of freedom' and has great constitutional significance. In the words of the well known adage, 'justice should not only be done but be seen to be done', the jury plays its part in ensuring openness and fairplay. It might be argued that use of the jury in criminal trials is one of the fundamental pillars of a free society and is of the same order of importance as the presumption of innocence and a right to remain silent before and during trial.

Blackstone described the jury as 'the bulwark of our liberties' and Lord Devlin in *Trial by Jury* as 'the lamp which 1986 shows that freedom lives'. On the other hand, some suggest that the jury has little, if any, useful part to play and that for those unfortunate to be called upon to serve on a jury it is an unwelcome public duty from which few are exempt or can be excused, although compensation is paid for travelling, subsistence and financial loss.

Juries are rarely used nowadays in civil trials although the most notable type of trial, namely defamation, where juries are used has received much criticism recently in the light of huge awards of damages. Some examples include civil claims by Jeffrey Archer, Lord Lindley, Ester Rantzen, Sonia Sutcliffe and Koo Stark. By s 8 of the Courts and Legal Services Act

1990, the Court of Appeal has a rule-making power to substitute awards of damages by a jury where that is found to be excessive.

Much of the criticism of the amounts of jury awards has resulted from comparisons between the awards of damages made in personal injury cases and those in defamation claims where the former relatively have been much lower. In 1993 an award in favour of Ester Rantzen was reduced from £250,000 to £110,000.

By the Administration of Justice (Miscellaneous Provisions) Act 1933 civil courts have a discretion to order the use of a jury where either party requests one in cases of defamation, malicious prosecution, fraud and false imprisonment unless there is good reason for not having a jury, for example where the case will involve scientific investigation or prolonged examination of documents.

Civil juries in the County Court comprise eight persons whereas in the High Court the jury has 12 members and majority verdicts are acceptable.

The main use of juries is in trials on indictment in the Crown Court where the jury has the function of deciding the guilt or innocence of the defendant. Jurors take an oath or affirm that they will 'faithfully try the defendant and give a true verdict according to the evidence'.

Twelve persons aged between 18 and 70 (those aged 65 and over may be excused under s 119 of the Criminal Justice Act 1988 which amends the Juries Act 1974) are selected at random from the electoral register. Those aged 18 registered as an elector who have been resident for five years are liable for jury service. *from age of 13.*

A distinction is made between exemption and excusal from *exemption-disqualified* *excusal - through rights.* jury service. The former allows those involved with the administration of justice such as judges, barristers and solicitors and others including clergymen, police officers and the mentally disordered to be exempt whereas the latter permits those who would find attendance at court difficult, to seek the permission of the court clerk to be excused. Those away on holiday or business or who have some other good reason, for example, doctors and members of the armed forces, must apply to the court clerk to be excused from the jury summons. Those with certain past convictions are disqualified as are those who have been on probation during the previous five years.

Those who attend are empanelled and become 'jurors in waiting'. A juror in waiting may be challenged for cause by the defence, for example, the person is known to the defendant or has knowledge of the case. 'Cause' is defined by a Lord Chief Justice Practice Note of 1972 and must be a good reason for a juror in waiting not being sworn in to sit on the jury to try that particular case. It follows that such a person may be called on to remain in the precincts of the court and to sit on a jury trying another case. By s 118 of the Criminal Justice Act 1988 the so-called 'peremptory challenge' was abolished. This permitted the defence to challenge up to three jurors in waiting without any reason. It was most often used to challenge those dressed smartly on the assumption that such an individual would be more likely to convict a defendant accused of theft or burglary. In trials involving offences against a woman it was usual for the defence to use its peremptory challenge to ensure representation of women on the jury. The prosecution can ask jurors in waiting 'to stand by for the Crown' and no limitation exists on the number of times it can be used.

The jury appoints a foreman from among its number to announce its verdict and to keep order during its deliberations following the trial when it goes into secret session. A unanimous verdict may be announced or by a majority of 10 to 2 providing the jury has deliberated for a minimum of two hours. Section 17 of the Juries Act 1974 as amended provides that a unanimous verdict of 10 to 1 may be given if 11 jurors only sit or 9 to 1 if 10 jurors sit. The minimum number of jurors is nine.

The jury is the arbiter of fact whereas the judge is the arbiter of law. At the conclusion of the trial the judge sums up the evidence to the jury and may direct the jury to acquit or convict. The judge is not empowered to order a jury to pronounce one way or the other as was clearly shown in the trial of Clive Ponting in 1985. Ponting was accused of offences under s 2 of the Official Secrets Act 1911 arising out of disclosures in the press on the sinking of the Belgrano during the Falklands conflict. The judge directed the jury to convict but this was ignored by the jury who acquitted the defendant on all counts.

By s 10 of the Juries Act 1974 (as amended) provision is made for the discharge of a jury or of an individual juror. A jury can be discharged, for example, where the defendant's previous convictions are disclosed or other information which might prejudice a fair trial.

Matters of law are for the judge and where counsel wishes to query a question of law the judge will order the jury to retire whilst that matter is dealt with. By s 122 of the Criminal Justice Act 1988, if a question arises as to whether the defendant has previously been tried for the offence for which he appears before the court (*autrefois acquit* or *autrefois convict*) this is a matter of law for the judge to decide in the absence of the jury. Individual jurors may be discharged at the discretion of the judge, for example, for illness, wrongful conduct or contact with the defendant.

Several issues concern the selection and effectiveness of juries in criminal trials. Firstly, selection is conducted secretly as is the way in which they work. By s 8 of the Contempt of Court Act 1981, jury members are under a duty not to disclose what happened during the course of the deliberations. This is an absolute duty which prevents research into the workings of the jury. Lord Runciman recommended that suitable research should be conducted and that s 8 should be amended so as to permit research into the influence that jurors with criminal records may have on verdicts.

Disadvantage + advice

Other recommendations include:

- removal of the exemption for clergymen and members of religious orders providing instead a right to be excused;

- in exceptional cases the prosecution or defence should be able to apply for selection of a jury to include up to three people from ethnic minorities and that either the prosecution or the defence should be able to argue that one or more of the three should come from the same ethnic minority group as the defendant or the victim;

- writing materials should be provided as standard and the judge should explain to the jury at the start of the trial the extent to which they might ask questions and that they have a right to take notes.

Another issue is that of jury 'nobbling' or the intimidation of jury members. Lord Runciman recommended that every effort should be made to protect jurors from intimidation. Sensitive cases should be assigned to courtrooms where the public gallery cannot be used for such purposes. For example, members of the public present will not be able to catch the eye of members of the jury. The Criminal Justice and Public Order Bill, presently before Parliament, follows this recommendation and includes a provision for a new offence of 'witness and juror intimidation'.

Another issue is that of 'jury vetting', whereby the prosecution seeks to check on, and then exclude from jury service, those who are considered undesirable. The Attorney-General issued guidelines on Jury Checks in 1980 (revised in 1988) which recognised the following general principles:

- Jury members are to be selected at random from the panel. The Juries Act 1974 lists those disqualified from, or ineligible for, jury service. The prosecution should only seek to exclude a member of the panel in open court by a request to 'stand by for the Crown' or, if necessary, to challenge for cause.

- Corrupt and biased jurors are provided for by way of majority verdicts and the provision that an unqualified person who sits on a jury commits an offence. Such persons can be removed as a result of searches by the police as the authorised body of criminal records.

- Further safeguards are needed to ensure the administration of justice where national security and terrorist cases are involved. In such cases it is permitted for the police to make a limited investigation of the panel to see whether any have criminal records.

- The Attorney-General can, in addition, authorise that Special Branch records be searched following an application by the Director of Public Prosecutions. These are known as 'authorised checks'. Following such a check a right to 'stand by for the Crown' should only be used if there is strong reason to believe that the juror in waiting might be a security risk or susceptible to improper approaches or be influenced in arriving at a verdict by way of improper influences. Prosecuting counsel has a discretion whether or not to disclose the nature and source of such information. Where a juror is not asked to 'stand by for the Crown' but is believed to be potentially a risk to the defence the latter should be given a general indication as to the reason why he may be inimical to their interests.

As already mentioned, the question of secrecy as to the deliberations of juries is of great concern and ensures that the debate concerning the effectiveness of the jury in reaching decisions is hampered. By s 8 of the Contempt of Court Act 1981 it is an offence to 'obtain, disclose, or solicit any particulars of statements made, opinions expressed, arguments advanced or votes cast by members of a jury in the course of their deliberations in any legal proceedings'.

This effectively prevents any intrusion on the independence of the jury but, as noted by Professor McConville, its secrecy suggests that it 'is a source of weakness, making it vulnerable to charges of stupidity, capriciousness and bias'. In an article in the *New Law Journal* (1991) Professor McConville describes the research conducted with the co-operation of the Lord Chancellor's Department by

'Twenty Twenty Television': 'Inside the Jury', where shadow juries sat alongside actual juries and whose deliberations were observed. In all respects the shadow juries emulated the conditions of the actual juries and this was also reflected in the similarity of the verdicts. Of the five trials shadowed agreement as to verdict was reached in four and in the other the actual jury convicted whereas the shadow jury failed to reach a verdict. Professor McConville suggests that we have every reason to be confident in the quality of decision-making by juries and that on the evidence of this experiment, the jury 'would survive any examination of its workings'.

In conclusion, use of the jury, particularly in trials on indictment in the Crown Court, is likely to be retained as it is considered that findings of fact should be decided by more than one person. Also it is considered important to have the involvement of the layperson in the administration of justice as it retains public confidence and provides a balance between the interests of the State and of the individual.

very important

However, many criticisms have been made of the jury and some of these were addressed by the Royal Commission on Criminal Justice. The facilities afforded to jurors are often rudimentary. For example, paper and pencils are not always provided and members of the jury may be overawed by the judge, counsel or simply the occasion. Jurors receive no training for their task and they may be young or inexperienced. They may also be unwilling participants and be either unable or unwilling to participate fully. They may well have to assimilate long and complex evidence or that which is harrowing or unpleasant. Members of the jury may be swayed by the persuasive arguments of counsel and in some cases, such as shoplifting, the defendant may elect for jury trial on the advice of counsel who considers that acquittal is more likely in the Crown Court.

no training
no experience
young
unwilling participants therefore no true cross section
prejudices of jury
Bad experience
persuade by counc

Other disadvantages include the threat of intimidation and the possibility of corruption; undue leniency; unrepresentative composition and the cost to the State of reimbursing juror expenses. We have mentioned above the secrecy which surrounds the workings of the jury system and the disadvantages this causes for effective research and possible reforms.

The Layperson and the Law

Lay magistrates

The appointment and functions of lay magistrates is considered as are the advantages and disadvantages of their dealing with some 95% of offenders. Their role in youth courts is mentioned and their relationship with the magistrates' clerk is considered in the light of proposed changes in the Police and Magistrates' Court Bill presently before Parliament.

Coroners

An office first established in 1194 to inquire into suspicious deaths and the ownership of unclaimed property. Their appointment is considered as is the assistance they derive from a jury of between 7 and 11 persons.

Lay assessors

Lay assessors use in tribunals, the Restrictive Practices Court and the Admiralty Court of the Queen's Bench is noted, as is s 14 Courts and Legal Services Act 1990 (amending s 63 County Courts Act 1984) for the appointment of lay assessors in the county court. The Roskill Committee on Fraud Trials recommended in 1986 the use of lay assessors in place of juries in complex fraud trials.

The jury

The role of the jury in criminal trials in the Crown Court is considered. Brief mention only is made of civil juries. Juries in criminal trials have a constitutional significance and have been described as the 'bastion of freedom for the citizen against the state'. The provisions of the Juries Act 1974 (as amended) regulating the number, age and other qualification of jurors is considered. Section 17 provides for unanimous verdicts and the role of the foreman. The jury comprises 12 persons aged 18 to 70 (those aged 65 and over may be excused under s 119 Criminal Justice Act 1988).

Selection is at random from the electoral register and a distinction is made between 'excusal' and 'exemption' from service. The rights of the defence to challenge jurors in waiting are discussed as are the right of the prosecution to ask a juror in waiting to 'stand by for the Crown'. Section 118 Criminal Justice Act 1988 abolished the 'peremptory' challenge.

The relationship of judge (arbiter of law) and jury (arbiter of fact) is considered, and reference made to the trial of Clive Ponting. The rules for the discharge of juries are noted, as are the recommendations for reform made by the Runciman Royal

Commission in 1993 including reform of s 8 Contempt of Court Act 1981. Jury 'nobbling' and 'vetting' are distinguished and the Attorney-General's Guidelines on Jury Checks explained. The advantages and disadvantages of jury trials are considered as are suggested reforms.

Chapter 6

Law Reform Agencies

In considering the question of change and reform of the law it is necessary to consider the agencies that facilitate change and the need for reform of the law. Before looking at each of the main agencies we will consider the need for change. If law is to meet the changing needs of society it not only needs to adapt to social change but also to anticipate change and in some cases to mould and shape social habits and attitudes.

'Change' and 'reform' should, however, be distinguished because reform implies change that is desirable and which improves the lot of members of society. Change, if it is too frequent and ill-thought-out may outweigh any advantages in seeking reform.

A fundamental tenet of law and of a developed legal system is the idea that there should be certainty in the legal rules and how they are applied so as to allow those subject to them to arrange their affairs in such a way as to comply. The 1980s and 1990s have seen much new legislation initiated by government to give effect to its policy of privatisation of public services and reform of many of the institutions of society including the legal system and legal profession. The last century also saw many legal reforms, culminating in the Judicature Acts 1873-75.

Some notable examples from this century include the Environmental Protection Act 1990, the Courts and Legal Services Act 1990, the Criminal Justice Acts 1988, 1991 and 1993 (to be followed in 1994 by the Police and Magistrates' Court Bill and the Criminal Justice and Public Order Bill).

This is not to suggest that the only means by which legal change can be effected is by way of statute, for the courts too have a role to play in developing the law. Theirs is, however, a much more limited role as we have seen when considering the sources of law.

Traditionally, the doctrine of the sovereignty of Parliament has limited the role of the courts and ensured that Parliament is the supreme law maker. The government of the day puts forward its legislative proposals and providing it has a strong majority in the House of Commons will expect to pass these into law. The courts will interpret the provisions contained in Acts of Parliament when and if a dispute arises concerning the meaning of the words used. The courts are also limited in

6.1   The background to change

developing the common law and are generally reluctant to extend the boundaries of the law beyond established precedent. The advantage of this is that the law will have some certainty but the disadvantage is that it may fail to take account of changing needs and attitudes. Policy is said to be the province of Parliament, and it will be for Parliament to promote major change in the law.

This is a relatively modern idea, for in the past the courts have taken it upon themselves to develop the law. This is clearly shown in the development of the law of tort, in particular the tort of negligence. However, some recent cases illustrate that the courts may yet demonstrate reforming zeal. The case of *R v R* (1991) where the House of Lords recognised for the first time that a husband could be guilty of the rape of his wife. In *Airedale NHS Trust v Bland* (1993) the House of Lords permitted the ending of treatment of a patient in a persistent vegetative state. *R v Brown* (1993) also demonstrates the willingness of the courts to take into account the wider issues and see the need for the law to cover new situations. In this case liability under ss 20 and 47 of the Offences Against the Person Act 1861 was imposed on those who had undertaken sado-masochistic acts in private.

On 30 March 1994 the Queen's Bench Divisional Court held that the rebuttable presumption that a child between the ages of 10 and 14 was incapable of committing a criminal offence was no longer part of English law. Lord Justice Mann said that the 'common law was not a system of rigid rules but of principles whose application might alter over time and should be renewed by succeeding generations of judges'. The court rejected three arguments for the retention of the presumption, namely the decision would have retrospective effect, change should only be made by Parliament or at least a decision of the House of Lords, and the court was bound by the doctrine of *stare decisis*. The judge also said that the presumption 'had no utility whatever in the present era and ought to go'. Appeal by way of case stated is to be made to the House of Lords so that a more authoritative statement of the law can be made.

.2   The Law Commission

Moving onto law reform agencies, the main body is the Law Commission established by the Law Commissions Act 1965, and appointed by the Lord Chancellor with five Commissioners appointed for up to five years and one consultant together with a legal support staff.

Two Commissions exist, one for England and Wales and the other for Scotland. The Commission for England and

Wales is chaired by a High Court Judge and the members are solicitors and barristers, judges and academics. No lay representatives sit on the Commissions. An annual report is laid before Parliament concerned with codification, repeal of obsolete and unnecessary Acts, reduction in the number of separate Acts (consolidation) and the elimination of anomalies.

The 1994 report concludes that of the 30 reports published since 1983 only one in five have been acted on by Parliament. It also states that the law should be made as simple, fair and cheap as possible and that there are far too many faults and flaws. Much of the blame for effective reform is to be laid at the door of Parliament and its antiquated procedures which are in urgent need of reform.

The Commission is charged with keeping under review the law of England and Wales 'with a view to its systematic development and reform, including in particular the codification of such law, the elimination of anomalies, the repeal of obsolete and unnecessary enactments and generally the simplification and modernisation of the law'. The extreme breadth of jurisdiction is limited in that the Commission may only work on topics approved by the Lord Chancellor. Its recommendations are, however, its own and are laid before Parliament. However, Parliament may decide not to give legislative effect to them and there is no duty in the Act on government to comment on such recommendations or the decision to legislate or not. Many of the recommendations made in the past have been adopted albeit in modified form.

Two areas which have been the subject of scrutiny by the Commission have seen its recommendations passed into law. The Unfair Contract Terms Act 1977 was passed as a result of the Commission's recommendations and also in the area of family and matrimonial provision its recommendations have been given legislative effect. Its proposal for a draft criminal code has, however, not met with wide support. In the light of many serious miscarriages of justice it might be argued that rather than devoting its attention to codification of the criminal law, time and resources would have been better spent investigating and proposing reform of the criminal justice system. This is particularly true now that it has become clear that the government has decided not to fully implement the recommendations of the Royal Commission on Criminal Justice in particular its decision to remove the right of silence of suspects.

A vital aspect of law reform is the process by which reform proposals are generated. An important preliminary to reform must be consultation with those affected by the proposals. This must include not only lawyers and judges but the general public and those whose interests would be affected. The Law Commission under the chairmanship of Lord Scarman developed the practice of issuing consultation papers (which became known as Green Papers due to the colour of their covers). The Commission researches a topic, sets out possible courses of action and their implications, the law as at the date of the Green Paper and any relevant practice from other jurisdictions. This is then published and responses are called for. A recent example is that of the Commission's consultation paper on administrative law entitled 'Administrative Law: Judicial Review and Statutory Appeals' (1993), in which the Commission considers the need for reform of the procedure for obtaining judicial review and the need for a general requirement for public decision-makers to give reasons for their decisions.

Other bodies now also prepare Green Papers including government departments. Another recent example is the Human Fertilisation and Embryology Authority established under the 1990 Act which has recently called for the views of all interested parties on the issue of the use of foetal tissue in fertility treatments.

| 6.3 | **The Law Reform Committee** | Another reform agency is the Law Reform Committee made up of judges and practising and academic lawyers. This was set up in 1952 and took over the work of the Law Revision Committee set up in 1934. It deals with civil law matters referred to it by the Lord Chancellor and is under a duty 'to consider, having regard especially to judicial decisions, what changes are desirable in such legal doctrines as the Lord Chancellor may from time to time refer to the Committee'. |

Some of the Acts which have resulted from its work include the Occupiers' Liability Act 1957, the Limitation Act 1939 and the Law Reform (Contributory Negligence) Act 1945. In 1966 its report on Transfer of Title to Chattels (Cmnd 2958) concluded that the interests of an innocent purchaser of goods should have precedence over those of the original owner and that the market overt exception to the *nemo dat* rule should be extended to cover all purchases from retail premises and auctions. This did not find favour with the government in 1966 but when Lord Renton put forward the Sale of Goods (Amendment) Bill in the House of Lords in January 1994 with the aim of abolishing the market overt exception it was rejected by the government pending publication of a Green Paper dealing with transfer of title.

So far as criminal law is concerned the Criminal Law Revision Committee oversees reform. This was established in 1959 as a standing committee and advises the Home Secretary of the need for reform. It is under a duty 'to examine such aspects of the criminal law of England and Wales as the Home Secretary may from time to time refer to the Committee to consider whether the law requires revision and to make recommendations'. Notable reports led to the Suicide Act 1961, the Theft Acts 1968 and 1978 and the Criminal Law Act 1967. This Committee has not been convened since 1985.

6.4   The Criminal Law Revision Committee

We have already mentioned the Royal Commission on Criminal Justice which reported in July 1993. This was set up in 1991 in response to several miscarriages of justice notably the 'Guildford Four' and the 'Birmingham Six' trials.

6.5   Royal Commissions and Advisory Committees

Royal Commissions are appointed by the Crown on the advice of a Minister who names a chairperson. Membership varies but reflects expert, professional and lay opinion. They have the aim of investigating a matter of public importance and take evidence and formulate recommendations. This may result in legislation following the usual process of Green Paper, followed by a White Paper containing the government's proposals, followed by a Bill and finally enacted by statute. However, invariably the recommendations are altered in part or not adopted at all.

It is instructive to trace the sequence of events which resulted in the Courts and Legal Services Act 1990. The Benson Royal Commission reported in 1979 and was followed by the Marre Report: 'A Time for Change' in 1988. This was followed by three Green Papers which in turn was followed by the White Paper: 'A Framework for the Future'. The Courts and Legal Services Bill followed and after amendment this was enacted in 1990 and brought into effect subsequently by means of regulations promoted by the Lord Chancellor.

The Lord Chancellor through his Advisory Committee on Legal Aid, Working Parties on Legal Services and Contingency fees also effects reforms. The recent report by Lord Justice Steyn for the Lord Chancellor's Advisory Committee on Education and Conduct recommended the abolition of the separate training of solicitors and barristers. The chairman of the Bar, Robert Seabrook QC has in response published a consultation paper and suggests that reform is timely. It is proposed that the Bar should not retain the monopoly over the training of barristers and that there should be a common vocational training of barristers and solicitors. The present time sees great pressure being applied to the existing system of training. The Lord Chancellor has given the Bar only another three years in which to continue with the existing system and the Director-General of Fair Trading wishes to see an end to the present monopoly. The latest embarrassment has been caused by the large number of applicants for places at Bar School who have been refused places, some of whom sought judicial review in the High Court. The proposed reforms are not without their critics from barristers and senior judges but the urgency for reform is such that it is inevitable.

6.6   Judicial inquiries

Another mechanism for reform is the judicial inquiry. Lord Justice Taylor has recently concluded his investigation of the 'Matrix Churchill (Arms to Iraq)' affair. It is likely that reforms will be instituted in the issue of public interest immunity certificates under the Crown Proceedings Act 1947 as a result of the criticisms that have been made of their use and the role of the Attorney-General.

Another notable inquiry was that of Lord Scarman into the Brixton Riots in 1981 which led to the Police and Criminal Evidence Act 1984.

6.7   Private Members' Bills

When considering the means by which law reform may be achieved, the role of the private member of Parliament should not be overlooked. If nothing else a bill promoted by a private member may well publicise the issues and even though not passed into law may create an opportunity for law to be passed in the future. Lord Stallard introduced a Crime of Vagrancy (Abolition) Bill which received its second reading in the House of Lords on 11 December 1993. If enacted it will repeal the Vagrancy Act 1824 apart from s 4 which prohibits indecent exposure in public. The effect of this reform will be to decriminalise begging and homelessness. Further progress through the Parliamentary stages will depend on it receiving government support and not being talked out of time.

This is illustrated by the Bill introduced by Dr Richard Berry in the House of Commons and which received its second reading on 11 March 1994 with the aim of outlawing discrimination against the disabled. There is no certainty that this Bill will become law given limitations on time imposed by the government.

There have been many notable Private Members' Bills including the Abortion Act 1967, the Video Recordings Act 1984, the Defamation Act 1952 and the Indecent Displays (Control) Act 1981. From the 1960's major reforms in the law have been made on moral issues including the Murder (Abolition of the Death Penalty) Act 1965, reform of the divorce law, abortion, suicide and homosexuality. A further change in the latter was recently seen as a result of an amendment proposed by Edwina Currie MP for the reduction in the age of consent for homosexuals from 21 to 18.

The part played by pressure groups should not be overlooked in bringing to the attention of the public and in lobbying MPs' need for reform. For example, Liberty (formerly the National Council for Civil Liberties), Justice, the Howard League for Penal Reform, the Legal Action Group and the Statute Law Reform Society are some bodies concerned with law reform.

6.8   Pressure groups and legislation

It is not always easy to distinguish 'pressure' and 'interest' groups. The former are those with a 'cause' such as prison reform, nuclear disarmament, protection of endangered species or divorce reform. The latter represent a body or group such as the Law Society, the TUC, the British Medical Council, Local Authorities, the RAC or AA or the CBI.

A recent Private Members' Bill sponsored by Alan Beith attempted to encourage energy conservation and had received the support of all the main conservation and environmental groups including Friends of the Earth. However, the government did not support the Bill (which would have imposed a duty on all local authorities to carry out an energy efficiency audit on all dwellings in their area) on the ground that it would have created an unnecessary burden on local authorities and increased costs on taxpayers. The junior environment minister, Tony Baldry, talked out the Bill by tabling some 200 amendments. The government assured the House of Commons that there were better ways of improving energy conservation and that Britain was on target to comply with the objectives agreed at the Rio Earth Summit in June 1992 on emissions into the atmosphere.

The issue of time and government control of business in the House of Commons (and to a lesser extent in the House of Lords) is an important one, not only in relation to Private Members' Bills but for legislation generally. Governments in recent years have controlled business by such devices as the guillotine which limits the amount of time devoted to debating the provisions of a bill. This is not the only way in which poorly drafted legislation might result. Sometimes government passes legislation to fill a gap or deal with an immediate problem. This was the case with the Insolvency (No 2) Bill 1994 which passed all its stages in one week from the announcement by the Secretary of State of the intention to introduce the Bill. The Act was passed to remedy the undesired effects of a judicial decision but it is now feared that the Act itself will give rise to interpretation difficulties not having been fully thought through.

As we have seen when considering statutory interpretation, the courts will have a role to play in interpreting legislation and following the case of *Pepper v Hart* (1993) Hansard, the Official Journal of proceedings in Parliament may be consulted in limited circumstances.

A distinction is usually made between 'codification' and 'consolidation'. The former involves re-writing a body of law (both statutes and case law), for example, the Sale of Goods Act 1893, the Theft Act 1968, the Bills of Exchange Act 1882 and the Partnership Act 1890.

Consolidation involves reducing the number of statutes on a particular subject to a more manageable number. An example is the Employment Protection (Consolidation) Act 1978 which has, of course, now been supplemented by later Employment Acts necessitating a new consolidating measure. The Consolidation of Enactments (Procedure) Act 1949 provides for consolidation measures.

6.9 The European context

Another means by which our law may be reformed is as a result of our membership of the European Union. A clear illustration following the *Factortame* case which demonstrates that European law takes precedence over domestic law is the case of *R v Secretary of State for Employment ex p Equal Opportunities Commission* (1994) where the House of Lords held that the provisions of the Employment Protection (Consolidation) Act 1978 applying to part-time workers were incompatible with European Union law and that the Equal Opportunities Commission was entitled to judicial review in the form of a declaration against the Secretary of State for Employment. The House of Lords decided that it was not necessary to refer the matter to the European Court of Justice under Article 177 of the Treaty of Rome but that it was competent to hear the matter. Other areas which have been subject to the influence of European Union law and policy include the protection of the environment and pollution and also regulation of companies, consumer and employee protection and quality standards for goods and services.

Reform may also be achieved as a result of the European Convention of Human Rights although as noted elsewhere this does not have binding effect in the UK. The continued failure of governments to ratify the Convention has given rise to calls for constitutional reform and the need for a written constitution or at least a Bill of Rights enforceable through the courts of the UK to protect the civil liberties of the citizen against governmental abuse of power. No such reform has been forthcoming in the face of arguments about the role of the courts and the doctrine of sovereignty of Parliament.

There are a number of other issues in need of legal reform and this will necessitate one or more of the reform bodies referred to preparing proposals and for Parliament then to pass legislation to give effect to them. It is unlikely that the courts will be able to effect such wide-ranging reforms given their traditional reluctance not to involve themselves with policy issues other than in extreme situations or where traditionally Parliament has not passed legislation.

6.10   Some areas in need of reform

One such issue concerns the '366 day rule' in the offence of murder, whereby if a defendant is to be successfully prosecuted it must be proved that his victim died within one year and a day of the commission of the injury. This has been referred to the Law Commission as a result of the improvements in medical science and treatment whereby victims are increasingly being kept alive on life-support machines but may well be pronounced dead some considerable time after the infliction of the injury.

Another issue is that of the defendant who is jointly accused of an offence with another and both refuse to assist the police in their investigations. The prosecution will fail in the absence of independent evidence to prove beyond all reasonable doubt the guilt of the accused. There have been several cases in recent years involving the deaths of children where joint suspects have refused to assist the police investigation and no other evidence exists as to who committed an offence. The result has been that the Crown Prosecution Service has not brought a prosecution in recognition of the right of an accused to remain silent and that in the absence of other evidence the presumption of innocence will ensure that the case will not succeed. It has been proposed that in this type of case that suspects, particularly those who have some family relationship with the victim, have imposed on them a duty to assist the police and that failure to comply would result in the court having a discretion to draw adverse conclusions.

The Law Commission has also had referred to it the question which has arisen following several decisions imposing sentences of five years on defendants found guilty of manslaughter. The Court of Appeal guidelines on sentencing suggests a sentence of five years where, for instance, death results from an act by a defendant who was not armed and there were no other aggravating circumstances. Victims' families have protested at the leniency of such sentences but the Attorney-General has refused to refer these cases to the Court of Appeal under ss 35 and 36 of the Criminal Justice Act 1988. The Law Commission has requested the views of all interested parties before October 1994 with a view to preparing proposals for reform thereafter.

We have already mentioned the Royal Commission on Criminal Justice which made 352 recommendations for reform of the criminal justice system in July 1993. The Criminal Justice Bill presently before Parliament contains in clauses 27 and 28 provisions for the removal of the right to silence. The Commission proposed retention of this right but the government has decided that on policy grounds the judge should be able to comment on a defendant's silence during investigation where, for example, the defendant attempts to rely on information known to him or her earlier. The right to silence has been described as a 'criminal's charter' and that those who have nothing to hide have nothing to fear from answering police questions. It remains to be seen what form the final provisions will take but critics suggest that any change will effectively dismantle the fundamental presumption that a person is innocent until proved guilty.

One reform proposed by the Royal Commission namely the creation of a criminal cases review body has come a stage closer to being implemented. The Home Secretary issued a consultation paper on 25 March 1994 inviting discussion as to the establishment of such a body to oversee alleged miscarriages of justice.

6.11 Conclusion

In conclusion, it can be seen from the above that reform of the law is often slow and piecemeal and that there is no one body charged with its reform and development. One thing that has become noticeable in recent years is that individuals or groups who wish to see reform of a particular area of law or the creation of law have become much more professional in their approach as to the means of achieving their aims. We have mentioned pressure and interest groups and it is useful also to note the efforts of investigative journalists who highlight flaws and failings in the law. It is through publicity that public awareness can be increased and for a debate to take place as to what end should be achieved and by what means.

Given that law is not an end in itself but rather a means to an end it is right that not only lawyers and judges should be concerned with law reform but also members of the public for whose benefit law exists. On a practical level law reform is essential to remove clutter and to ensure that finding and understanding the law is as straightforward as possible.

In a common law system where there is no reliance on codes and which is based on judicial precedent one of the major criticisms is that the law has become too complex not only in substance but also in its form. Consolidating statutes should reduce this problem but lack of Parliamentary time is often mentioned as a reason for the few consolidating measures passed. The judges also have limited powers to reform the law given their adherence to *stare decisis* and the fact that legislation is only interpreted when a dispute brings the meaning of a provision into doubt. We do not have a constitutional court with the power to measure legislation against the principles of a written constitution and thereby ensure that changes in the law are in line with the constitution. We have noted, however, that in the past much of the developments in the law arose as a result of judicial decisions and that this is still the case in special circumstances where the court feels compelled to break new ground on a serious issue rather than wait for Parliament to pass legislation. The judges are, however, guarded in the use of such power often stating that Parliament determines policy as the representative of the general public and that the courts are ill-suited to this task. Residual power may, however, exist in the courts to reform the law in pressing cases and where Parliamentary action is not likely.

Law Reform Agencies

Change and reform are distinguished and the various agencies concerned with reform are considered including Parliament, the courts, and bodies such as the Law Commission and pressure groups. The need for reform is mentioned and that this must be balanced with certainty.

The background to change

Commissions for England and Wales and Scotland were established by the Law Commission Act 1965 to review the law in their respective countries and ensure its development and reform, codification, repeal of obsolete measures and for its simplification and modernisation.

Appointment of Commissioners by the Lord Chancellor is noted as are its functions, procedure and effectiveness.

The Law Commission

The Law Reform Committee comprises judges and academic lawyers who review civil law matters referred to it by the Lord Chancellor.

The Law Reform Committee

The Criminal Law Revision Committee is a standing committee charged with examining criminal law matters referred to it by the Home Secretary. It has not been convened since 1985.

The Criminal Law Revision Committee

Two examples of Royal Commissions (which are appointed by the Crown) are the Runciman Commission on Criminal Justice which reported in July 1993 and the Benson Royal Commission Report on Legal Services in 1979.

The Lord Chancellor appoints Advisory Committees, for example, on legal aid and legal education to advise him on reform.

Royal Commissions and Advisory Committees

A notable recent example of a judicial inquiry is that of Lord Justice Scott's inquiry of the 'Matrix Churchill Affair', concerning the sale of arms to Iraq. Reforms are likely in the issue of public interest immunity certificates under the Crown Proceedings Act 1947.

Judicial inquiries

Even if a Private Members' Bill fails to become law (and private members have to compete for limited time and resources to promote a bill) the publicity and possible

Private Members' Bills

embarrassment to the government may be sufficient to ensure that legislation is promoted by the government at a later time.

The procedure for promoting such a bill has recently come to public attention as a result of the bill introduced by Richard Berry aimed at outlawing discrimination against the disabled.

Pressure groups and legislation

Some notable pressure groups include 'Liberty', 'Justice', the Howard League for Penal Reform and the Legal Action Group.

The distinction is made between 'pressure' and 'interest' groups, and the limitations which exist on Parliamentary time are noted. These include pressure of government business and devices such as the guillotine which curbs the amount of time spent on debating measures. Codification and consolidation are noted.

The European context

The recent case of *R v Secretary of State for Employment ex p Equal Opportunities Commission* (1994) is discussed, where the House of Lords held that a preliminary reference under Article 177 of the Treaty of Rome was not necessary, and that it was competent to decide that provisions of the Employment Protection (Consolidation) Act 1978 conflict with European Community law. The Commission was entitled to a declaration against the Secretary of State in a judicial review application.

Reference is also made to the European Convention of Human Rights and its effect on English law.

Some areas in need of reform

The following are mentioned:

- The '366 day rule' in the offence of murder whereby the victim must die within 'a year and a day' of the injury if the defendant is to be charged with murder. Improvements in medical care may ensure a victim survives longer on a life-support machine.

- Where a defendant is jointly accused with another and both refuse to assist the police in the absence of other sufficient evidence a prosecution will fail. In such a case it is suggested that both defendants should be under a duty to assist the police.

- The leniency of sentences for manslaughter.

- Clauses 27 and 28 of the Criminal Justice and Public Order Bill, removing the right to silence.

- The creation of a criminal cases review body to oversee alleged miscarriages of justice.

Reform is slow and piecemeal and no one body exists to effect reform. The role of pressure and interest groups is noted as is that of investigative journalists in publicising defects in the law. The limitations of Parliament in effecting reform suggest that the courts have residual power to effect change in some circumstances albeit that the UK does not have a constitutional court.

Conclusion

Chapter 7

Alternatives to Court Action

In this chapter we will consider some of the alternatives available, or which are proposed, for the settlement of disputes other than the traditional means by way of adjudication in a court of law.

It has long been established that disputes may be settled by way of adjudication by courts of law and in more recent times by tribunals. Tribunals took on much of their present day importance following the post-war Welfare State reforms. They were set up by statute to adjudicate disputes between the citizen and the State on such matters as welfare benefits, rates, taxation and land disputes. Some, including industrial tribunals, adjudicate disputes between individuals but where the State regulates the relationship of the parties by legislation, for example, pay and conditions of work, redundancy, maternity rights and unfair dismissal.

Tribunals may provide an alternative to a court of law in the sense that statute may provide that a certain type of dispute shall be adjudicated on by a tribunal rather than a court. This should not, however, be confused with a concept from America and countries of the Commonwealth known as 'alternative dispute resolution' (often abbreviated to ADR) and which is still in a developmental stage in the UK.

Alternative dispute resolution covers forums for the settlement of disputes by way of negotiation, conciliation, mediation and mini-trials and which emphasise settlement by agreement rather than adjudication where the emphasis is on finding in favour of one party and against the other. ADR may precede litigation as a way of establishing the common ground between the parties and the points on which they cannot agree. It must be noted that in any dispute litigation will usually be a last resort and legal advisers will attempt to negotiate a settlement.

In some disputes settlement may not take place until just before or even after the case comes to court. This is known as a settlement 'at the door of the court 'and has the advantages for the plaintiff that he or she does not have to prove their case before a court together with the attendant delay, cost and the possibility of losing the case and being responsible for not only their costs but those of their opponent. The advantages for a defendant may be similar and another advantage is that no precedent will be set and this is particularly useful for an institutional party such as an insurance company faced with a personal injury claim.

Terminology is not necessarily well defined and it is not always easy to distinguish between, for example, 'mediation' and 'conciliation'. The former involves an impartial independent third party who attempts to bring the parties to agreement but who does not put forward solutions. It is used in family disputes and is the less formal. Conciliation on the other hand may go further in an attempt to effect a reconciliation and a non-binding opinion may be given as is the case with court conciliation schemes which can then lead to a settlement.

Another means of settlement which can properly be included under ADR is arbitration. This is the most formal and a decision is made by an umpire appointed with the agreement of both parties which will be binding and is usually enforceable by the court. Given that arbitration is a well established means of settling disputes and results in an adjudication, albeit not by a judge sitting in that capacity we shall consider its main uses, then move on to consider the role of tribunals and then consider the developing use of alternative dispute resolution.

7.2   Arbitration

Both parties agree to submit to the procedure and decision of an arbitrator who will usually be a person with both legal knowledge and specialist knowledge of the subject-matter of the dispute. Arbitration is most often used in landlord and tenant disputes, commercial and shipping claims and where a contract provides that settlement shall be by way of arbitration. It is also used in the High Court where judges of the Commercial Court can act as arbitrators under s 4 of the Administration of Justice Act 1970, having obtained the permission of the Lord Chief Justice that pressure of work in the High Court and Crown Court is not such as to prevent his availability.

The judge when acting as an arbitrator sits in private and in any place convenient to the parties. Conduct of the hearing is informal and the award is private and so is not published as is a court judgment. The Arbitration Acts 1950, 1975 and 1979 regulate the procedure and powers of the arbitrator and provide for the enforcement of the award by the court.

Arbitration is also used in the County Court by way of the 'small claims procedure' involving claims of up to £1,000 (or more where both parties agree). At present there is an exception in respect of personal injury claims and other unliquidated claims, but it has been proposed by the Lord Chancellor to change the rules so as to include personal injury claims and other unliquidated claims and generally to increase the value of small claims from £1,000 to £2,500.

Small claims are heard by the district judge and parties usually represent themselves. In any event, no order for the costs of a legal representative can be made but some people choose to have the assistance of a 'McKenzie Friend' or adviser who offers a party to the proceedings support and advice. By the Lay Representatives (Rights of Audience) Order 1992 passed under ss 11 and 120 of the Courts and Legal Services Act 1990 lay representatives have rights of audience in small claims where the client he or she represents attends the hearing.

The advantages of arbitration are often said to be speed, cost, lack of formality, a binding decision which can be enforced by the court with the minimum of publicity and also the absence of a binding precedent for similar cases. However, in recent times the cost, time and complexity of arbitration proceedings have certainly increased but it remains a favoured option for it is still relatively cheaper and quicker than litigation, particularly in commercial matters.

It is usual for parties to a contract to include a term known as a 'Scott v Avery' clause after the case of that name in 1856, stipulating that in the event of a dispute arising it will be referred to arbitration and only if this is not successful will application be made to the court. This is permissible unlike a provision which attempts to oust the jurisdiction of the court altogether, that is, prevent a claim from ever coming to court. For businesses the main advantage of arbitration is that no binding precedent results so that if more than one claim arises, each will have to be settled separately.

Before moving on to consider tribunals, it is worth mentioning here the work of ACAS, the Advisory, Conciliation and Arbitration Service, which is an independent body which promotes good industrial relations by way of the voluntary co-operation of employers, employees and their representatives. Its services are free and it comprises a council with a chairperson and members drawn from employers, trade unions and employees. The main functions it performs are to provide advisory and information services, conciliation in trade disputes, arbitration services at the request of both parties, mediation and conciliation in individual cases of complaint, for example, where unfair dismissal or discrimination is alleged. Arbitration awards are not binding in law and normally attempts to settle a dispute by conciliation should be made before resort to arbitration.

7.3 Tribunals	Since tribunals are so varied in composition, appointment of members, procedure and functions, it is not possible to provide a satisfactory classification.

Many examples of statutory tribunals can be found, including the Social Security Appeals Tribunal, Medical Appeals Tribunal, Mental Health Review Tribunals, Industrial Tribunals, Pensions Appeal Tribunal, Immigration Appeals Tribunal, Agriculture Land Tribunal, the Lands Tribunal, Plant Varieties and Seeds Tribunal, Commissioners of Income Tax, VAT Tribunals, Rent Tribunals and Data Protection Tribunal.

As a general rule, tribunals comprise three members one of whom is appointed chairperson and who is legally trained. The other two members are drawn from the area or areas of concern. For example, with Industrial Tribunals one member will have knowledge and experience as an employer and the other as an employee. In some cases as, for example, the Lands Tribunal one member sits alone.

Before looking more closely at some of the statutory tribunals we must mention 'domestic' tribunals which regulate disciplinary matters of trades and professions and also sporting activities. Some examples include the General Medical Council, the Solicitors' Disciplinary Tribunal of the Law Society, the Inns of Court, the Jockey Club and the General Nursing Council. Some have been set up by statute or Royal Charter and others by way of contracts entered into between members and the association.

We will consider later the extent to which such tribunals are regulated by the courts. Statutory tribunals are subject to the supervision of the High Court under Order 53 of the Rules of the Supreme Court whereby if they act *ultra vires* or in breach of the rules of natural justice the prerogative orders of *mandamus, certiorari* and *prohibition* will lie so as to correct the excess of power. In addition, a person aggrieved by the decision of a tribunal may seek an injunction or declaration of his or her rights and where a private law right has been broken a claim for damages may be made.

7.4   Some examples

In this section the role of four administrative or statutory tribunals will be considered.

7.4.1   Social Security Tribunals

Procedure is governed by Schedule 8 of the Health and Social Services and Social Security Adjudications Act 1983 amending the Social Security Act 1975. On refusal of a claim for benefit such as employment benefit by the Social Security Office application is made to the local administration officer. Appeal lies to a local Social Security Appeal Tribunal with three members: two non-lawyers and a legally qualified chairperson. A further appeal lies to a Social Security Commissioner with leave. These are appointed from barristers or solicitors of not less than 10 years standing, and since the Courts and Legal Services Act 1990 eligibility will be extended to those with rights of audience. Further appeal lies to the Court of Appeal with leave of the court or the Commissioner and then to the House of Lords.

Procedure is governed by rules made by the Lord Chancellor. Hearings are in public in various parts of the country and there is a right for claimants to be legally represented and to receive legal aid. Decisions are written and full reasons are given. The tribunal deals with valuations of property, for example, for compulsory purchase compensation claims. Appeal lies to the Court of Appeal on points of law. The tribunal is presided over by a President who will have held high judicial office or will have been a barrister of at least seven years' standing (or equivalent). Other members will either hold legal qualifications or have experience in land valuation.

7.4.2   Valuation and Lands Tribunals

Industrial tribunals hear claims concerning contracts of employment, unfair dismissal, redundancy, equal pay and sexual and racial discrimination in employment. The chairperson will have been a barrister or solicitor of at least seven years' standing appointed by the Lord Chancellor. The other two members will have expertise of employment matters, one as an employer and the other as an employee. They are selected by the President on Industrial Tribunals appointed by the Lord Chancellor from a panel compiled by the Secretary of State for Employment. Legal aid is not available although it is on appeal to the Employment Appeal Tribunal. The legal advice scheme will permit initial advice to be given and a claimant may wish to have the assistance of a 'McKenzie Friend' during the tribunal proceedings.

7.4.3   Industrial tribunals

The Employment Appeal Tribunal is a superior court of record governed by the Employment Protection (Consolidation) Act 1978 which hears appeals on points of law. Appeals are heard by a High Court judge or a judge of the Court of Appeal and two or four appointed members with special knowledge or experience in employment. A majority decision may be made and hearings are usually in public except where questions of national security or trade secrets are raised. Appeals lie to the Court of Appeal and then to the House of Lords. Leave is required in both cases.

The recent House of Lords decision in *R v Secretary of State for Employment ex p Equal Opportunities Commission and Another*

(1994) illustrates not only that where domestic legislation (in this case the provisions of the Employment Protection (Consolidation) Act 1978 concerning the rights of part-time workers) conflicts with European law the latter takes precedence but also that a body such as the Equal Opportunities Commission has a sufficient interest in challenging legislation to seek judicial review under Order 53. The court dismissed an appeal by a private individual on the ground that she was not entitled to seek judicial review as hers was a private law claim against her employer in the Industrial Tribunal (at first instance) and thereafter by appeal to the Employment Appeal tribunal and then to the Court of Appeal and House of Lords in appropriate cases.

7.4.4   Mental Health Review Tribunals

The Mental Health Act 1983 permits the detention of persons in secure hospitals in certain circumstances. A person who considers that he or she is entitled to be discharged may apply for release to the above tribunal. The tribunal may order conditional or unconditional discharge. The tribunal is staffed by a chairperson who must be legally qualified and two other members, one of whom must be a medical doctor and the other a person considered by the Lord Chancellor to be suitable given knowledge or experience. Where a restricted patient does not apply for release those who have charge of him or her are under a duty to do so at prescribed frequencies and in any event the Secretary of State has power to refer cases to the tribunal. With effect from 11 April 1994 the Advice by Way of Representation scheme has been extended to cover all applications to this tribunal.

7.4.5   Domestic tribunals

As we have already mentioned, domestic tribunals, such as the General Medical Council, regulate the standards of members of the trades, professions or activities and enforce the rules amongst their members. In law, domestic tribunals are treated as private associations based on contract and so are not subject to the prerogative orders under Order 53 of the Rules of the Supreme Court. This was established in the case of *Law v National Greyhound Racing Club* (1983) and subsequently followed in *R v Football Association Ltd ex p Football League Ltd* (1993) where it was held that the Football Association was a domestic body whose powers derived from private law and that in general it was not susceptible to judicial review.

However, it has been recognised that the courts do have a limited jurisdiction over domestic tribunals. Thus, the court may grant a declaration of rights as in the case of *Lee v Showman's Guild of GB* (1952). Alternatively, the court may grant an injunction to ensure that an association interprets its rules and applies the rules of natural justice correctly. The courts have prohibited the wrongful expulsion of members, refusals to admit to membership, refusals to admit women and restrictions improperly placed on members.

Prior to 1986 the law was quite clear and judicial review would be available where an organisation derived its powers from statute or the Royal Prerogative. If the source of power was from contract entered into between the organisation and its members the courts only had a limited jurisdiction. In *R v Panel on Take-overs and Mergers ex p Datafin* (1986) the Court of Appeal decided that this body was susceptible to judicial review even though its powers were not derived from either statute or the prerogative. The panel exercised public functions in the City of London and these functions gave rise to public law consequences. Thus, in addition, to the source of power it was essential also to consider the nature of the functions performed. In later cases, however, the courts have retracted from this bold approach and have emphasised the need for the public function to have some relationship with government.

In *R v Chief Rabbi ex p Wachmann* (1992) the court stated that judicial review was only available where the source of the public function was the government. This was followed in *R v Disciplinary Committee of the Jockey Club ex p Aga Khan* (1993) where it was held that although governmental functions were performed the club derived its powers from contract and so judicial review was inappropriate. The case of *R v Insurance Ombudsman Bureau and Insurance Ombudsman ex p Aegon Life Assurance Ltd* (1993) comes full circle in that the court held that where power derives from contract judicial review will not lie even where governmental functions are performed.

Two further cases illustrate the distinction between contractual source of power and that derived from statute or the prerogative. In *R v Visitors to the Inns of Court ex p Calder & Persaud* (1993) it was held that the visitors to the Inns (judges of the High Court who adjudicated in matters of discipline) were only subject to judicial review in limited cases namely where the visitor had acted outside his jurisdiction or had abused his power or had acted in breach of the rules of natural justice. This had long been established in educational institutions founded by Charter or by way of contract or charitable trust and further authority is to be found in *Page v Hull University* (1993) where a lecturer who had been made redundant claimed that under the University statutes he could only be dismissed for good cause and that none had been shown. The University visitor found that the dismissal was *intra vires*. It was held on the facts there was no jurisdiction to hear an application for judicial review.

However, in *R v Manchester University ex p Nolan* (1993) which concerned a student who was alleged to have cheated at examinations the statutory source of the powers of the University was noted (as a new University it was set up as a result of the Education Act 1988) and despite contractual elements in the relationship of student and University judicial review was available without the limitations placed on Charter institutions. The anomaly has been commented on by Professor Wade and others who suggest that it is time for reform in this area.

7.5 Control of administrative tribunals

We have already noted that tribunals may be controlled by means of the supervisory jurisdiction of the Queen's bench Divisional Court under Order 50 of the Rules of the Supreme Court as provided for in s 31 of the Supreme Court Act 1981. It has often been said that as tribunals are created by the State to adjudicate on disputes between the citizen and the State there is a tendency for them to find against the individual.

In addition to the control by way of judicial review control is also imposed by the Council on Tribunals established as a result of the Franks Committee Report in 1957 by the Tribunals and Inquiries Act 1958. This Act has subsequently been amended by the Act of 1971 and both have been replaced by the 1992 Act of the same title.

The Council gives advice to the Lord Chancellor on the workings of administrative tribunals and reports to Parliament annually. It keeps under review the constitution and workings of tribunals and has power to examine rules of procedure used by a tribunal. The Franks Committee Report concluded that the system of administrative justice should achieve the aims of 'openness, fairness and impartiality' and if these were to be achieved tribunals should give reasons for their decisions (so as to facilitate appeals in appropriate cases) and a right of appeal should exist to the High Court or Court of Appeal.

Following the Franks Report, chairmen of tribunals are selected by the Secretary of State from a panel of persons appointed by the Lord Chancellor. It is usual for chairmen to be legally qualified. Legal representation is usually allowed but a major drawback is the lack of legal aid availability except in the Employment Appeal Tribunal and the Lands Tribunal. The ABWOR scheme has, however, now been extended to hearings before the Mental Health Review Tribunal. Hearings are normally in public unless, for example, the interests of national security are paramount. Although the rules of evidence are relaxed it is usual for all documents to be disclosed to the other side and reasons for the decision are given at the request of the parties. Appeal lies to the High Court or where statute provides to the Court of Appeal.

It is useful to mention here the role of inquiries which are also governed by the Tribunals and Inquiries Act 1992. In some areas of administration, notably town and country planning and compulsory purchase of land, no right exists for an aggrieved individual to have resort in the first instance to a court or tribunal. Statute, and in the case of planning provisions, this is the Town and Country Planning Act 1990, provides for an administrative appeal to the Secretary of State who appoints an inspector to conduct a public local inquiry into the grievance. It might be that an applicant for planning permission has been refused consent by the local planning authority for his or her area or, having been granted permission, has had conditions attached which the applicant finds unsatisfactory. The inspector hears evidence and then prepares a report for the minister who then makes a decision. Only then does a right of appeal lie to the High Court and, in some cases, it may be appropriate to seek judicial review of a planning decision where it is alleged that the decision-maker acted *ultra vires* or in breach of the rules of natural justice.

It is usual where major developments are planned, for example, highways or an airport, for the Secretary of State to call a public inquiry so that all those who have some interest in the proposed development have the opportunity to air their views. It is not only residents of an area which is the subject of a proposed major development that may put forward their views but also those who represent interests which may be adversely affected such as environmental and conservationist bodies, eg Friends of the Earth, the National Trust or the Council for the Conservation of Rural England.

Before concluding our discussion of tribunals it is necessary to briefly sum up with some of their main advantages and disadvantages. Following the post-1947 governmental intervention into social welfare and administration a need arose for quick and cheap means of adjudicating disputes. The courts were not considered suitable to handle the detailed provisions of such legislation and delegated legislation and in any case could not have coped with the volume of claims. Tribunals offered a means of adjudication in an informal setting where the rules of evidence were relaxed and compared with the courts were cheap, quick and located locally. They also provided knowledge and expertise from those selected for their connection with the subject-matter in dispute.

7.6 Advantages and disadvantages of administrative tribunals

Tribunals are primarily concerned with the proof of fact and are not bound by previous decisions although, in applying the law, must take account of superior court decisions. Tribunals are firmly embedded into dispute resolution but they are not without criticism either generally as a system or in relation to particular tribunals or decisions. One criticism is that they tend to find in favour of the government view although this should be checked by the supervisory jurisdiction of the High Court and the Council on Tribunals. Another criticism is the lack of legal aid and a further criticism is that there is no uniform procedure regulating all Administrative Tribunals and no one appeal procedure.

It has been suggested that there should be established an Administrative Court to hear all appeals from tribunals and replace the present jurisdiction of the High Court and Court of Appeal. Some argue that resort to tribunals is justice on the cheap, particularly as there is no choice as to forum and that, consequently, tighter procedures should be instigated so as to ensure a high quality of decision-making including the automatic giving of reasons and legal aid. A criticism made in recent years has been that the idealism of the Franks Report has been lost and that tribunals are no longer so cheap, quick and informal as they once were and that in fact they have become subject to delay and complex procedures with no overall pattern of procedure or control.

The industrial tribunals are a good illustration where it may take up to a year for a case to be heard and in some 22% of applications parties are legally represented. This increases the chance of success for those represented but the compensation awards are low and legal aid is not available. One other factor is the increased amount of legislation that has to be taken into account emanating from the European Union and also precedent.

7.7 Alternative dispute resolution

In this section we shall consider recent developments to encourage the use of non-adversarial procedures in the settlement of disputes including mediation, conciliation and mini-trials. The most formal type of ADR, arbitration, has already been considered. On consulting a dictionary, this phrase is used to describe 'conciliation, mediation and mini-trial procedures for the resolution of disputes without recourse to litigation'.

It has been in use in America and Australia, Canada and New Zealand for some time and has found favour there in family and sporting disputes, and has been endorsed by the Lord Chancellor in the light of major criticisms as to the effectiveness of the civil justice system and the pressures on legal aid. A court decision offers certainty and finality (subject to rights of appeal) but these are often outweighed by delay, cost and the stress of undertaking litigation.

ADR attempts to involve the client in the process of resolving the dispute. It does not rely on an adversarial approach but rather on reaching an agreement. Each case is decided on its merits without reference to previous cases and the common ground between the parties can be emphasised rather than points of disagreement. It offers a confidential process and the outcome will not be published without the consent of both parties. Resolution of a dispute can be quicker and more straightforward and hearing times and places are at the agreement of the parties. As we have already noted, negotiation before undertaking litigation is a recognised procedure in an attempt to settle the matter amicably. However, it will be important for each party to preserve his or her position should litigation not be avoidable. It is usual to state that all correspondence is 'without prejudice' so that statements made during negotiation cannot be relied on by the opponent at the trial.

7.7.1   Mediation

This involves a neutral third party acting as a 'go-between' so as to facilitate co-operation and agreement. Where the relationship between the parties needs to be preserved, for example, in family disputes or those involving commercial matters, mediation ensures that the relationship is not soured as it would be by litigation. It is a voluntary process and, should it fail, the parties will have preserved their positions. The procedure is informal and involves an independent third party discussing the matter in dispute with each party in separate rooms. The mediator is independent and assists the parties to negotiate with each other on points in dispute. Parties feel in control and mediation is much used in America in family and corporate disputes. It can be used to settle priorities before the start of litigation or in some cases in place of litigation. However, its use presupposes a degree of co-operation between the parties and one of the major criticisms is that where parties are entrenched mediation will not be appropriate.

Commercial mediation is used in the UK and has been promoted by companies such as International Dispute Resolution Europe Ltd who predict that before long lawyers will adopt mediation as it is being demanded by commercial clients who see as its advantages speed, cost, simplicity and the preservation of goodwill. Its mediators are lawyers with mediation training. The Centre for Dispute Resolution founded in 1990 under the auspices of the Confederation of British Industry and commercial law firms also offers commercial mediation. The National Association of Family Mediation and Conciliation Services offer mediation in family disputes. Some 57 local agencies offer support to those who wish to conduct their own negotiations and only refer to lawyers in an advisory capacity. Some 300 mediators throughout the country offer family counselling and legal advice. The mediators are trained solicitors and counsellors and the aim is to arrive at a mutually agreed settlement.

The Lord Chancellor published a Green Paper in 1993 proposing radical reforms in divorce law. The sole ground for divorce would be 'irretrievable breakdown' but only after 12 months' reflection time. Divorce settlement would be taken out of the courts and instead family mediation centres would be established throughout the country. It would be compulsory for all parties to attend such a centre for an hour-long interview with the aim of saving those marriages which have not irretrievably broken down. The Lord Chancellor has also indicated that the annual £180 million Legal Aid Bill for divorce must be reduced. Those who refuse mediation could be denied legal aid.

A variation known as Med-Arb is also used in America. If both parties agree mediation is used with the option of resorting to arbitration where appropriate.

| 7.7.2 | Conciliation |

Conciliation is a half-way house between arbitration on the one hand and mediation on the other, the former being the most formal and the latter being the least formal. The conciliator offers a non-binding opinion which may lead to settlement.

In 1985 the Lord Chancellor's Department commissioned a report by the Conciliation Project Unit at Newcastle University to investigate the cost-effectiveness of conciliation in the County Court and in the settlement of matrimonial disputes. The Civil Justice Review of 1992 highlighted the often costly and bitter litigation resulting in such disputes and recommended reform. However, it must be noted that where ADR is used in conjunction with litigation the result will be an increase in cost and delay in some cases.

| 7.7.3 | Mini-trials |

This is another practice much used in America to settle commercial disputes. Lawyers representing the parties present the arguments in the case to the parties themselves and a neutral adviser who may be a judge or senior lawyer. In the words of the Beldham Report this will enable the parties 'to assess the strengths, weaknesses and prospects of the case, and then have an opportunity to enter into settlement discussions on a realistic, business-like basis'. The neutral adviser has a vital role to play and may offer an opinion on the case having knowledge or experience of the matter in dispute.

In 1992 the Hart Workshop at the Institute of Advanced Legal Studies carried out a debate on civil justice and its alternatives. Several points were made including that conciliation procedures first started to be used in the UK in the 1970s and that it had already been much used abroad particularly in commercial disputes.

The aim of ADR is to facilitate settlement whereas the aim of litigation is to obtain judgment. Judges are increasingly becoming involved with ADR as are solicitors and barristers. This may well have the disadvantage of clouding the perception of their roles by the lay client. In addition, it will create tensions between lawyers and other professionals who might expect to offer services such as counsellors and social workers. Proper training is essential but to date little has been done to provide public funding for such services and where litigation follows ADR the costs of both will have to be met.

In 1993, a practice statement was issued by the Commercial Court on ADR to the effect that parties should be encouraged to consider using ADR as an additional means of settling disputes. Judges of the Commercial Court cannot offer ADR, but the clerk to the court retains a list of bodies offering mediation, conciliation and other ADR services although it would be for the parties or their legal representatives to approach such bodies.

The Report of the Committee on Alternative Dispute Resolution established by the General Council of the Bar and chaired by Lord Justice Beldham was published in 1991 and supported the notion that the courts should embrace ADR in order to support the judicial process. This is a widely supported idea and involves potential litigants undertaking ADR processes before resorting to litigation.

Several experiments have been conducted in the English courts, for example, in the divorce county courts in property and children proceedings. There is no one pattern but they range from meeting with the parties to draw their attention to the advantages of settlement to encouragement for further negotiations leading to settlement. In some courts the judge or court welfare officers act as mediators or refer the parties to an outside agency. In others a 'pre-trial' review is held at which conciliation on property matters is encouraged leading to settlement. The Beldham Report recommended that such preliminary procedures should be used generally in civil disputes and proposed that pilot projects be set up in both the county court and High Court. The scheme could be either entirely voluntary or, in suitable cases identified by the judge, mediation could be suggested. The mediator would be selected from lawyers with at least seven years' post-qualification experience. At least two concerns have been identified with court-linked ADR namely the clouding of the perception of the roles of judges and lawyers and the position of weak parties who may find themselves manipulated by the other party and the mediator. Some would go so far as to say that compromise of a dispute is not as effective as allowing a person his or her 'day in court' and that ADR is a poor substitute for having one party win and the other lose in open court. The Beldham Report assumes that lawyers with long experience will make competent mediators but this is unproven and there would seem to be a serious conflict in the roles of a neutral adviser and that of a representative of a claimant.

The Law Society's Guide to the Professional Conduct of Solicitors states that mediation is a separate professional activity and not part of a solicitor's practice. In any event there are others who are already able to offer ADR services including social workers, accountants, family counsellors, architects and surveyors.

In concluding our discussion of ADR we must note in passing the role played in settling disputes of administrative agencies such as the Citizens' Advice Bureaux, the Advertising Standards Authority, trade associations such as the Association of British Laundry Cleaning and the National Association of Retail Furnishers and ombudsmen schemes such as the Estate Agents Ombudsman and the Office of the Banking Ombudsman.

Ombudsmen in the public administration field were set up as a result of the recommendations of the Justice Report in 1960. The Parliamentary Commissioner for Administration and Local Government Commissioners were established under the Parliamentary Commissioner Act 1967 and the Local Government Act 1974 respectively to review malad-ministration in the conduct of public powers and duties. In 1987 the Health Services Commissioner was set up with power to review the workings of the national health service. Under the Courts and Legal Services Act, ss 21 to 26, the Legal Services Ombudsman oversees the workings of the Solicitors' Complaints Bureau which deals with complaints against solicitors not involving allegations of professional negligence. The Ombudsman also reviews complaints against barristers and other professionals such as legal executives and licensed conveyancers.

Alternatives to Court Action

Overview

The existing and proposed alternatives to adjudication as a means of settling disputes are considered, together with the reasons for the shift towards finding alternatives and their advantages and disadvantages.

Arbitration, tribunals and types of alternative dispute resolution (ADR) are taken in turn.

Arbitration

The appointment and functions of an arbitrator are explained, and examples given including the small claims procedure and appointment of High Court Judges from the Commercial Court under s 4 Administration of Justice Act 1970.

The advantages of arbitration are speed, cost, lack of formality, enforcement by the court, little publicity and the absence of a binding precedent.

The Arbitration Acts 1950, 1975 and 1979

Arbitration is most often used in commercial disputes and the parties may include a clause in their contract providing for settlement of disputes by arbitration. '*Scott v Avery*' clauses are noted. The role of the Advisory, Conciliation and Arbitration Service (ACAS) in the settlement of employment disputes is also noted.

Tribunals

Classification is not easy given the varied composition, appointment of members, procedure and functions of the many tribunals in existence. Some examples are given, ranging from the Mental Health Review Tribunal to the Lands Tribunal to the Social Security Appeals Tribunal.

'Statutory' tribunals are distinguished from 'domestic' tribunals, that is, those regulating disciplinary matters in trades and professions for example the Solicitors' Disciplinary Tribunal.

The supervisory jurisdiction of the High Court is also noted.

Domestic tribunals

R v Football Association Ltd ex p Football League Ltd (1993)

Lee v Showman's Guild of GB (1952)

R v Panel on Take-overs and Mergers ex p Datafin (1986)

R v Chief Rabbi ex p Wachmann (1992)

R v Disciplinary Committee of the Jockey Club ex p Aga Khan (1993)

R v Insurance Ombudsman Bureau and Insurance Ombudsman ex p Aegon Life Assurance Ltd (1993)

R v Visitors to the Inns of Court ex p Calder & Persaud (1993)

Page v Hull University (1993)

R v Manchester University ex p Nolan (1993)

Social Security Tribunals

Schedule 8 Health and Social Services and Social Security Adjudications Act 1983 governs procedure. Appeals lie to the Social Security Appeal Tribunal and then with leave to a Social Security Commissioner who is legally trained. Further appeal to the Court of Appeal and then to House of Lords.

Valuation and Lands Tribunals

Valuation and Lands Tribunals deal with valuations of property and the Lord Chancellor makes rules governing procedure. Appeal lies to the Court of Appeal on points of law. The President of the tribunal holds legal qualifications.

Industrial tribunals

Industrial tribunals decide employment disputes including unfair dismissal, redundancy and sexual and racial discrimination claims. The chairperson, who is legally qualified sits with two others (one with knowledge as an employer and the other as an employee) and is appointed by the Lord Chancellor. Appeal lies to the Employment Appeal Tribunal and then to the Court of Appeal and then the House of Lords. (*R v Secretary of State for Employment ex p Equal Opportunities Commission and Another* (1994)).

Mental Health Review Tribunals

ABWOR was extended to cover all applications to this tribunal in April 1994. It can order the detention of those found to be mentally ill under the Mental Health Act 1983. The chairperson must be legally qualified and one of the other two members must be a medical doctor.

Control of Administrative Tribunals

The two main types of control are judicial review under Order 53 of the Rules of the Supreme Court and by the Council on Tribunals established under what is now the Tribunals and Inquiries Act 1992. The use of inquiries particularly in town and country planning matters is also mentioned.

Advantages and disadvantages of Administrative Tribunals

The main advantages of tribunals are speed, cost, informality, knowledge and expertise and being situated locally.

Criticisms include their tendency to take the government view, the lack of legal aid and the absence of a uniform procedure. The proposal to set up an Administrative Court to hear appeals from all tribunals has not been taken up.

The use of alternative dispute resolution (ADR) in the UK is still in a developmental stage but is much used in America, Canada, Australia and New Zealand.

This term covers a range of techniques which provide an alternative to adjudication of disputes and attempt to involve the parties in the settlement process. The three main types are outlined.

- Mediation

  A neutral third party acts as a go-between to facilitate agreement between the parties. Its use in commercial and family disputes is mentioned, as is the Lord Chancellor's Green Paper on divorce reform published in 1993 recommending the use of family mediation centres.

- Conciliation

  A 'half way house' between arbitration (the most formal, and which is binding) and mediation (the least formal).

  The conciliator offers a non-binding opinion to assist in settlement.

- Mini-trials

  An American practice used to settle commercial disputes where a neutral adviser (a judge or senior lawyer) hears the arguments of both sides and then attempts to have the parties settle points in issue.

Various initiatives are noted which investigate and encourage the use of ADR. These include the practice statement of the Commercial Court in 1993 and the Beldham Committee Report published in 1991, which supported the use of ADR in the judicial process. Experiments have been conducted in the use of ADR in divorce county courts following the Beldham Report.

The roles of administrative agencies including the Citizens' Advice Bureaux is noted as is the role of Ombudsmen in public administration and commercial activities.

Chapter 8

Civil Proceedings – In Outline

Civil disputes involve a wide range of matters including claims for faulty goods and services, trespass to property, personal injury claims, disputes over the ownership or disposition of property. Taking a case to court will be the last resort in the majority of disputes and this is just as well if for no other reason that if everyone with a legal claim wished to litigate the courts would be unable to cope with the demand.

Most claims are settled before they reach court and it is a requirement for the legal representatives of both parties to try to negotiate a settlement at the outset. What is known as 'a letter before action' is sent by the claimant or his or her lawyer setting out the position and how it might be settled. It is usual to conduct negotiations by inserting into correspondence the phrase 'without prejudice' so as to preserve the position of the writer and prevent the contents of letters being called in evidence without their consent.

It may be that alternative dispute resolution (ADR) is available and allows the parties to settle the issue by agreement rather than resort to litigation. This takes various forms as we have seen in the chapter on 'Alternatives to Court Action', including arbitration, mediation and conciliation. It may have the advantages of speed and cost and avoid the stress of appearing in court and preparing for a trial.

We will consider first the procedure for bringing a claim in the High Court and then in the county court. It may appear odd to have two courts with jurisdiction to hear civil claims at first instance but this has been due mainly to their historical development. The High Court was created by the Judicature Acts 1873-75 with originally five divisions: Chancery, Probate, Divorce and Admiralty, Queen's Bench, Common Pleas and Exchequer. The Common Pleas and Exchequer Divisions were merged with the Queen's Bench Division a little later and in 1970 the Family Division was created from Probate, Divorce and Admiralty Divisions. The county courts were created in 1846 as a system of small claims courts dealing mainly with debt enforcement.

Although both have developed along different paths (High Court procedure is regulated by the 'White Book' or by its full title: 'The Supreme Court Practice' and the Supreme Court Act

8.1   Civil disputes

8.2   High Court proceedings

1981 (as amended) and the County Court by the 'Green Book', that is the 'County Court Practice' and the County Courts Act 1984 , differences have largely been ones of detail rather than substance.

Thus, terminology differs as do the forms used and some means of enforcing judgments. As we shall see later, however, as a result of the Civil Justice Review leading up to the Courts and Legal Services Act 1990, points of difference have been further reduced.

3.2.1   Underlying principles

It is worth mentioning here some of the main features of the civil justice system. The underlying principle of any system, whether criminal or civil, must be the attainment of justice.

One means by which this can be assured is equality of access regardless of means. In addition to substantive rules of law there must also be fair rules of procedure and requirement for proof of facts alleged. Ours is an adversarial system likened to a battle between two adversaries only one of whom can be adjudicated the winner. The judge is usually the arbiter of both fact and law and makes a decision following the presentation of evidence by oral testimony. The plaintiff has the burden of proof, 'on a balance of probabilities' (ie 'more likely than not') and usually decisions are made in open court where the result can be published and to which members of the public can be admitted. A decision will be final except where an appeal is permitted and in some cases this may only be on questions of law or where leave is given.

3.2.2   Procedure in the High Court

(a) Pre-trial Proceedings

Proceedings are commenced either by writ or by originating summons or motion. Any action may start by writ and some must. The originating summons or motion is only used where a question of law is in point such as the construction of an Act or other document such as a will.

The writ must issue from the court and until the action is heard the procedure is at an 'interlocutory' stage. To issue a writ the plaintiff takes two copies (and as many additional copies as there are defendants) to the Central Office of the High Court in London or a local District Registry. One copy, signed by the plaintiff or his solicitor, is sealed, stamped and filed at the court. The second is sealed and returned to the plaintiff. The writ remains valid for 12 months and must be served on the defendant within four calendar months of the date of sealing. Service may be made post or personally on the defendant. Included with the writ is either a Statement of Claim or a brief statement of the nature of the claim and remedy sought. A fee is payable and the legal aid certificate, if appropriate, must be produced.

On receipt the defendant has 14 days within which to acknowledge service of the writ. If he fails to do so or if he has no defence, the plaintiff may obtain judgment 'in default'. If the defendant wishes to contest the claim and has acknowledged service the pleadings are prepared by both parties. The plaintiff submits a statement of claim (if not in the writ) and is required to do so within 14 days of the date of the defendant's acknowledgement. This outlines the facts on which the plaintiff relies and the remedy sought. Failure to do so permits the defendant to apply for dismissal of the claim for 'want of prosecution'. The time periods are intended to speed up the proceedings but can be extended by the mutual agreement of the parties.

On receipt of the statement of claim the defendant replies by entering a defence denying or refusing to admit the allegations. Failure to do so results in admission of liability. Alternatively, the defendant may wish to make a full admission and the plaintiff then proceeds to enter judgment.

The plaintiff may issue a reply to the defence but is usually presumed to deny the allegations in the defence. Either party may then apply to the court for further and better particulars to clarify any issues arising from the pleadings.

The defendant may include in his defence a counterclaim or, if it is a money claim, a 'set-off'. A counterclaim raises a separate issue from that raised in the plaintiff's claim, for example, if P sues D for breach of contract for non-payment for goods D may counterclaim that P is liable to him as the goods supplied were faulty. A 'set-off' allows a claim for money to be cancelled out, so if P sues D to recover a loan of £5,000 D may attempt to claim a set-off against a debt owing to him by P.

Pleadings then close although the writ or pleadings may be amended at any stage providing leave of a Master is granted for substantial changes and for those after close of pleadings. A Master may order further and better particulars so as to clarify any issues and the answers are attached to and become part of the pleadings.

Within 14 days of the close of pleadings both sides send to the other a list of documents. These fall into one of three categories:

- those in possession which will be produced to the other side;

- those in possession but to which the party objects to producing and his reasons (for example, that they are 'privileged');

- those no longer in his possession.

The Master may order discovery of documents if full disclosure is not made or objections to disclosure are inadequate. Failure to make discovery may result in the claim or defence being struck out.

Either side may serve a notice on the other to admit facts appearing on the face of the pleadings. Alternatively, or in addition, written questions may be served on the other with the Master's leave. These are called 'interrogatories' and their purpose is to prove a fact peculiarly within the knowledge of the other party. They are a type of discovery (of facts, not documents) for example, establishing a person's handwriting by comparing samples. There is a duty to answer by way of sworn statement (an 'affidavit').

Within one month of close of pleadings the plaintiff must take out a Summons for Directions (this is the final interlocutory stage and when completed the parties are ready for trial). When the Master is satisfied of compliance with the 29 matters in Order 25 on which directions may be sought he notes on the summons the time and place of trial.

Order 14 provides for summary judgment for the plaintiff where the defendant has no answer to the claim. This is not appropriate in defamation, malicious prosecution, false imprisonment or fraud claims. Where the defendant shows he has a case the Master grants leave to defend and gives directions for trial.

Where judgment is granted this will be final for liquidated claims but only interlocutory for unliquidated claims, where the final award is decided at trial.

(b) Costs

The general rule is that 'costs follow the event', so that the loser will expect not only to meet his own costs but also those of the winner (subject to one or both being legally aided). Where the winner is legally aided the judge will normally order the loser to pay all costs except, for example, in matrimonial matters. If the loser is legally aided he or she may only be ordered to pay 'a reasonable amount' depending on all the circumstances of the case.

Reference to the rule that 'costs follow the event' implies that all costs are recoverable by the successful party but this is often not the case. In contentious matters the court oversees the amount of costs that can be recovered (called 'taxation' of costs) and any shortfall must be met by the winner. Two bases for assessment are used which can undoubtedly lead to unfairness. The solicitor charges on an 'indemnity' basis (all costs except those unreasonably incurred or are of an unreasonable amount) whereas the court taxes on a 'standard' basis (a reasonable amount of all the costs reasonably incurred).

A tactical move by a defendant may be to make a 'payment into court' during the course of the interlocutory proceedings in a bid to settle the matter. If the plaintiff recovers no more than the sum paid in he will only be able to recover his costs up to the date of payment in and will have to pay the defendant's costs thereafter.

Another means of encouraging a plaintiff to settle is for the defendant to send what is known as a 'Calderbank' letter (*Calderbank v Calderbank* (1976)) where an offer to settle is made 'without prejudice except as to costs'. If the plaintiff rejects the defendant's offer and goes to trial once all issues have been decided the letter can be brought to the judge's attention if the plaintiff has failed to recover more than that offered in the letter. It then follows that the judge may order the plaintiff to pay all costs from the date of the letter.

(c) The Trial

A single judge determines issues of fact and law and it is rare for juries to be called except, for example, in defamation claims. The plaintiff's counsel will open as 'he who claims must prove' that is the burden of proof lies with the plaintiff.

His case must be proved by adducing evidence to prove the facts relied on on 'a balance of probabilities'. Evidence may be in the form of witnesses giving oral testimony having made an Oath or affirmation, by way of documents, or objects. Witnesses are called first by the side who relies on their testimony ('examination-in-chief'), then by their opponent ('cross-examination') and may be 're-examined' where it is thought necessary to clarify a point in issue.

Once the plaintiff has called his evidence the defence may make a submission of 'no case to answer'. The judge rules on this only where the defence does not wish to call evidence. If the defence wishes to call evidence it must proceed to do so. Again witnesses are examined in chief, cross-examined and re-examined if appropriate.

The judge then sums up and makes a decision. If he finds for the plaintiff, he grants a remedy and makes an order for costs. If for the defendant, he dismisses the claim and makes an order for costs. Enforcement of judgments will be briefly mentioned at the conclusion of the next section.

8.3 County court proceedings

As we have already noted, the procedure in the county court is governed by the 'Green Book'. The plaintiff files a request for a default summons with particulars of claim (for claims for a sum of money, both liquidated and unliquidated) or a fixed date summons with particulars of claim (for other than money claims such as for possession or for the return of goods). Copies and fees accompany the request. The court then issues a plaint note and a default summons or a plaint note and a fixed date summons. This is then served on the defendant by the court by way of bailiff or postal system or by personal service by the plaintiff. Service must be made within four months of the issue of the summons. Accompanying the summons will be a form of admission, defence and counterclaim together with the particulars of claim.

8.3.1 Default summons

The defendant has 14 days within which to deliver a defence or counterclaim. Pleadings close 14 days after delivery of a defence (28 days where a counterclaim is also served). Automatic directions for trial then take effect subject to exceptions such as where the defendant makes a part-admission which is not accepted by the plaintiff or the claim is referred to arbitration.

In exceptional cases the matter is referred to a pre-trial review which is equivalent to a summons for directions in the High Court. The directions regulate discovery and inspection of documents, the calling of expert witnesses, setting down for trial and its expected length.

If no defence or counterclaim are filed the defendant may have paid a sum into court or filed an admission. If he has not, judgment will be entered if the sums claimed are liquidated or interlocutory judgment ordered for unliquidated claims. If he has, and the plaintiff accepts, then judgment is entered. If the plaintiff does not accept, the matter is disposed of. Where the defendant admits only part of the claim a pre-trial review date is agreed. The review is then followed by the trial by the district or circuit judge or by way of arbitration.

8.3.2 Fixed date summons

The defendant has 14 days within which to deliver a defence or counterclaim. If he does, he is given directions for trial as above. If not, but he files an admission which the plaintiff accepts, judgment is given. If the plaintiff does not accept, the matter is disposed of, or if part only is admitted then a pre-trial review is held followed by the trial. If the defendant does not file an admission then trial is ordered, or if both parties agree, arbitration is ordered (the 'small claims' procedure).

In both the High Court and county court a successful party may have to seek enforcement of an award or other order of the court where the other party defaults. A judgment debtor may be called before the court and, on oath, asked questions about his or her finances so as to determine what assets may be used to meet the claim. This is called an 'oral examination'. Goods, leases and cheques may be made subject to a writ of *fieri facias* in the High Court (a 'warrant of execution' in the county court), land, stocks and shares may be made subject to a charging order, bank accounts and other debts due to the judgment debtor may be made subject to a 'garnishee' order. A receiver may be appointed and bankruptcy proceedings commenced.

In the county court an 'attachment of earnings' order may be made, so that payments of salary due to the judgment debtor are paid to the judgment creditor to meet the claim. High Court claims are transferred to the county court.

8.4   Enforcement of judgments

Lord Hailsham, the then Lord Chancellor, set up the Civil Justice Review to investigate improvements that might be made in the machinery of civil justice – jurisdiction, procedure and court administration, reduction in delays, cost and complexity. Five areas were studied: personal injuries, small claims, the Commercial Court, the debt enforcement process and housing cases. In each area a consultation paper was prepared in 1986/87 setting out the options for reform and preferred solutions.

In March 1987 the Lord Chancellor's Department issued a General Issues Paper identifying common problems and proposing changes in jurisdiction, procedure and administration. Three aims of the civil justice system were identified:

8.5   Reform of civil litigation

- a high quality of justice including fair procedures and adjudication methods;

- limitation of delay and cost, both to the parties and the court service, proportionate to the subject matter; and

- an effective system able to respond to the types of business, changing needs and convenience of the parties.

The Paper recommended a single unified system to replace the High Court and county court. Two models were suggested. Either a single civil court with two levels of judiciary equivalent to judges from the High Court and Court of Appeal or a single court with an integrated judiciary.

The Law Society supported the idea of a single unified court but the Bar did not, for in its view this would jeopardise barristers' monopoly over rights of audience. It was also suggested that the courts should work longer hours and have an extended legal year.

In June 1988 the Final Report was published and implemented by Part I of the Courts and Legal Services Act 1990 and the High Court and County Courts Jurisdiction Order 1991 with effect from July 1991. The High Court and County Court were to remain separate with no upper limit on County Court jurisdiction. A lower limit of £25,000 for High Court cases with all cases below £25,000 to be heard in the County Court unless public law, specialised or unusual complexity involved. Cases of £25,000 to £50,000 to be heard in either court . All personal injury cases to start in the County Court. Registrars to be called district judges and their jurisdiction to be increased to £5,000.

Thus, cases are allocated according to substance, importance and complexity. Generally, cases below £25,000 are heard in the County Court; cases above £50,000 in the High Court and those between £25,000 and £50,000 in either, depending on the above criteria and judicial availability. Personal injury claims are to start in the county court unless above £50,000 and claims under £25,000 in the county court unless transferred to the High Court on above criteria. Claims under £25,000 commencing in the High Court are to remain there if these criteria are met.

Another criticism concerns the arrangements for handling family disputes and the need for a Family court. The Finer Committee as long ago as 1974 recommended a family court comprising three tiers:

- circuit judges, lay magistrates and registrars;

- appeals on questions of fact from tier 1 to circuit judges and two magistrates;

- reserved categories of work for High Court judges.

No reforms have been made and the High Court, county court and magistrates' court have jurisdiction in family matters.

8.5.1   Integrating the courts

In 1983 the Lord Chancellor issued a consultation paper proposing integration of the High Court and county court work (no mention was made of the magistrates' court) equivalent to the Crown Court. Alternatively, the identity of both was to be retained but transfers of cases and allocation of judges between them was to be permitted. Lord Hailsham favoured the former option.

A further consultation paper followed in May 1986 which noted five criticisms of the present system:

* fragmentation and overlap of jurisdiction;

* lack of transfer facilities;

* less expertise due to fragmentation;

* delay and expense;

* different remedies in different courts.

It was also noted that the system was too adversarial, too formal and the magistrates' court was associated with criminal cases. Three options were proposed:

* a revised structure;

* a unified court based on the High Court and county court;

* a wholly new court structure and judiciary.

No changes have been made largely due to the cost of implementing change. In 1989 the Children Act was passed (under the supervision of Lord Mackay), providing for concurrent jurisdiction between the magistrates' courts and the High Court, allowing for transfer of cases and uniformity by way of Regulations. A separate Family Court was not introduced by Part I of the Courts and Legal Services Act 1990 but the recent Green Paper of the Lord Chancellor proposes use of mediation in the settlement of matrimonial matters.

Other recommendations of the Civil Justice Review which have come to nothing, include:

* the replacement of the Lord Chancellor's Department with a Ministry of Justice for civil matters (and of the Home Office for criminal matters); and

* the establishment of a separate small claims court and limitation of litigation costs.

The latest development in reforming the civil justice system further is the appointment by the Lord Chancellor of Lord Woolf to review the rules and procedures of the civil courts in England and Wales in order to improve access and to create one set of procedural rules. Lord Woolf is assisted by a team of experts and is expected to report in 1996.

Civil Proceedings – In Outline

Civil disputes involve a wide variety of claims and litigation should be as a first resort. The parties will be encouraged to settle out of court or by way of ADR. Letters before action and 'without prejudice' clauses are noted.

Civil disputes

The historical development of High Court and county court is noted as are the differences in terminology, forms and procedure. The White Book governing High Court procedure is mentioned as is the Green Book which governs county court procedure.

High Court proceedings

The main features of the civil justice system are noted including its adversarial nature and the burden and standard of proof.

Underlying principles

The three main aspects of procedure are:

Procedure in the High Court

- pre-trial proceedings;

- costs; and

- the trial.

The sequence of events from the issue of the writ are explained. Payment into court is mentioned as is the use of a 'Calderbank' letter to encourage a plaintiff to settle.

The procedure and forms used are outlined and the differences between a default summons and a fixed date summons is explained.

County court proceedings

Following a successful claim, a plaintiff may need to have the court enforce its judgment. The methods of enforcement are noted as are the differences between High Court and county court.

Enforcement of judgments

The Civil Justice Review is outline together with subsequent developments culminating in the Courts and Legal Services Act 1990 and the High Court and County Courts Jurisdiction Order 1991. The Finer Committee recommendation for a Family Court has not been implemented.

Reform of civil litigation

Integrating the courts
The 1983 Consultation Paper proposing integration of the High Court and county court is noted together with subsequent developments. Lord Woolf has recently been appointed by the Lord Chancellor to review the procedure of the civil courts and is due to report in 1996.

Chapter 9

Criminal Proceedings

9.1 Introduction

In this part we will deal with trials in the magistrates' courts and the Crown Court mentioning only briefly police powers in investigating offences. Sentencing powers of the courts and police powers have been dealt with in greater detail elsewhere. We will conclude by mentioning the major proposals for reform of the criminal justice system.

9.2 The investigation of offences

The police are the chief agents of law enforcement with extensive powers of arrest, to question suspects, to enter premises, to search persons and property and to seize property. In contrast, the citizen has very limited powers of arrest under s 24(4) of the Police and Criminal Evidence Act 1984 (PACE), but may be called on to assist the police in effecting an arrest or preventing the commission of an offence. The citizen also has a limited right to bring a private prosecution but the Attorney-General may issue a nolle prosequi ('no prosecution') to prevent it from continuing.

The prosecution, brought by the Crown Prosecution Service (CPS) under the Prosecution of Offences Act 1985, has the burden of proof (beyond all reasonable doubt). Sections 76-78 of PACE permit exclusion of evidence at the judge's discretion where it has been obtained unfairly. Involuntary confessions must be excluded.

Section 1 of PACE allows a person to be stopped and searched (although there is no general power) where a police officer reasonably believes he is in possession of stolen or prohibited articles. Once arrested a person may be searched under s 32 if reasonable grounds exist for believing that he or she may present a danger to himself or others, for anything which might be used to escape or which might be evidence of an offence.

No general power exists to enter private property but the police may do so with the owner's consent. Reasonable force may be used to gain entry to effect an arrest under warrant or to arrest for an arrestable offence under s 17. This is also permitted to prevent a breach of the peace, to recapture a fugitive and to prevent serious injury or damage.

On arrest a person's property can be searched if relevant to the alleged offence, and also his or her premises and premises where he or she was arrested belonging to another person.

Evidence obtained during an unlawful search may be admissible at the discretion of the judge. Other Acts such as the Theft Acts permit magistrates to issue warrants to enter and search premises.

By ss 24 and 25 of PACE the police are empowered to arrest suspects. Arrest deprives a person of his or her liberty and may involve physical restraint or simply a restriction on freedom. Police wishing to question a suspect must effect an arrest unless the suspect voluntarily consents to assist them. Following arrest a suspect must either be charged with an offence or released. Magistrates may issue a warrant for the arrest of a suspect. Only reasonable force should be used and reasonable force may be used to resist an unlawful arrest.

Section 28 of PACE stipulates that the person arrested must be informed of the reason for arrest and civil law remedies will be available for wrongful arrest including assault and battery and false imprisonment.

Detention should only normally arise on arrest and then only for up to 24 hours. For serious arrestable offences this can be extended to 96 hours subject to conditions. Once charged, a suspect should be brought before the magistrates either the same day or the next day.

Part IV of PACE and the Codes of Practice (which replaced the Judges' Rules 1964) regulate the making of confessions, the giving of cautions, the right of the police to question a suspect, the defendant's right to remain silent, the taking of statements and the right of the suspect to be informed of his or her right to a solicitor.

The suspect has a right to have one named person informed of his arrest and whereabouts, without delay, unless this is necessary in the interests of the investigation or prevention of crime. Evidence of identification may be obtained by way of an 'ID parade', fingerprints and photographs. Section 61 requires authorisation for the taking of fingerprints by a police superintendent when satisfied that reasonable grounds exist (or the suspect consents).

The case of *R v Smurthwaite & R v Gill* (1994) illustrates the discretion that the court has in holding evidence to be inadmissible. It was held that s 78 of PACE was to be given its natural meaning and the court was to have regard to 'the circumstances in which the evidence (relied on) was obtained' and to exclude it, but only if it 'would have such an adverse effect on the fairness of the proceedings that the court ought not to admit it'. Where evidence was obtained by entrapment or by an agent provocateur or by a trick this did not of itself require the judge to exclude it. If in all the circumstances he considered that the means by which it was obtained would have an adverse effect on the fairness of the trial he should exclude it. 'Fairness of the proceedings' referred to fairness to the accused and to the public. The judge should take into account all the circumstances including whether the police officer was acting as an agent provocateur (that is, enticing the accused to commit an offence he would otherwise not have done), the nature of the entrapment, whether the evidence consisted of admissions to a completed offence or the actual commission of an offence, how active or passive the officers' role was in obtaining the evidence, whether there was an unassailable record of what happened or whether it was strongly corroborated. Suspects should not be questioned by under-cover detectives in abuse of their role or deprived of the protections of PACE and the Codes of Practice. The judge should rule evidence obtained in this way inadmissible.

Before considering the trial process, we will mention the right of a suspect to bail. This is governed by the Bail Act 1976 as amended by the Bail (Amendment) Act 1993. By s 4 there is a general right to bail from a court (the police need only allow bail under the Magistrates' Court Act 1980, s 43 if it is impracticable to bring the suspect before a court within 24 hours and the offence is not a serious one).

9.2.1   Bail

The effect of PACE is that the police need only allow bail after either of the extended periods of detention. On issue of a warrant for the arrest of an accused it may be 'backed for bail'. This instructs the police to release the accused on bail to attend court. Conditions may be attached, for example, for the provision of sureties. The police lose their powers to grant bail from the moment that the accused appears in court. It is then for the court to decide whether bail should be granted.

Court bail need not be granted where:

- the defendant is accused or convicted of an imprisonable offence and

   (i)   the court is satisfied that substantive grounds exist for believing that the defendant would fail to surrender to custody or commit an offence or interfere with witnesses or otherwise obstruct the course of justice;

   (ii)   the defendant is a prison fugitive, bail absconder or is charged with treason;

   (iii)   the court has insufficient information to decide;

   (iv)   it is for the defendant's protection; or

- the defendant is accused or convicted of a non-imprisonable offence if he has previously been granted bail and failed to surrender and in view of that, the court believes he would do so again or for his own protection.

In deciding whether to grant bail the court considers the nature and seriousness of the offence, the character, antecedents and associations and community ties of the accused, his or her bail record, the strength of evidence and any other factors which appear relevant.

Sureties may be required that is a person or persons to stand 'guarantee' for a sum of money which will be forfeited to the court if the accused absconds. Conditions may be imposed, for example, that the accused attends a police station at stated intervals or resides at a named address.

If an accused absconds whilst on bail he or she commits an offence unless able to prove a reasonable cause and surrenders as soon as possible.

If bail is refused, the accused is remanded in custody and the maximum period is eight days, but the magistrates can order further periods of eight days indefinitely. In cases of excessive custody an accused can apply to the Queen's Bench Division of the High Court for bail. Legal aid is available for all bail applications.

Section 4 of the Bail Act and the presumption in favour of bail does not apply to bail applications where a case is adjourned due to illness or absence of witnesses, for example, nor where a defendant wishes to appeal against conviction and /or sentence or where he is committed for trial or sentence to the Crown Court. The court will decide such applications on their merits.

By the Criminal Justice and Public Order Bill there is a provision which will reverse the s 4 presumption in favour of bail where the defendant is charged with a serious offence.

9.3   The trial process

The procedure for summary trials and committals in the magistrates' courts and Crown Court trials is considered altogether with the possible outcomes and differences.

9.3.1   The magistrates' court

The vast majority of all criminal cases start in the magistrates' court. They have two main roles in criminal cases: as examining justices to decide if the defendant should be committed for trial to the Crown Court (trial by jury), or by hearing the case summarily and making a decision.

Each case starts as a result of the prosecution (this is the Crown Prosecution Service in most cases), 'laying an information', a statement of the alleged offence and the name of the accused. The information can be in the form of an oath, in writing or oral (unless statute stipulates a prescribed form).

The defendant may have been summoned to appear before the court following an information put before a magistrate or magistrates' clerk. This is most often used for motoring offences and the summons requires the defendant to attend court on a stated date (the 'return' date). Alternatively, a warrant may have been issued for the defendant's arrest following a written and sworn information against him. This is used for indictable and imprisonable offences or where the defendant's address is unknown or where he has failed to answer to a summons. A defendant may also appear as the result of a charge following arrest without warrant for an arrestable offence or offences under ss 24 and 25 of PACE.

The magistrates' have to decide whether the defendant is to be tried summarily or committed for trial to the Crown Court. This will depend on both the class of offence and the wishes of the defendant, prosecution and the magistrates.

In indictable offences the magistrates must commit the defendant for trial to the Crown Court. In summary offences the magistrates must try the case. Only in offences which are 'triable either way' has the defendant any choice as to mode of trial. He or she has a right to elect jury trial in cases of theft, burglary and damage to property, referred to in Schedule 1 of the Magistrates' Courts Act 1980.

9.3.2 Indictable offences

Here the magistrates must determine the mode of trial for defendants aged 17 and above. By the Magistrates Court (Advance Information) Rules 1985 the magistrates must satisfy themselves that a person who is subject to the rules is aware that he may ask for advance information before mode of trial is decided (or before plea for youths).

9.3.3 Offences triable either way

The prosecution is under an obligation to give written notice to the defence setting out this obligation and an address to which a request for information may be made. Service must be as soon as is practicable after charge or summons. Material parts of all written statements to be relied on by the prosecution must be given to the defence or a summary of all facts on which it is proposed to call evidence.

Withholding information is permitted where the prosecution is of the opinion that it might lead to intimidation or attempted intimidation of witnesses or the course of justice would otherwise be interfered with. Notice of this must be given to the defence and an adjournment may be ordered where the prosecution fails to comply with a request for information without good reason.

The magistrates must take account of the following matters: whether the offence appears more suitable for summary trial

9.3.4 Mode of trial

or trial on indictment; representations made by prosecution and defence; whether the offence a serious one in the light of its circumstances; whether the sentence imposed by the magistrates would be sufficient in all the circumstances; any other relevant circumstances.

Where the Attorney-General or the Director of Public Prosecutions initiate a prosecution he can require that trial is on indictment.

Where summary trial appears more suitable, the charge is read to the defendant and his right to elect jury trial is explained together with the fact that if he is tried summarily he may be committed to the Crown Court for sentence if the powers of the magistrates are insufficient. The defendant makes known his choice.

Where trial on indictment appears more suitable the defendant is informed of this and may make representations for summary trial. However the defendant cannot insist on summary trial.

9.3.5   Criminal damage

Special rules apply to a charge of criminal damage. If the value of the property exceeds £2,000 the offence is treated as triable either way. If it is less than £2,000 the magistrates treat the case as if it were triable summarily and the defendant cannot elect jury trial. The maximum sentence is three months imprisonment or a fine of £2,500, and there is no power to commit for sentence to the Crown Court under s 38 of the Magistrates' Courts Act 1980. If the value of the property is in doubt then the defendant is asked to consent to summary trial and if he does so it must be explained to him that he will be sentenced by the magistrates and cannot be committed for sentence to the Crown Court.

9.3.6   Committal proceedings

When magistrates act as examining justices they have a duty to decide whether the defendant should be committed for trial to the Crown Court on indictment. In other words the prosecution must establish a prima facie case against the defendant.

There are two types of committal, a 'new style' (or 'paper') committal and an 'old style' (or 'full') committal, where the magistrates consider the evidence against the defendant. New style committals are still known as 'section 1' committals (after s 1 of the Criminal Justice Act 1967 despite this having been replaced by s 6(2) of the Magistrates' Courts Act 1980).

- New style committals

  Certain conditions must be met for a new style committal to be used, namely that the defendant must be legally represented, evidence must be in the form of written statements, the defendant's representative must not wish to argue that the prosecution have insufficient evidence for committal.

The order of events is such that the prosecution informs the court that all the evidence is in the form of written statements and have been supplied to the defence. The statements are presented to the court and the prosecution indicates the type of witness order required. The charge is read to the defendant and the defence is asked whether there is any objection to the written statements, whether the defence wishes to call evidence and whether it wishes to argue that the prosecution have insufficient evidence. If the answer to all these is 'no' then the committal proceeds as a new style committal, otherwise an old style committal is ordered.

The defendant must be given, where appropriate, an 'alibi warning' both orally and in writing when committed for trial. That is, he is informed that he will not be able to rely on an alibi at trial unless he gives particulars to the magistrates and to the prosecution within seven days. Questions as to the extension of legal aid to the Crown Court, bail and costs are then considered.

- Old style committals

The prosecution opens the case by outlining the charge and the facts. Evidence in support of the facts is presented either orally or in writing. Oral testimony is given on oath (or by way of affirmation) and witnesses are examined in chief, cross-examined and re-examined if necessary. The magistrates are also able to ask questions of witnesses. Notes are taken by the clerk and these are then read over to each witness who signs them. The magistrates sign a certificate authenticating the evidence and this is known as a 'deposition' and is an exhibit at the trial.

Written statements must comply with the requirements as for new style committals but in some cases the rules may be relaxed, for example, for child witnesses in sexual abuse cases.

The defence may submit that there is 'no case to answer' in that the evidence is insufficient on which to commit the defendant for trial either because the prosecution has failed to prove an essential element of the offence charged or the evidence is weak or has been discredited and no reasonable jury could convict the defendant. If the magistrates agree, the case is dismissed. If not, the case continues.

Assuming the latter course, the charge is then read to the defendant by the clerk. The defendant is informed of his or her right to remain silent but that anything he or she wishes to say must be given on oath (or by way of affirmation) and will be subject to cross-examination. The alibi warning is then given together with an alibi notice.

The defence can then open its case and the defendant and at least one witness gives evidence followed by the prosecution closing speech (if the defence has made an opening speech). The defence then makes a closing speech addressing the court and arguing that the evidence is insufficient to prove a case against the defendant. Usually these steps are omitted as the defence will normally reserve its case for the trial.

The magistrates decide whether to commit or not, and if committal is ordered the application for legal aid, bail and costs are decided.

In committing the defendant for trial to the Crown Court several matters are taken into account in selecting the Crown Court, including the convenience of defendant, prosecution and witnesses, the class of offence and the need to expedite trial.

There are four classes of offence ranging from the most serious, eg murder, tried only by a High Court Judge, to the least serious usually tried by a circuit judge or recorder but power of the High Court Judge to try must be taken into account in addition to the three tiers of Crown Court.

9.3.7   Summary trial

If the defendant pleads guilty, the magistrates then pass sentence. If he or she pleads not guilty, or there is some doubt as to the plea, the magistrates hear the evidence and decide guilt or innocence. The order of events is as follows:

- The defendant's identity is checked by the clerk.

- The plea is entered.

- The prosecution opens its case by stating the charge and outlining the evidence.

- Oral testimony and other evidence is given. Witnesses are examined-in-chief, cross-examined and re-examined if appropriate. The clerk makes notes of the evidence.

- The defence may submit no case to answer.

- Assuming this is not accepted, the defence opens its case.

- The prosecution may call evidence in rebuttal on matters arising unexpectedly in the course of the defence case. If this is not done, the closing speech is made.

- The defence makes its closing speech.

- Either the prosecution or the defence may address the court with leave. If one does so the other has a right to do so also.

- The magistrates decide guilt or innocence.

- If the defendant is found guilty, the magistrates pass sentence. For any one offence the maximum penalty is generally six months imprisonment and/or a fine of £5,000, although in some matters the fine can be much greater. For example, in some food safety cases the penalty can be as much as £20,000.

For summary offences punishable with not more than three months imprisonment, a defendant may plead guilty by post providing he or she has been served with the summons, statement of facts and an explanatory note and he or she sends to the court a written guilty plea. The court will take note of the statement of facts and any written comments of the defendant in mitigation. The defendant may be convicted and sentenced in his or her absence.

9.3.8   'Guilty by post' pleas

The defendant must be present when 'arraigned' (naming of the defendant, reading to him the indictment and a request as to how he or she pleads) so as to plead to the charge in the indictment (the formal document setting out the alleged offence or offences). The defendant may represent himself, seek the services of a 'McKenzie Friend', or be represented by a lawyer (with or without legal aid). The trial is in public with reporting in the press unless restrictions apply as, for example, in official secrets trials or those where delicate personal matters are dealt with.

9.3.9   The Crown Court

The jury is empanelled before the start of the trial, but remain outside the courtroom until the defendant is arraigned and has pleaded. This ensures the impartiality of jurors and challenges can then be made subject to conditions noted in the chapter on Laypersons.

The prosecution opens its case, calls witnesses and the usual order of examination-in-chief, cross-examination and re-examination is followed. The defence then opens its case and the defendant may decide to give evidence on oath and on which he or she may face cross-examination by the prosecution.

The prosecution then sums up followed by the defence. It is then the turn of the judge to sum up to the jury after which the jury retires to consider its verdict. From amongst its number a foreman is appointed to deliver the verdict. Following a guilty verdict the judge passes sentence whereas if the defendant is acquitted he or she is discharged. Each count on the indictment is tried separately and a separate verdict is given.

- Appeals

  Appeals from Crown Court trials on indictment lie to the Court of Appeal against conviction and/or sentence. Section 11 of the Criminal Appeal Act 1968 provides that the trial judge must grant a certificate of suitability and leave of the Court of Appeal is needed in appeals against sentence. For an appeal to be successful it must seen to be too severe in all the circumstances and wrong in principle.

  Appeals against conviction may concern due process (fairness of trial process) or miscarriages of justice (was the result right?). The defendant may appeal as of right on questions of law or with leave of the Court of Appeal where the trial judge certifies that the case involves a mixed question of fact and law or of fact alone. Section 2(1) gives three grounds of appeal:

  (a) the conviction is unsafe or unsatisfactory in all the circumstances;

  (b) the trial judge made a wrong decision on a question of law; and

  (c) a material irregularity arose in the course of the trial.

  If one of these three grounds is proved, the Court of Appeal must allow an appeal unless it considers that there has been no miscarriage of justice.

  The Court of Appeal has been reluctant to apply this 'proviso' since it involves the court attempting to put itself into the position of the jury who tried the case. In allowing an appeal the Court of Appeal may quash the conviction, admit fresh evidence, order a retrial, or, in certain circumstances, convict on an alternative charge.

- Other powers of the Court of Appeal

  Section 17 of the Criminal Appeal Act 1968 allows an appeal at any time to be made to the Home Secretary who may refer the case to the Court of Appeal. Section 36 of the Criminal Justice Act 1972 provides for a reference by the Attorney-General on a point of law to the Court of Appeal following acquittal for an opinion on the state of the law.

  This must not be confused with the power under ss 35 and 36 of the Criminal Justice Act 1988, whereby the Attorney-General may refer an unduly lenient sentence to the Court of Appeal which may quash the original sentence and replace it with one considered appropriate up to the maximum available in the Crown Court.

Following review by the Court of Appeal either party may, subject to a Court of Appeal certificate and leave of Court of Appeal or House of Lords, refer the case to the House of Lords for an opinion on a point of law of general public importance.

Consideration of criminal appeals would be incomplete without mention of appeals by way of case stated, the rights of prosecution and defence to appeal to the House of Lords from the Court of Appeal with leave on a point of law under s 1 of the Administration of Justice Act 1960 and exercise of the royal prerogative of mercy by the Home Secretary. Section 133 of the Criminal Justice Act 1988 introduced a right for defendants wrongly convicted to seek compensation from the Home Secretary.

9.3.10 Youth court

Formerly called juvenile courts, youth courts deal with offenders aged up to 18 years inclusive (Criminal Justice Act 1991, ss 68 and 70). Special rules apply at the police station, during detention pending first appearance at court, courtroom procedure and sentencing. By s 24(1) of the Magistrates' Courts Act 1980, a juvenile must be tried in a youth court (or an adult magistrates' court if jointly charged with an adult) unless charged with homicide or charged jointly with an adult who is to be tried on indictment, and the magistrates consider it is in the interests of justice to commit both for trial, or the juvenile has reached the age of 14 and is charged with a grave offence.

Trial in the youth court necessitates that magistrates are drawn from a special panel and the court should sit in a room not used for an adult court in the previous hour. The public are not admitted and the magistrates should comprise at least one woman. Reporting restrictions apply unless necessary to avoid injustice and the procedure is less formal. There is no dock and the magistrates sit at the same level as the juvenile who is seated with his or her parents.

9.3.11 Reform of the criminal justice system

The Royal Commission on Criminal Justice (chaired by Lord Runciman) reported in July 1993, and made 352 recommendations for improvements in the criminal justice system.

The Commission took two years to report and followed some notable miscarriages of justice including the 'Guildford Four', the 'Birmingham Six', the 'Maguire Seven', Judith Ward, the 'Tottenham Three' and Stefan Kiszko. These cases illustrated some very important failings in the system including how easily convictions can be secured as a result of fabricated evidence, how vulnerable suspects are accused and found guilty of offences they have not committed, and the near-impossible means by which wrong decisions can be rectified.

The overriding conclusion was the inadequacy of the judicial process in detecting and dealing with major shortcomings arising during and as a result of the investigative process. The court and the jury can only be as good as the evidence put before it, given that ours is an accusatorial and not an inquisitorial system.

Thus the due process of law remains above reproach and, where it is found wanting, an appeal may lie to the Court of Appeal to correct the error. This was recently demonstrated in the case of *R v Whybrow and Saunders* (1994), where the Court of Appeal held that although the trial judge should prevent the trial from becoming protracted he should not attempt to cross-examine the defendant or show disbelief of the defendant's evidence since this would prevent the defendant from receiving a fair trial.

Commentators suggest that we must reform our present system in order to have an independent investigative process charged with finding the truth rather than leaving the police to conduct the investigations alone. Michael Mansfield QC in 'Presumed Guilty' proposes that the accusatorial system be retained but that a judge should conduct an independent investigation along the lines of the French Juge d'instruction into the truth and who is not concerned with finding evidence to prove a theory or hunch as to who committed the offence. The prosecution should also be obliged to reveal to the defence (if not the court) all evidence collected whereas under the present system the prosecution need only disclose evidence on which it intends to rely at the trial. The risk that in some cases the guilty will go undetected may be an acceptable price of justice but it is not acceptable that the innocent should be wrongly convicted. If this happens then at least there should be speedy and effective means of rectifying mistakes.

Two fundamental principles lie at the heart of the criminal justice system namely the presumption of innocence and the right to elect trial by jury. Some would add the right to remain silent in the face of questioning by the police and at trial but this is under serious threat from clauses 27-30 of the Criminal Justice and Public Order Bill.

Some major defects in the criminal justice system have been identified which lead to the acquittal of the guilty and the conviction of the innocent.

We have mentioned the role of the police in conducting investigations and the allegations of bias, presumption of guilt, stereotyping and targeting of those with records. This has led to calls for independent supervision of police investigations. The Police Complaints Authority has also been the subject of much complaint in failing to win the confidence of the public. The Crown Prosecution Service has not only been much criticised in failing to disclose all evidence in its possession but also for its policy of initiating prosecutions and then in some cases offering no evidence on reaching trial.

The limitations placed on granting bail have been criticised and its availability is further under threat as a result of the Criminal Justice and Public Order Bill now before Parliament.

The Forensic Science Service is a State run monopoly largely benefiting the prosecution and it has been suggested that this should be made freely available to the defence. The need for this will no doubt increase given advances in new technology and DNA profiling and wider police powers.

Other criticisms concern the ineffectiveness of the jury system, the need to reform the judiciary and legal profession and court procedures so as to ensure that it is a challenging forum in which to decide the guilt or innocence of an individual.

Reform of the appeals system is also needed with replacement of the Court of Appeal by an independent review body.

The main recommendations of the Royal Commission on Criminal Justice were:

9.3.12   Recommendations of the Royal Commission on Criminal Justice

- The decision whether a defendant should be tried by jury should rest with the magistrates so as to ensure 'a more rational division of triable either way offences between the magistrates' court and Crown Court.

- The right of silence in police stations to be retained; adverse inferences not to be drawn; retention of caution and trial direction on silence.

- An independent review body to be set up to investigate alleged miscarriages of justice and to refer appropriate cases to the Court of Appeal. Section 17 of the Criminal Appeals Act 1968 (power to refer cases to the Court of Appeal) should be replaced by a review body to be chaired by a person appointed by the Queen on the advice of the Prime Minister. Other members are to be appointed by the Lord Chancellor. No appeal would lie from its decisions nor would judicial review be available.

- The Court of Appeal to be enabled to overturn unsafe verdicts and to order retrials where practicable – Criminal Appeal Act 1968 s 2(1) to be redrafted providing a single broad ground for a retrial or an appeal where a decision 'is or may be unsafe'.

- Pre-trial defence disclosure be required and subject to adverse inferences by the jury for non-disclosure.

- Video surveillance of police custody suites and of police interviews of suspects be introduced.

- The abolition of committal proceedings, but submission by the defence of 'no case to answer' to remain.

- The defendant to have an enforceable right of access to forensic evidence held by the prosecution.

- The judge should warn the jury regarding the dangers of uncorroborated confessions and the need for independent evidence.

- Sentence discounting should be allowed – earlier pleas would receive higher discounts;

- The guidelines issued in the 'Judith Ward' case on disclosure of evidence by the prosecution should be narrowed.

- Increased use should be made of DNA profiling by the police (for example saliva samples).

- A forensic science advisory council should be created and both prosecution and defence should have access to the public sector forensic laboratories

- Improvements should be made in standards for those attending to offer advice to police suspects.

- The present low level of fees for criminal work is adverse to the quality of service required.

- Prosecution counsel's opening speech should last no longer than 15 minutes, unless the judge gives leave.

- Opening speeches should be confined to an explanation of the issues in question.

- The recommendations concerning juries have been mentioned in the chapter on Laypersons.

3.13 Reactions to the proposals

Generally, the recommendations have been said not to be far-reaching enough, and unlikely to reduce significantly the risks of wrongful convictions.

Outrage was expressed at the proposal to abolish the defendant's right to elect jury trial. This was seen as merely a cost-cutting exercise and not done in the interests of justice.

However, the proposals to retain the right of silence, appointment of an independent review body and the proposed changes in the functions of the Court of Appeal were welcomed together with a mixed reception for most of the other recommendations.

In the result, the report was not followed by a Green Paper and then a White Paper but by the Criminal Justice and Public Order Bill and the Police and Magistrates' Courts Bill (mentioned in the chapter on Laypersons) both now before Parliament.

The main provisions of the former concerning the criminal justice system include an end to the right to silence allowing the court to draw inferences from the defendant's failure to answer police questions; creation of offences of witness and juror intimidation; the ending of the presumption in favour of bail for those charged with serious offences and police powers to take DNA samples and to examine suspects' mouths.

It remains to be seen what form clauses 27-30 of the Criminal Justice and Public Order Bill, permitting adverse inferences to be drawn from a defendant's silence will take, but the Lord Chief Justice has spoken out against the proposal that the judge should formally call on the defendant to take the stand. Lord Taylor supports the proposal that in specified cases adverse inferences should be drawn but has suggested that the defendant should be warned of the consequences of failing to give evidence by his own lawyers. Doubt also surrounds the form that the proposed review body will take and it is likely that it will not be introduced before at least 1996.

Criminal Proceedings

The powers of the police under the Police and Criminal Evidence Act 1984 are outlined and the Prosecution of Offences Act 1985 is noted as is the case of *R v Smurthwaite* and *R v Gill* (1994) on admissibility of evidence.

The investigation of offences

The right of a suspect to bail under the Bail Act 1976 is outlined.

Bail

- The magistrates' court

The trial process

  The two main roles of magistrates as examining justices for offences which may be committed to the Crown Court and in trying cases summarily are noted as is the procedure followed. The differences between indictable offences, offences triable either way and summary offences are explained as is the procedure in determining the mode of trial for triable either way offences. The provisions of the Magistrates' Court (Advance Information) Rules 1985 are noted along with the provisions concerning criminal damage. The procedure for committal proceedings is explained as is the difference between new style and old style committals provided for in s 6(2) of the Magistrates' Courts Act 1980. Summary trial procedure is outlines and the provisions for pleading guilty by post.

- Trials in the Crown Court

  Procedure is outlined including the arraignment of the defendant, calling of the jury and the order of events.

  (a) Appeals

  Sections 2(1) and 11 Criminal Appeal Act 1968 – powers of the Court of Appeal.

  (b) Other powers of the Court of Appeal

  Section 17 Criminal Appeal Act 1968

  Section 36 Criminal Justice Act 1972

  Sections 35, 36 and 133 Criminal Justice Act 1988

  Section 1 Administration of Justice Act 1960.

- Youth Court

  Sections 68 and 70 Criminal Justice Act 1991

  Section 24(1) Magistrates' Courts Act 1980.

Reform of the criminal justice system

The background to the Runciman Royal Commission on Criminal Justice 1993 is noted as is the distinction between miscarriages of justice arising from defects in the investigative process and failures of due process (*R v Whybrow and Saunders* (1994)). Proposals for reform and criticisms of the present system are noted including the inadequacy of the Police Complaints Authority and the Forensic Science Service, limitations on bail and the need to reform the jury and appeals system. The threat to the right to silence by clauses 27-30 of the Criminal Justice and Public Order Bill is noted as are the fundamental principles of the presumption of innocence and the right to elect jury trial.

Recommendations of the Royal Commission on Criminal Justice

A summary of the main proposals is given including abolition of the defendant's right to elect jury trial, the abolition of committal proceedings, the use of DNA profiling, the use of video surveillance in police custody suites, the right of the defendant to have access to forensic evidence and services, curtailment in the length of trials, retention of the right to silence and the establishment of an independent review body to investigate alleged miscarriages of justice.

Reactions to the proposals

The reactions to the proposals were mixed and in the result the government has not published a Green or a White Paper but has put before Parliament the Criminal Justice and Public Order Bill and the Police and Magistrates' Courts Bill. The most controversial provisions are those in clauses 27-30 of the former Bill removing the right to silence.

PART TWO
GENERAL PRINCIPLES OF ENGLISH LAW

Chapter 10

Rules

Defining a rule is not an easy task, but it is useful to attempt a definition since this concept forms the basis of social behaviour. Rules govern a person's relationships with others and this concept is fundamental to the study of law and the legal system.

The lawyer asked to advise a client will be expected to offer advice as to the client's legal position taking into account the appropriate legal rules. The judge, in reaching a decision in a case, will apply the law to the facts to arrive at a reasoned decision and not one based on whim or bias.

Rules are a phenomenon of society regulating the conduct and relationships of people, so that whenever one person comes into contact with another their dealings, whether of a social or business nature, may well be governed by a rule or more likely a set of rules. It is useful, therefore, to be able to distinguish rules from other social phenomena such as habits and to consider the sources from which a rule may derive, for example, religion or morality.

An essential feature of most, if not all societies, is that of institutions – the family, schools and colleges, the workplace and financial bodies to name but a few. Such institutions and the groups and individuals who exist within them operate by way of rules. Similarly, clubs and societies operate by rules and the State itself is regulated through a constitution, both in its parts and its relationship with the citizen, by way of rules. Rules will usually be written but this is not essential to the definition of a rule. Some rules as with custom will invariably be unwritten.

Another useful illustration is that of sports and games where not only the players need to be aware of the rules but also spectators and those vested with authority to enforce the rules. The interpretation and use of the rules will determine whether the game or sport is being played properly and the consequences that will or could follow from breach of a rule. This may range from a reprimand to the imposition of a penalty such as a fine or disqualification. Usually, the rules will be contained in a 'rule book' and this may also contain provisions for their enforcement and amendment.

Alternatively, the rules may change over time by accepted practice or in particular instances players may agree on a particular set of rules or an interpretation of the rules.

10.1   What is a rule?

This brings us to a broad definition of rule as a norm or guide regulating social conduct. It is a measure or standard by which conduct is gauged and which may give rise to a consequence such as a penalty when not complied with.

We can say that rules are imperative in that a person who is the subject of a rule does not usually have any choice as to whether or not he or she complies. This is not to say that there may not be exceptions to a rule or that a person cannot be exempted from a rule but both of these should be provided for in the rule itself or by the rule making body.

As already noted, rules may be written or unwritten. Legal rules, with only the exception of customary law, are written and derive from a formal source vested with authority within the State. On the other hand, other types of rule such as moral rules will tend to be unwritten and there may be no consensus as to their scope and effect and no formal mechanism for their enforcement.

Some rules are expressed in negative and others in positive terms. An example of the former is 'do not walk on the grass' and an example of the latter 'pedestrians must use the pavement'.

Some examples illustrate the points made so far:

- Operators of a car park are authorised by law to levy charges and to provide in other ways for vehicles parked on their property. A rule requiring the display of a valid ticket is expressed in positive terms and on breach a fine may be charged.

- The above rule could just as easily be expressed in the negative that is a car parked without displaying a valid ticket will be subject to fine.

- It is usual to associate the notion of 'penalty' with the concept of rule in that the rule is attempting to ensure compliance. Thus, if a rule is not complied with, some consequence should follow to 'punish' the rule breaker and to deter him or her and others from future breaches.

  Thus, those who park without a valid ticket may be liable to a fine. The consequence may be stated as part of the rule itself or in a subsidiary rule.

- Some rules are categorical commands, for example, vehicles must stop at a red light, the speed limit is 30 mph or vehicles should not stop on the hard shoulder of the motorway except in an emergency.

- Most rules will have exceptions where the otherwise regulated conduct will be permitted or prohibited in special defined circumstances. Using the above scenario of a car park, an example might be that vehicles parked in the car park on a Sunday are not required to display a ticket.

  Some conduct may be exempt entirely from the application of a rule, for example, invalid carriages are not subject to any charge for parking on any day of the week.

Let us now consider more fully how a rule can be identified and distinguished from other social phenomena. Twining & Miers in 'How to Do Things With Rules' (3rd ed) define rules as 'a general norm mandating or guiding conduct or action in a given type of situation'. They explain that rules have four aspects:

10.2   Rules distinguished from other social phenomena

- Rules guide or lay down standards of behaviour.

- Rules are normative in that they prescribe (or proscribe) desirable (or undesirable) conduct, that which is valid, good or lawful and are not optional but imperative requiring compliance, expressed in terms that a person must/must not, shall/shall not, ought/ought not conduct him or herself in a certain way.

- Rules provide justification for a decision or course of action and its source can persuade a person to obey. Some would argue that the law is the most authoritative of rules ultimately deriving its authority from the State and where the most far reaching of penalties can be imposed. Rules have general effect and govern a situation which has arisen in the past and which is likely to arise again. A novel situation cannot be said to be governed by a rule but following recurrence a rule may develop which guides or regulates future conduct.

The concept of a norm is a wide term, and as a result, Twining and Miers are able to include within their definition of rule 'precepts, regulations, conventions, principles and guiding standards'.

Other writers, notably HLA Hart in *The Concept of Law*, have also analysed the concept of rule and distinguished it from 'habit, prediction, practice, command and value'.

A broad definition is useful in that it can cover the various social phenomena referred to by Twining and Miers which often overlap and which may change over time. Writers and jurists may not always be exact in the use of language and it is common for judges to use the term 'principle' interchangeably with 'rule'.

At one extreme a rule may be formal, having derived from an authoritative source, and may set out clearly what is to be done or not to be done. In addition, it may be provided as part of the rule, or separately in another rule, the consequences for non-compliance. Legal rules will often fit into this category.

At the other extreme, conventions, for example, suggest that a course of action is to be preferred or not but which may have no clear statement as to consequences of breach or authoritative or written source. These will have developed over time and be passed down from one generation to another. Social conventions regulate etiquette and good manners, for example, replying to a letter or acknowledging a friend or acquaintance in a public place.

Returning to Twining and Miers' definition of rules as including 'precepts, regulations, conventions, principles and guiding standards', we will take each in turn and then consider more fully Professor Hart's distinction between rules and 'habit, prediction, practice, command and value'.

10.2.1   Precepts

'Precepts' are maxims or principles related to issues of justice, fairness or morality. Often such terms as 'rules', 'principles' and 'standards' are interchangeable and this is so with the terms 'precepts' and 'principles'. We may say that the fundamental principles of a criminal justice system should be a presumption of innocence, a right to remain silent during police questioning and during trial, that the burden of proof should rest with the prosecution and that the standard of proof should be beyond all reasonable doubt and that defendant's should have in serious criminal cases a right to jury trial. These principles are basic or fundamental to the system and equally may be described as precepts. In the case of *Airedale NHS Trust v Bland* (1993) Lord Browne-Wilkinson analysed what he described as the moral precept which requires 'respect for the sanctity of human life'. He concluded that the role of the judge in developing the law was a limited one and that it was for Parliament to address itself to the 'moral, social and legal issues raised ...'.

However, in the exceptional circumstances of this case the declaration to cease treatment was to be granted as this was on both medical and ethical grounds in the best interests of the patient.

10.2.2   Regulations

'Regulations' is a term often used interchangeably with, or in addition to, the term 'rules'. It implies an official body empowered to lay down a code or set of rules. In law it may have a technical meaning referring to law made by those to whom power is delegated by Parliament. Thus, government ministers may be able to make rules, regulations or orders under an enabling Act of Parliament. The collective term for such provisions is 'delegated' or 'subordinate' legislation.

'Convention' or, as it is sometimes called, 'usage' refers to proper modes or standards of conduct by which an individual will feel bound. The degree to which conventions may be enforced resulting in some penalty may be limited and non-compliance tolerated.

10.2.3   Convention

It is often difficult to distinguish conventions and custom although custom (not to be confused with customary law as described in the section on Sources of Law) are rules which are considered (by those to whom they apply) as generally obligatory. Social customs may regulate etiquette and good manners but more generally are concerned with folklore and the traditions which have been passed down from one generation to another. In Derbyshire, for example, annual well-dressing festivals take place and the customary May celebrations held to welcome the coming of Spring at Helston and Padstow in Cornwall are well known. Other customs that come to mind include the carrying of the bride over the threshold, eating pancakes on Shrove Tuesday, never opening an umbrella indoors and avoiding walking under ladders.

Over time, a course of action which has been customary may become more fluid and be considered to be no more than a convention. Traditionally, it was customary for a man to doff his hat to a lady. This has become outdated for the majority of people, partly because few men wear hats and partly because women generally do not wish to be treated in this way.

The term 'convention' may be used generically to refer to morality, custom, ethics, religion and rules of etiquette. Constitutional conventions are those practices which develop and which are considered binding by those who are the subject of the rule. They often supplement the official rules making the latter more workable.

In the constitution of the UK, by convention, the Monarch does not refuse her assent to bills which have passed all stages in the House of Commons and House of Lords. In law the Queen might refuse her assent but since the 18th century the practice has developed whereby it is understood that no such refusal will occur.

In non-developed societies social regulation may be by way of custom and this may take the form of law in that it is officially recognised and enforced by those with power and authority who can impose sanctions or penalties for breach. In studying the history and development of the common law the importance of custom will be seen. The origins of the common law are said to be those local customs collected and moulded by itinerant justices into a common, uniform body of precedent.

10.2.4   Principles

'Principles' are not always easily distinguishable from 'rules' and certainly judicial statements suggest that these terms are synonymous. We might talk of the 'rules of natural justice' but equally they may be referred to as 'principles'. We have already referred to fundamental precepts such as the presumption of innocence but this can just as correctly be referred to as a principle.

A principle may be open-ended and take the form of a maxim or wise saying. Thus, the principles that 'no man should profit from his own wrong' or 'the polluter pays principle' or that 'he who comes to equity should come with clean hands' suggest an essential truth or grain of wisdom but do not suggest the type of conduct which is prohibited or the consequence which will follow non-compliance.

This is not to suggest that a rule will always provide for a consequence for non-compliance but rules will often be more precise as to the situations in which they are to apply.

Principles may conflict as was shown in the *Airedale* case already referred to where the House of Lords had to decide whether to grant a declaration permitting treatment of Tony Bland to cease. The court was faced with the dilemma that the principle of the sanctity of human life was said to conflict with the principle of having regard to the quality of life. The court held that these principles did not so much conflict but that they complemented one another and it was for the court to arrive at a balance.

As we shall see later, Professor Dworkin disagreed with Professor Hart's narrow definition of law to include only rules and suggested that law is a 'rich fabric' including rules and non-rule standards that is principles and policies. In Professor Dworkin's view rules apply in an all-or-nothing fashion whereas principles may conflict and will have to weighed by the judge in reaching a decision.

This is borne out when considering the development of the common law in that a judge may be bound by a decision of a higher court. In other words he or she will have to comply with the rules unless there are means of avoiding the rule for example by way of distinguishing. If on the other hand the court is not bound by previous decisions it may reach its decision by calling on principle as noted by Lord Slynn dissenting in *R v Brown* (1993). The court may also seek assistance in reaching a decision by referring to the public interest or public policy as illustrated by the majority in *Brown*.

'Guiding standards' may be even more fluid than conventions and their source will determine the extent to which they may be binding. A useful example is that of the Highway Code and others can be found in the various Charters recently established including the Citizens' Charter, Rail Passengers' Charter, Students' Charter and Taxpayers' Charter.

10.2.5   Guiding standards

It is not only in the area of public administration that charters are being adopted but commercial and educational organisations are also preparing charters setting out the minimum standards to be expected by those who are customers or members of such organisations. Some provide for compensation for breaches in the guidelines as, for example, the Passengers' Charter whereas others do not.

It has become fashionable for government departments and other bodies to issue guidelines, circulars and policy notes so as to assist in the interpretation of legal rules. These will not form part of the law but may assist in determining its scope and effect.

The Highway Code is an example of a Code of Practice breach of which does not automatically result in breach of a legal rule. However, breach of the code may be used in evidence in a court of law to prove breach of a legal rule, for example, failure to comply with a traffic signal may be used to prove that a driver was negligent in a civil claim for damages and/or in a criminal prosecution for careless or dangerous driving.

We will now move on to consider some of the distinguishing features of habits, predictions, practices, commands and values.

10.2.6   Distinguishing features

Rules can be clearly distinguished from habits in that a person who acts out of habit does so without any sense of obligation. An habitual course of conduct may be undertaken regularly but one which arises either by way of accident or convenience. If I always take a particular route on my way to work or I always wear a red hat on Fridays or I eat an apple each day for lunch these actions can be described as habits.

One is neither compelled to do them nor obliged to do them in compliance with a rule. As Professor Hart noted, habits, practices and predictions are capable of verification and are concerned with types of behaviour. The individual who behaves in these ways may not do so out of any sense of duty or from any wish to act correctly.

Rules, commands and values, however, involve some internalisation and each attempts to regulate and control behaviour. Some rules may develop from habits and practices but they take on a normative form, for example, an 'ought' and the original reasons for their existence may be lost.

Rules differ from predictions in that a prediction is nothing more than a forecast of behaviour and factually the prediction may be shown to be true or false. I may attempt to predict the weather for the coming week. I may be shown to be correct or incorrect in my prediction. Rules do not attempt to predict how people will behave but rather provide guidelines or standards to regulate their behaviour.

This is not to say that those involved in advising others about the application of a rule (and most often this arises where the lawyer offers advice to the client as to how the legal rules which govern the client's situation will affect him or her) will not attempt to predict how a particular rule will apply to an individual. The lawyer asked to advise a client will base his prediction of the extent of the client's liability or the likely success of the client's claim on his estimation of how the court will interpret relevant legislation or apply case law to the problem. The prediction will be based on an estimation of how the courts have decided past cases in accordance with the rules of precedent or how a statutory provision will be interpreted by the court.

Commands may overlap with rules but there are important differences. A command may apply to a purely novel situation whereas rules will apply in general. Some rules command the doing of something (or refraining from doing something) but others attempt to encourage or facilitate a course of action.

The notion of a command implies a person or body able to command. As we will see later, John Austin devised a command theory where he suggested that legal rules were commands emanating from a sovereign power. He subscribed to the 'positivist' school of legal philosophy whereby the validity of the law was to be measured not in terms of its moral content but rather by the process required for a rule to become law. The process by which law came about was a formal one recognised as having authority to compel the citizen to comply with the commands of the sovereign body.

Perhaps the most difficult distinction to draw is between 'rules' and 'values'. It is clear that values underlie most rules and it can be argued that rules are the means by which social values are achieved.

Thus, values are ends in themselves and are concerned with right and wrong. Values are closely linked with ideals and these may often be unattainable but provide standards towards which people strive. The embodiment of values into rules may necessitate the rule having more limited effect than the value which underlies it and limitations may have to be placed on the rule.

Values are most often associated with morality and what is considered to be right or wrong conduct. The 'natural law' school of thought suggests that legal rules should be judged by standards of fairness, equality or justice and that a rule which fails to meet such a standard at best need not be obeyed and at worst is not to be classed as law. The 'utilitarian' view measures rules according to their consequences. If a rule maximises happiness or well-being or some other effect which is deemed good it will be justifiable. Some suggest that the correct approach is to combine both these theories with the effect that if a rule achieves a moral principle or value and has utility it is justifiable.

Having considered the definition of rules and compared rules and other social phenomena it is time to classify types of social rule. Traditionally, rules have been classified into legal rules, religious rules, ethical rules, moral rules, rules of etiquette, and customary rules.

10.3   Classification of rules

However, these are not hard and fast categories and there may be considerable overlaps between one or more. In addition, it is worth reminding ourselves that the concept of a 'rule' may be defined narrowly or widely depending on context with the effect that conduct governed by what one person considers to be a rule may be thought of by another as no more than convention or values.

Attempting to classify rules serves to illustrate their origins and other distinguishing features such as the effects of breach, the form a rule takes and whether a mechanism exists for their enforcement. It must be stressed, however, that at different times in history in one society, or between different societies, particular conduct may be regulated by one or more types of rule and that legal rules may well have a special relationship with one or more types of rule.

Legal rules are the most formal and in developed societies are invariably written. In the UK the main sources of law are statute and case law together with law emanating from the European Union. Other sources of law include custom and what are known as subsidiary sources of law including ecclesiastical law, Roman law and learned works. Only customary law is unwritten but once it has been relied on in a

10.3.1   Legal rules

dispute decided by the higher courts it will be recorded in the law reports. It does not, however, depend on being so recorded for its validity.

Legal rules exist as part of a system with machinery for enforcement and amendment of the rules. Agencies such as the police and courts will be vested with legitimate authority to enforce the law in the case of criminal law and prosecutions will be brought in the name of the Crown or State or, in some jurisdictions, the people. The civil law provides means by which individuals may enforce their rights against others whether it be in contract or the commission of a tort, a family dispute or dispute over property rights. An important constitutional principle is that of the 'rule of law' – the citizen cannot 'pick and choose' which laws to obey but is obliged to obey all rules which have been made by a properly constituted authority.

Where no moral consensus exists as to the worth of a particular law, how that law is viewed by both the enforcer and those who are subject to the law are of crucial importance. If law is to be obeyed it will need moral authority and on principles of justice will have to be seen to be fair not only in how it is applied but also in its content. The imposition of heavy criminal penalties may simply have the effect of 'increasing the stakes' whereby the offender will feel justified in risking a more serious offence or, in the words of the adage, the offender might as well 'be hanged for a sheep as for a lamb'.

We will look more closely at the definition of law and the different approaches of the 'positivist' and 'natural law' schools to this question in a later section.

10.3.2	Religious, ethical and moral rules

Religious, ethical and moral rules are often difficult to differentiate and may well have a common root. Those who adhere to a religion will often derive from it their moral code. Christians will look to the Bible for guidance on what is right and what is wrong. Muslims look to the Koran and Jews to the Torah. Religion will often involve much more than just a moral code for it is concerned with spiritual matters and the after-life and the relationship of humans with God.

Ethical rules are a branch of morality and usually regulate the conduct of professional people such as doctors, lawyers and teachers and their dealings with patients, clients and students. Ethical codes will be administered by a governing body, for example, the Law Society or General Council of the Bar or the General Medical Council with the aim of ensuring high standards of conduct in relationships where the recipient of the service may be vulnerable and where the provider of the service exercises authority and power and is in a position of trust. Terminology can sometimes be confusing and the term ethics may be used simply to refer to an individual's or group's moral code and professional ethics may be referred to as 'professional etiquette'. In considering the relationship of solicitors and barristers and their dealings with clients it is usual to refer to the respective rules of etiquette enforced by the Law Society or Bar Council.

Morality as we have noted may be founded in religious belief but for some people their moral code is based on humanist principles or the fundamental principle 'do as one would be done by'. The political debate initiated by John Major in 1993 under the slogan 'back to basics' raises the question as to what is meant by a moral code. Some suggest that morality is purely a private matter for the individual and that what he or she does in private is the sole concern of that person.

This so-called private morality is to be distinguished from public morality where those who hold public positions may be accountable for their actions in so far as they affect the carrying out of public duties. Others suggest that there is no such distinction and that morality affects all aspects of ones life, private and public, and that, for example, when a public figure breaks a promise made to a member of his or her family or commits adultery or engages in sharp financial practice or has a child outside wedlock this is of relevance in judging his or her suitability to carry out public or commercial activities.

It is, of course, convenient for public figures or those in positions of authority or trust to distinguish between what they do in their private lives from their public position but such a distinction sits uncomfortably with the notion that morality is all-encompassing in regulating a person's dealings with others. It has been argued that morality has a narrow scope regulating sexual conduct and controlling violence both to humans and animals. Certainly any reference to morality brings these two areas to mind. Thus the acceptability or otherwise of homosexuality, abortion, pornography, incest, extra-marital relationships, bigamy, euthanasia, divorce, cohabitation, vivisection, sado-masochistic practices, human embryo experimentation involve moral issues and some have been legalised and others not. This last point suggests that even where a moral consensus on a particular issue exists, and in many cases this may not be so, law does not always follow and reflect moral values.

Abortion is one such case where the Abortion Act 1967 permits abortion where specified conditions are met but where extremes of opinion exist as to whether abortion is 'right' or not. At one extreme is the view that life starts at conception and the human person who results should have the full protection of the law and at the other extreme there is the view that it is the pregnant woman who should be able to decide whether to abort or continue with the pregnancy.

It is to be noted that this debate has taken a new turn in the light of the scientific developments which suggest that aborted foetuses will in two or three years time be able to be used in fertility treatments and the Human Fertilisation and Embryology Authority established under the Act of 1991 has called for public discussion of the moral, ethical, social and legal issues involved before proposals are made on changes in the law.

We shall consider later the questions whether, on the one hand, legal rules should reflect moral rules and on the other whether legal rules should shape and influence moral values.

Law and morality may overlap and this is mostly true of the criminal law based as it is on moral and religious principles of wrongdoing, fault, punishment and retribution, guilt and the attainment of justice. In other instances law and morality diverge and in some cases the law regulates neutral conduct which has no moral element. We shall also consider the extent to which law which fails to comply with moral principles and which is considered to be 'bad' law can be said to be law at all.

10.3.3   'Natural' and 'positivist' law

The 'natural law' school of thought suggests that 'bad' law either need not be obeyed or is not law at all, whereas the 'positivist' school of thought hold that no matter how bad a law is, or the system by which it is made, if the recognised procedures for law-making have been complied with 'the law is the law' and in legal terms should be obeyed.

It will be a separate issue, and one with which the jurist is not concerned, as to whether, as a matter of conscience, a citizen will be morally justified in not obeying such a law. It will be for the citizen to decide the extent of his or her moral responsibility not only to obey but also to bear any penalty exacted for breach of the legal rule.

Before concluding our remarks on classification of rules we must briefly mention rules of etiquette and custom. We have already mentioned that the term etiquette may be used to refer to professional codes of conduct but in a general sense the word denotes good manners and common courtesy. However, in a narrow sense, etiquette has overtones of class division whereby social inferiors are required 'to keep their place' and show subservience to those who consider, or who are considered to be, socially superior. The old ways die hard and a person may be 'judged' according to his or her table manners, the manner of his or her dress, accent and social connections and may still be required to do 'the right thing' on social occasions such as bowing or curtseying to members of the Royal Family or complying with a dress code to enter the Royal Enclosure at Ascot.

In its widest sense, etiquette remains essential in an increasingly crowded world. Good manners and politeness towards others help to give meaning to the notion of a civilised society as one where its members show care and concern for others and at the same time enhance conditions for all.

When discussing conventions earlier we compared this with the notion of custom and noted that it is not always easy to distinguish between the two. Customs tend to be more fixed than conventions and are generally obligatory. Both regulate social conduct and breach may result in disapproval, gossip, ridicule or ostracism. This distinguishes custom and law in that breach of the latter results in a penalty imposed by or with the authority of the State.

It is not possible to distinguish law and custom by means of the type of action since an action in one society may be a breach of custom and in another a breach of law. In less developed societies there may be a dependence on custom in that this passes from one generation to another and the rate of change may be relatively slow. In complex societies, however, custom gives way to more formal rules and mechanisms for change. Vestiges remain, for example, social customs, local customary law and the customs and practices of the constitution.

10.4   Why have rules?

In concluding this section on rules we may well ask what purposes are served by rules. Given the social nature of humans and that people operate in groups and institutions and enter into relationships with others for the fulfilment of needs and wants we need standards and guides to behaviour. We need to know what is socially acceptable and the consequences of participating in socially unacceptable behaviour.

Although most rules may be in written form, mechanisms for change are provided and rules may well form part of a network or system. We may well ask why people obey rules and some answers might be fear of a penalty, internalisation of the 'rightness' of rules, acceptance with or without questioning and a sense of obligation. We will consider later some of the theories as to why law is obeyed including that of Professor HLA Hart, Professors Robert Summers, Farrer and Karl Llewellyn.

Rules

Definition of a rule is useful but not always easy. Rules form the basis of social behaviour governing a person's relationships with others. Society is made up of institutions such as the family, schools and associations and these operate by way of rules. The State also operates by way of rules in the form of a constitution.

A broad definition of a rule is 'a norm or guide regulating social conduct breach of which invariably gives rise to a social consequence such as a fine, imprisonment or censure'.

Rules are imperative – the subject has no choice whether or not to comply although there may be exceptions and, occasionally, a person may be exempted from a rule altogether.

Rules may be written or unwritten but legal rules will usually be written and derived from an authoritative source and supported by a formal process of enforcement.

Rules may be expressed in negative or positive terms and may prohibit certain behaviour or permit or command that certain things are enacted.

Rules have four characteristics:

- they guide or lay down standards of behaviour;
- they are normative and either prescribe or proscribe conduct;
- they are imperative and require compliance;
- they provide justification for a decision or course of action.

A broad definition will include within the term 'rule' such phenomena as 'precepts, regulations, conventions, principles and guiding standards' as noted by Twining and Miers in their book *How to Do Things With Rules*.

On the other hand, as noted by HLA Hart in *The Concept of Law*, rules are to be distinguished from 'habit, prediction, practice, command and value'.

The lawyer is concerned with the definition and application of the law and this is generally defined as a body of rules satisfying the above criteria and others mentioned below. Writers such as Professor Dworkin adopt a wide definition of law to include rules, principles and policies.

What is a rule?

Rules distinguished from other social phenomena

Classification of rules

Rules are a social phenomenon traditionally classified as legal, religious, ethical, moral, rules of etiquette and customary rules.

The categories are, however, not rigid and considerable overlaps may exist. Classification illustrates the origin of rules, the effects of breach and the mechanism, if any, for enforcement.

Legal rules are the most formal and are usually written. They form part of a system in which agencies such as the police and courts have authority to enforce the law and in given circumstances provide for its development.

Why have rules?

Rules perform a social function regulating conduct and providing standards and guides to behaviour. Linked with the question 'why have rules?' is the question 'why are rules obeyed?'. This may be out of fear of a penalty, internalisation of the rightness of a rule, acceptance or out of a sense of obligation.

Chapter 11

Rules that are Laws

We have already defined law as 'a system of rules imposed by the State or those having authority which give rise to sanctions or penalties when legal rules are not complied with'. We have to bear in mind that the concept of a 'rule' may have a wide definition to include principles, guiding standards and regulations.

Several questions arise when analysing the nature and characteristics of law. Firstly, its role in society and the purposes law serves, secondly, the reasons why people obey law, thirdly, its relationship with morality and, lastly, its relationship with justice.

Some of the roles attributed to law are to maintain order (and this may well involve in some societies or at some times repression of groups or interests within society), to regulate conduct both by means of the criminal and civil law and to provide a means of settling disputes which arise or ensuring that people can order their affairs so as to avoid disputes. Professor Atiyah suggests that this has its drawbacks in that it suggests that law is an end in itself; that it has a mind whereas law, like other concepts, is an abstract social construct made up of 'rules, principles and ideas'. Its purposes or functions are those of the people who make and enforce the law and it is necessary to analyse the principles and policies underlying legal rules if one is to appreciate their effect. Principles and purposes may conflict and a law may not have been clearly thought through or its possible effects considered. In any event circumstances may change and a law may be adapted to meet new needs which are outside of its original purposes. This is most often associated with the extent to which the judge has an active role in law-making so as to develop the law by taking into account the purpose he or she considers that the law ought to serve.

The accepted approach is that the judge must give way to Parliament, which, as the elected representative of the people, is the arbiter of policy issues. The role of the judge is a limited one concerned with interpreting statutory provisions and developing the common law within the confines of binding precedent. Where the judge is confronted with a hard case and no binding precedent exists he or she should look to principle to assist the reaching of a decision. If in so doing the judge

11.1   The nature of law

11.1.1   The accepted approach

extends the boundaries of the law beyond that which is acceptable it is for Parliament to pass legislation to achieve acceptable policy objectives.

In discussing the functions of law what law is supposed to do and how effective it is in achieving those purposes must be distinguished. The former concerns the theories that have been devised about the functions of law and the latter with how law in practice works. Both are useful in that the former may be used as a measure of the effectiveness of law in society.

As we have noted, one of the main functions of law is said to be to resolve (or provide mechanisms for the avoidance of) disputes. The UK has an adversarial system as opposed to an inquisitorial one. The parties to a dispute 'do battle', and it is for the plaintiff to prove his or her case.

1.1.2   Resolution of disputes

'Resolution of disputes' properly refers to civil claims where the standard of proof on the plaintiff is on a balance of probabilities. In criminal cases the prosecution must prove the defendant's guilt beyond all reasonable doubt. Only in a very wide sense is there a dispute, rather it is the State imposing a penalty on a defendant found guilty of an act or omission which is considered sufficiently serious as to warrant a fine, imprisonment or other penalty.

So far as effectiveness is concerned several questions arise. Firstly, whether the adversarial system is more effective than an inquisitorial one? Secondly, given the pressures on the civil law system regarding unmet need for legal services and reductions in legal aid and advice provision, whether alternatives to traditional court settlement of disputes should be promoted such as arbitration, mediation and conciliation?

1.1.3   Regulation of conduct

Another function of law is the regulation of conduct and the entering into of relationships. Thus, the law might be a means of defining and regulating marriage and divorce, the relationship of parent and child, the ownership and use of property and its disposition by will or on intestacy, the making of contracts, the entering into of business and commercial relationships and that of employer and employee to mention but a few.

Some or all of these may give rise to sensitive issues and bring into question the extent to which law should be used to regulate such relationships. Other means of social control such as morality or religion might be argued to be more effective. A balance between the interests of the individual to own and use property, to marry and have children or decide not to do so, to be free to enter into contracts and so on and the interests of others and society in general has to be struck.

Some would argue that the law should protect individuals in their relationships with others, particularly those who are young, weak or vulnerable. Others suggest that the role of law is a limited one particularly in matters which are more properly the concern of private morality such as sexual relations, the age of consent and abortion. Again, the distinction between judge-made law and that passed by Parliament has to be borne in mind in that some take the view that if law is to regulate matters it must take the form of legislation and not the decisions of judges made piecemeal as and when a dispute arises.

In some societies the law has not been an instrument to protect or facilitate social arrangements but rather as a means of giving recognition to the actions of a ruling class with power and authority. The legal system and the laws made by it are a means of repression not only of those who present a threat to the existing order but of the mass of people. This then ensures continuance of the existing order. Recent history has shown that the use of law as a means of repression is possible despite more enlightened views as to its purposes. The Nazi Regime is an oft-quoted example of a system of law which was enforced by judges in courts of law and where rules were duly passed in accordance with recognised procedures but which in its content and effect was cruel and barbaric. Professor Hart described such laws as too evil to be obeyed.

We will now turn our attention to some theories which explain what law is and the purposes it serves. The main distinction as to what law is between the positivist and natural law schools of thought. The latter went into decline in the 19th century but saw somewhat of a revival in the 20th century.

The proponents of modern positivism are Professor HLA Hart and Hans Kelsen, but in the 19th century John Austin and Jeremy Bentham put forward positivist theories of law. We will briefly consider the main principles put forward by Austin and Bentham and then those of Hart and Kelsen.

11.1.4 Austin's theory

John Austin in *The Province of Jurisprudence Determined*, published in 1832, stated that law was the command of a sovereign power within the State enforced by coercion.

Thus, in the UK, law was made by the Queen in Parliament and the breach of law gave rise to the imposition of a sanction. The study of law was to be distinct from historical or sociological inquiry and there was no necessary connection between law and morality. The jurist was to confine his study to what law is and not what it ought to be as measured against some value judgment which unlike fact could not be substantiated by proof.

He recognised that law is normative that is it requires obedience and there may well be both a legal and a moral obligation to obey. Austin was concerned with an analytical study of law and the legal system including what law is, how it is made and by whom.

11.1.5   Bentham's theory

Jeremy Bentham's writings lay undiscovered for more than a century after his death in 1832, but were published by Professor Hart in 1970. These revealed Bentham's criticism of the common law. He described precedent as 'dog's law' and proposed urgent reforms so as to de-mystify the legal system.

His theory of law was founded on the principle of 'utility' and he said that the legal system should be rational and accessible and that law should be contained in a code permitting the judge to adjudicate in disputes rather than having power to interpret the law.

Austin had been Bentham's disciple and both defined law as the commands of a sovereign power. Bentham wished to move away from the 19th century natural law doctrine which measured man-made law against Divine law or the law of nature and concluded that law which conflicted with a higher law was either not law at all or need not be obeyed.

11.1.6   Hart's theory

Professor HLA Hart in *The Concept of Law* in 1961 (which has recently been republished and continues the debate between Hart and Professor Dworkin), recognised five main components of positivism namely:

- law as a command enforced by coercion;

- law and morality are essentially separate;

- that a legal system is based on logic so that correct decisions can be deduced from legal rules;

- analysis of legal concepts is distinct from historical and sociological studies and moral judgments cannot be proved by rational argument.

Hart stated that law is concerned with what is, whereas morality is concerned with what ought to be but recognised a core of indisputable truth in 'natural law' doctrine. Unlike Bentham and Austin, Hart stated that law is a social phenomenon and not a command of a sovereign backed by coercion. Law is a system of rules which he analysed into primary and secondary rules.

Primary rules proscribe basic anti-social behaviour such as theft, the use of violence and fraud. Secondary rules are of three types: rules of change, rules of adjudication and rules of recognition.

Rules of change apply to both primary and secondary rules and permit changes to be made by Parliament and the courts to the law or legal system. Rules of adjudication confer power on the courts to decide when breaches have occurred in criminal and civil matters. Rules of recognition form the bedrock of a legal system and provide criteria for determining the validity of the system and rules made within it. Officials concerned with the administration and adjudication of the law have to adopt 'an internal point of view', that is, to accept secondary rules. Citizens need to obey primary rules and should do so from a sense of obligation.

Hans Kelsen, in the *Pure Theory of Law*, took a scientific approach to the study of law and stated that law is a system of 'oughts' or 'norms' which describe human conduct. The function of law is the use of force to ensure compliance with a rule. A rule would be expressed in terms of: 'if X, then Y'. The consequence of breach is the imposition of a sanction.

11.1.7   Kelsen's theory

Law is distinct from morality and was to be analysed in terms of a pyramid at the apex of which was the 'grundnorm' (basic norm) whose validity was presupposed and based on efficacy.

The basic norm provides the reason why law is obeyed but is neutral and is not founded in morality.

Extensive criticism has been made of the positivist' approach including that it was an over-reaction to the natural law doctrine drawing on 19th century distinctions between 'is' and 'ought'. It has been said that it takes no account of values and fails to contemplate a connection between law and morality, the emphasis on sanction is not a true representation of law as some laws impose no sanction and others impose a sanction in the absence of a legal duty. Other laws are power-conferring and it is far fetched to define sanction as including, for example, nullity following a failure to make a will in accordance with the proper rules.

11.1.8   Criticism of the positivist approach

We need to turn our attention now to the natural law doctrine. This analyses the point at which law and morality coincide. It is concerned with what should or ought to exist and measures man-made law against a Divine or higher natural law. If the former offends the latter St Thomas Aquinas was of the opinion that the law lost its moral binding power and that the citizen might be justified, in some cases, in not obeying the law. On the other hand, St Augustine, Plato, Cicero and Aristotle considered that such was not law at all and was not binding. Depending on one's stance this may well affect not only ones perception of law but also whether it is to be obeyed or not.

The positivist would argue that in legal terms all law, no matter how bad, must be obeyed but morally it will be for the individual to decide whether to do so or not. The natural lawyer argues that 'bad' law is either not law at all and need not be obeyed or that although law, morally it need not be obeyed, but that the citizen must expect imposition of a penalty for non-compliance.

Sir William Blackstone in *Commentaries on the Laws of England* stated that a conflict between positive law and God-given principles would nullify the positive law.

11.2   The functions of law

Having considered some of the theories defining law we will now move on to consider some theories which attempt to analyse the purposes of law.

11.2.1   Techniques of law

Robert Summers devised a 'techniques of law' theory in which he set out five techniques or aims of law. Professor Farrer subsequently added another two techniques, that of constitutive and fiscal functions.

Those noted by Summers were as follows:

- grievance-remedial;
- penal;
- administrative/regulatory;
- conferral of social benefits; and
- private arrangements.

This theory emphasised the role of the law-maker and the techniques available to give effect to social policies. Those who interpret the law will either have to apply the literal meaning of the words used or may have to look behind the rules to find their meaning so as to apply the law to given facts to arrive at a solution.

11.2.2   Law jobs theory

Karl Llewellyn constructed a 'law jobs' theory. In any group, certain needs will have to be met or, as he referred to them, certain jobs will have to be done. Rules are one of the main ways in which such needs are met although it is to be noted that law is not the only means of achieving social ends.

Llewellyn was a member of the 'American realist' school of thought which like the positivists was concerned with law as it is rather than with law as it ought to be. Law as an institution performs various jobs including allocation of authority, determination of disputes, the adjustment to change and, by far the most important, the disposition of 'trouble cases' or how officials deal with disputes.

Brief mention must be made here of the 'sociological' school of thought, which treats law as a social phenomenon and only one way of social control.

Writers such as Roscoe Pound, Emile Durkheim, Max Weber and Karl Marx put forward sociological views of law and the functions it performs.

Pound said that law-makers and lawyers were engaged in 'social engineering' and that the law identified and protected various interests by way of rights and duties. He identified three types of interest:

- those of the individual including personal, domestic and property interests;

- the public interest of the State as the guardian of the third type; namely

- social interests – including general morals, social institutions, security and order.

Law provides the means by which such interests are secured. Should interests on the same level conflict they must be weighed against one another with the aim of ensuring that as many as possible are satisfied. Interests on different levels cannot be weighed against one another so, for example, individual interests should not be weighed against public or social interests.

Emile Durkheim put forward the proposition that society was held together by social solidarity. Law had a central role to play in the transition from a simple system in which law was repressive (mechanical solidarity) to a more complex system based on the division of labour and secularism where law is restitutive (organic solidarity).

Weber took a traditional positivist approach to law and defined law in terms of an order imposed by those with recognised authority and one in which coercion would be applied where law was broken. He analysed different systems of law and the ways in which law is made and considered how justice could be achieved.

Marx saw law as a means simply of class domination and oppression. Law was a necessary evil in capitalist society whereas in a classless society there would be no need for law for the means of production would be equally shared amongst all members of society.

Before considering the relationship of law and morality and whether one is shaped by the other and the extent to which one should shape the other we need to consider what is meant by 'morality'.

Earlier we attempted to distinguish between rules and other social phenomena and between legal rules and other types of rule including moral rules. We noted that morality may be described as a body of rules but equally it may be described as a set of values, beliefs or tenets which govern a person's or group's behaviour. Religion, ethics and morality are intertwined and may be relative according to time and place. However, they are concerned with what is right and wrong and operate on a different level from custom.

To tell lies or act dishonestly is generally considered to be wrong and may offend against not only morality, but also religion and in some cases, the law, as with fraud or when taking an oath. Customs concern practices which have grown up over time and which are passed down from one generation to another. Failure to comply will rarely give rise to an allegation of guilt or fault or a sense of wrongdoing which is associated with moral rules.

Other types of conduct which are generally considered to be immoral include the killing or injuring of another person, to steal or damage another's property, to commit adultery, to commit incest, to take advantage of another person, particularly one who is vulnerable or weak, and to mistreat animals.

The essence of attributing to some action or omission that it is immoral is blameworthiness, opprobrium and that it ought not to be done. There is a transgression, and invariably it involves a curb on behaviour rather than a positive duty to act. It follows that those who believe in freedom of choice and the ability of freely consenting individuals to do as they please in private resent any attempt to enforce moral ideals subscribed to by the wider society or so-called 'do-gooding' individuals such as Mary Whitehouse or Lord Longford.

On the other hand, it might be argued that the law must take a lead either from the wider society and what public opinion suggests is wrong or in some cases from the enlightened few in that it commands authority and respect sufficient to warrant obedience. In the minds of some only when a law is passed prohibiting certain conduct will this warrant compliance. It necessitates the authority of the law to ensure that such conduct is not permitted.

Furthermore, implicit in the notion of freedom is knowledge and understanding. For one thing, not everyone is of the same level of intelligence and some by reason of age, disability or education may be vulnerable and easily lead by those more able, persuasive and without scruples or who are driven by money. Thus, the law may seek to protect people from others or from themselves.

Caution is needed, however, concerning the question of whether the law should reflect morality. There may be no one moral standard to be applied by the law. It appears that this is certainly true of modern day Britain and there may be no agreement as to whose 'job' it is to enforce moral principles. This ranges from organised religion, the home and the school to the government of the day.

The present Conservative government seems to have got itself in a hopeless mess over its 'back to basics' campaign which at first some thought was the promotion of 'old-fashioned' principles in both public and private spheres and which the Prime Minister has subsequently attempted to limit to standards in education, law and order and the provision of public services. The debate which has resulted also highlights the question of the suitability of elected representatives to make law concerning moral issues. Simply to follow the majority view holds dangers in that there is no guarantee that the majority reflect any standard other than one which promotes their interests best. If law is to reflect morality and the legislators are not the best equipped, this leaves the judges.

Arguments for and against leaving moral issues in the hands of the judges can be put forward. On the one hand, they are appointed and not accountable to the people and therefore should not attempt to impose their views on others whereas, on the other, it can said that as they are independent they can develop the law in an objective way without giving way to popular fashion or whim. Development of the law may well involve the judges in questions of public policy and this, it can be argued, is the province of Parliament where all relevant issues can be debated before law is enacted.

We will now move on to consider more fully the relationship of law and morality. Law and morality in some places and at some times overlap and sometimes diverge. This can be represented two partly intersecting circles. At the point of intersection law and morality regulate social conduct and at the points where they do not intersect conduct may be regulated by one and not the other. It should be noted, however, that even when they intersect they may not be identical and that the law may be more specific and allow exceptions whereas the moral rule may be all-embracing as, for example, with abortion where a person's morality may permit of either abortion on demand or not in any circumstances. The Abortion Act 1967 as amended by the

11.3.1   The relationship of law and morality

Human Fertilisation and Embryology Act 1990 permits abortion in specified circumstances.

Another area of overlap is the criminal law where the State imposes sanctions for the commission of offences considered sufficiently serious as to warrant loss of freedom or fine or other punishment. The offender must 'pay his or her debt to society', and the law attempts to deter the offender and other members of society from such a course of action. The criminal law may also attempt not only to punish but rehabilitate the offender so as to re-enter society better able to contribute to it.

The criminal law adopts terminology suggesting wrongdoing and censure such as guilt, offence, prosecution, sentence, and it regulates conduct which by any standards should be considered to be wrong or anti-social. Serious offences come readily to mind including murder, rape, burglary, theft and robbery – but these are not absolutes and although founded in a society's values and ideology and the need to protect fundamental principles and standards of conduct the law develops the meaning and effect of such offences.

Take murder for example, this is not defined in the same way as killing another person. In some cases killing another person can be lawful, as was the case before The Murder (Abolition of the Death Penalty) Act 1965, where a person convicted of murder was sentenced to death and this was carried out in the name of the Crown. The moral rule, however, may prohibit all killings and this may be widely interpreted to include the foetus (from the moment of conception), to the person being kept alive artificially, to the person who is in great agony and wishes to take his or her own life or have another dispense a lethal drug to end life. Some would argue today that the death penalty for murder of police officers and others should be reinstated so as to give effect to the moral opinion that taking the life of another is not acceptable and deserves the ultimate of penalties. However, Parliament has resisted various attempts to change the law so as to give effect to this suggestion.

The question has to be asked whether Parliament is correct in not passing a law to reinstate the death penalty if the majority of the population hold views whereby it is considered the best course of action. One counter argument to such a change is that, given the numbers of miscarriages of justice which have been proved to have occurred in recent years through abuses of the criminal justice system, no convicted person should be sentenced to death. One other argument might be that Parliament as the elected representative of the people need not, or should not, give way to a majority view of the moment but should attempt to set standards reflecting fundamental principles which apply long-term and transcend mere fad or fashion.

The former appears on the surface to be an argument based on expediency or practicality whereas the latter is based on morality or what ought, or ought not, to be done. However, it can be said that to discover at a later date that a person who had been hanged for an offence he or she did not commit is in itself repugnant to moral principles.

As we have already mentioned, the law in certain circumstances permits abortion and it is no longer a criminal offence to commit suicide (although it is to aid or abet another in an attempt to commit suicide), euthanasia is not permitted by the law as was shown in the unreported case involving Dr Cox in 1992 who was convicted of the attempted murder of a patient to whom he had administered a lethal dose of saline solution to end her life. This was commented on by the House of Lords and Court of Appeal in *Airedale NHS Trust v Bland* (1993) where it was decided that a patient in a persistent vegetative state, for whom there was no medical hope of recovery, could have his life-support treatment stopped, resulting in his death. The House of Lords stated *per curiam* that positive steps to end life were unlawful and that doctors should seek the guidance of the courts before ending life-support treatment because every case would be different. Lords Browne-Wilkinson and Mustill stated that 'the moral, social and legal issues' should be considered by Parliament.

Thus, the law draws the line between taking steps to end life and discontinuing treatment which prolongs breathing artificially when the medical evidence shows that brain death has occurred. To kill another person may be morally wrong but translated into law may be permitted in defined cases.

In other societies or at other times taking the life of another may be more widely permitted by the law so as to reflect the moral attitude to human life. In the *Bland* case both the Court of Appeal and House of Lords discussed the moral dilemma between the sanctity of human life and the quality of life. Both recognised that these were complementary and that in the absence of legislation the court's function was to balance the two. The House of Lords concluded that it was right to allow someone in the position of Anthony Bland who was adult, had not expressed any wish as to what should be done if such circumstances befell him and for whom there was no medical hope of recovery, to die naturally following removal of life-sustaining treatment.

When considering the issue as to how far the law should attempt to reflect morality on the question of life and death it is instructive to bear in mind the debate about the imposition of life sentences for murder. In the House of Lords case of *R v Secretary of State for the Home Department ex p Doody* (1993) mandatory life prisoners claimed judicial review of the Home Secretary's decisions as to the length of imprisonment they were to serve. Amongst other things the case illustrates that although the only sentence for murder is life imprisonment, in practice it is rare for a prisoner to remain in prison for his natural life. It is at the discretion of the Home Secretary how long is served. The court ruled that in the exercise of this power the Home Secretary is obliged to give such prisoners reasons but that there is to be no automatic right of challenge simply because a prisoner disagrees with the conclusions reached.

The independent Committee of Inquiry chaired by the former Lord Chief Justice, Lord Lane, reported in December 1993 recommending abolition of the mandatory life sentence for murder. In its place a life sentence would be the maximum sentence reserved for the most wicked and those who posed a continuing danger. In other cases of murder the judge should be free to decide the appropriate remedy on the merits of each case and a decision made in open court.

Under the present system all categories of murderer (and in the words of the Report) 'from the "mercy killer" and the battered wife to the terrorist and armed robber' are sentenced to life imprisonment and it is then for a member of the Executive, the Home Secretary, behind closed doors, to decide on the length of sentence. This brings into question not only moral issues but those of justice which will be considered in the next section.

Given that law and morality may overlap on a particular issue but that the scope and effect will not always be identical, it must be noted that often they diverge. This may be because law is used to regulate types of conduct which have no moral element, for example, minor traffic offences, or simply because no moral consensus exists so that the law is either not used at all or it reflects only one view current within society.

It might be that law is used in an attempt to change the general moral view and represents what those in authority consider to be appropriate or representative of an enlightened view. Morality may be unable to keep up with rapid medical, scientific or technological change and it will be for the law to give effect to such changes. In any event, over-regulation of every aspect of a person's life by law cannot be desirable and, for good or bad, people must be left to make choices as to personal behaviour even though this is not for their good or that of society generally.

Whether or not law should reflect and reinforce morality depends on one's view of law and the purposes it serves in society. Whether law should go even further and attempt to change attitudes and give a moral lead is more problematic and may result in the law and legal system losing some of its authority and respect.

11.3.2   Should law influence or merely reflect morality?

In discussing these questions we need to take account of the 'natural law' school of thought which we have already briefly described. This emphasises the close relationship of law and morality and a logical conclusion of the theory is that where law fails to accord with moral principles either such rules are not properly classed as law or that the citizen is not morally bound to obey such law.

Even proponents of the 'positivist' school such as Professor Hart recognised a core of moral principle in law and concluded that the Nazi regime was so morally indefensible that the citizen was not morally bound to obey. Professor Dworkin, on the other hand, considers that law is not only made up of rules but non-rule standards and in deciding a hard case the judge calls on moral and political standards (principles and policies). Rules and principles form part of the law and dictate, guide or influence a result. These are properly the province of the judge whereas policies are the province of Parliament since they set out a goal to be achieved in social, political or economic matters or which are deemed to be desirable but not necessarily on grounds of morality. The role of the judge is to find the one right answer, not to make law. A judge formulates principle and if it exceeds the limits it is for Parliament to state the policy to which the law should give effect.

Present day exponents of natural law doctrine include Professor Fuller who in *The Morality of Law* spoke of the law's 'inner morality' which he formulated in terms of eight procedural requirements including generality, promulgation, non-contradiction, clarity, non-retroactivity, constancy, the possibility of compliance and congruence between a declared rule and official action. He considered that Nazi law could not be considered to be law. Professors Hart and Fuller entered into what has become known as the Hart-Fuller debate on the morality of law whereby the former put forward positivist views and the latter the natural law view that law and morality are inextricably mixed.

11.3.3   The Hart-Fuller debate

Similarly, Lord Devlin stated that law, and in particular the criminal law, is based on moral and religious principles. Ultimate standards of right and wrong exist. In other words, society is held together by a binding moral code and the role of the judge is to ensure continuance of this code as a guardian of morality. The judge has to put himself in the position of the reasonable man so as to gauge what is in the public interest. The suppression of vice was the 'business of the law' and consent and prevention of public immorality was insufficient.

This attitude is clearly shown in the cases of *Shaw v DPP* (1961), *DPP v Withers* (1974) and *Knuller v DPP* (1972). Shaw has become known as 'the ladies directory' case where prostitutes advertised in magazines and where the publishers were convicted of the offence of 'conspiring to corrupt public morals'. In *Knuller* the publication of advertisements inviting homosexual contacts were said to be undesirable on grounds of public policy and were prohibited as in *Shaw*. In *R v Gibson* (1991) where a model's head was displayed at a public gallery and attached to the head were earrings made from freeze-dried foetuses of three to four months gestation it was held that the common law offence of 'outraging public decency' had been committed.

It may be argued that these cases are outdated in their approach and that judges are not suitable to decide such sensitive issues. If they are not to be left to individual discretion and choice it is for Parliament alone to lay down the ground rules. Professor Hart took a libertarian stance following John Stuart Mill that the 'individual is sovereign'.

An issue recently before Parliament was the question of the age of consent for homosexual men. The Sexual Offences Act 1967 provides that two consenting males aged 21 or over who participate in homosexual practices in private commit no criminal offence. The amendment proposed by Edwina Currie MP to the Criminal Justice Bill permitting reduction in the age of consent to 18 was approved, although the proposal to reduce the age of consent to 16 was rejected.

Critics of this proposal suggested that the law should protect young men from unscrupulous members of society and themselves at a time when they may be impressionable and vulnerable. Proponents of this measure suggested that this should be a matter for the individual and it is not the place of the law to intervene in private matters or seek to enforce a particular pattern of behaviour. At the extremes there are those who promote complete freedom of the individual and at the other those who wish to see the law impose limits. This raises the question as to where the line is to be drawn – no restrictions, or if so, how much, and by what means?

The Wolfenden Committee Report in 1957 on 'Homosexual Offences and Prostitution' made the following statement on the function of the criminal law:

'... to preserve public order and decency, to protect the citizen from what is offensive and injurious and to provide sufficient safeguards against exploitation and corruption of others especially the vulnerable that is the young, weak in body or mind, inexperienced or those in a state of physical, official or economic dependence. The law should not intervene in the private lives of citizens or seek to enforce any particular pattern of behaviour further than necessary to carry out the above purposes'.

This statement has recently been considered in the case of *R v Brown* (1992) where the House of Lords by a 3-2 majority held that where the defendants had committed sado-masochistic acts in private and their 'victims' had consented, public policy demanded that such acts be treated as unlawful under ss 20 and 47 of the Offences Against the Person Act 1861. Lord Mustill, dissenting, took the view that this Act did not cover the defendants' actions and thereby make them unlawful although clearly such actions were immoral. Where the parties had consented to sado-masochistic practices these did not fall within the provisions of ss 20 and 47 of the 1861 Act. These provisions made duelling and prize-fighting unlawful but were not appropriate to the facts of this case. He did not endorse a libertarian view and considered that right and wrong could be distinguished. However this was a matter of private morality and not the function of the criminal law to impose standards on the individual. The individual should be governed by his or her own moral standards or be subject to the pressures of religion or other community to ' whose ethical ideals he responds'. State intervention in the lives of individuals should not be more than is necessary to ensure a proper balance between the interests of the individual and those of the community in which he lives. It was for Parliament to decide where the public interest lay.

Lord Templeman, in the majority, asked whether the defence of consent should extend to sado-masochistic practices. This was to be decided on the basis of 'policy and public interest'. A line had to be drawn by the courts and, rightly or wrongly, it had become established that boxing was a lawful activity as is surgery, ritual circumcision, tattooing and ear piercing. Such activities are lawful and where practised with consent actual bodily harm, wounding or serious bodily harm do not give rise to criminal liability. Unlawful activities include duelling and prize-fighting and consent cannot legitimate such activities.

Lord Jauncey, also in the majority, drew the line between common assault where consent provides a defence and offences under ss 20 and 47 of the 1861 Act where consent is not available as a defence unless the circumstances fall within accepted exceptions such as sporting contests, chastisement or surgery. The creation of new exceptions was a matter for Parliament following a full review of the moral, social, medical and other issues.

Thus, the majority of their Lordships took the view that all acts above common assault are unlawful, and consent is no defence, unless statute permits such actions. It was not for the courts to allow a defence of consent and make such actions lawful. Lords Mustill and Slynn, dissenting, considered that the 1861 Act did not apply to these actions, although clearly they were morally wrong, and so it was for Parliament to prohibit such actions if this was desired.

Following this judgment, protests were raised by civil rights campaigners who demanded a right of privacy to be enshrined in law so as to comply with Article 8 of the European Convention on Human Rights. It was also alleged that the sentences of imprisonment were excessive, that questions of morality were for Parliament and not the courts which are unrepresentative of the population at large and are only able to make decisions after a dispute or question arises. As the case involved the consent of the parties involved who were adults conducting themselves in private the court had imposed an unacceptable limit on personal freedom. A line had to be drawn between the acceptable and the unacceptable. To torture a person and thereby cause his or her death and then plead consent would be unacceptable but Parliament should determine the proper place of consent, not the courts. The decision was reached by a 3-2 majority which suggests that in reality little consensus exists on such issues and for the majority to suggest that it is for Parliament to legitimise such activity if thought necessary and for the minority to suggest that such actions are lawful until Parliament prohibits them is equally unsatisfactory.

In 1991 the House of Lords made a landmark decision in respect of rape within marriage.

In *R v R (a Husband)* (1991) the principle established by Sir Matthew Hale in *History of the Pleas of the Crown* (1736), whereby a husband could not be guilty of rape committed on his wife 'for by their mutual matrimonial consent and contract the wife hath given up herself in this kind unto her husband which she cannot retract' was rejected.

On the facts of the case the parties had been separated some 22 days before the alleged rape but there had been no legal separation or court order prohibiting the husband from molesting his wife. The court held that the time had come to remove Hale's proposition altogether rather than create further exceptions to the rule. Its terms no longer accorded with what was considered acceptable behaviour. It was never any more than a 'legal fiction' and had been overtaken by events. In the words of Lord Lane, the Lord Chief Justice at the time, 'a rapist remained a rapist subject to the criminal law, irrespective of his relationship with his victim', the common law fiction had become 'anachronistic and offensive' and it was the duty of the court to remove the immunity created by it.

Lord Keith said that the common law could change and evolve in the light of social, economic and cultural developments. The status of women today is radically different from that in Hale's time and the institution of marriage is seen as a partnership of equals where a wife is no longer the subservient chattel of her husband.

The Law Commission in its final report recommended that rape in marriage be a criminal offence and that a wife who alleges rape against her husband be a compellable witness for the prosecution against her husband. Prosecutions should be brought with the consent of the Director of Public Prosecutions.

Legislation is still awaited in the light of this recommendation and the House of Lords' decision. It is needed so as to clarify the extent of the rule and the loss of immunity it gives rise to. It is likely to apply to all women including those still living with their husbands but legislation would define the extent of the law.

We have already referred to the case of Anthony Bland and the issues raised by the case. It is useful to note here the role of the Attorney General as *amicus curiae* (friend of the court). Given the public importance of the case and the serious medical, moral and ethical questions raised it was essential that those interests be put before the court. The case was novel in that it was the first time that the English courts had had to deal with such a question concerning life and death. Furthermore, Tony Bland was not a child or ward of court, he was immune from pain and had given no instructions concerning treatment in the event of his becoming such a patient. In the Court of Appeal Hoffman LJ stated in such an area as this there should be no difference between the law and what is morally right. The court's decision should be based on accepted ethical values. Both the Court of Appeal and the House of Lords made much use of persuasive authorities from Commonwealth and other jurisdictions in assisting them in reaching the decision that treatment should cease.

The case of *Re J (a Minor) (Medical Treatment)* (1992) was referred to in the *Bland* case. This concerned a severely handicapped baby whose doctor considered that mechanical ventilation procedures would not be appropriate. An injunction was sought to order the carrying out of such treatment but the court held that in the best interests of the child this was not to be granted. The court adopts the role of *parens patriae* in respect of minors as illustrated in the case of *Re J (a Minor) (Inherent Jurisdiction; Consent to Treatment)* (1992) where the court held that a 16-year-old does not have complete autonomy to refuse medical treatment. The court was also of the opinion that the 'Gillick competent', that is a child of sufficient intelligence and understanding, could not refuse treatment. In *Gillick v West Norfolk and Wisbech AHA* (1985) it was held that at common law 'the Gillick competent' could consent to treatment without the need for parental consent or even in the face of the parents express prohibition. The court can, therefore, override parental refusal of treatment and a child's refusal of treatment.

The conclusion may be drawn, therefore, that the court can protect children and others who are vulnerable or weak from themselves or others, although the jurisdiction of the court in respect of minors has always been considered special. It might be argued that where Parliament has failed to legislate it is for the courts to adopt what some might describe as a paternalistic approach in the meantime and then, if the decisions of the courts are unacceptable, for Parliament to set the limits of the law.

Other issues, which we can but mention and which have a moral dimension, include that of women over the child-bearing age giving birth to test-tube babies; sterilisation of the mentally and physically handicapped; surrogate motherhood and the use of foetal tissue in embryo experimentation.

Other issues which have come to prominence recently include the defence of provocation for women with violent partners. The present law is said to be to the advantage of men who react in a moment of passion or anger whereas women who are driven to retaliate against partners, often following many years of violence, do only after a time in which they plan their actions. Consequently, the defence of provocation is rarely available to such women and this needs to be changed.

The question of the extent to which morality plays a part in the decisions of local authorities to ban hunting over their land has recently come before the High Court on an application for judicial review of a decision by Somerset County Council to ban hunting. It was held that moral issues should play no part in such decision-making and that the ban was *ultra vires* in this case.

Two other issues and their regulation by law, have yet to be decided, namely whether the law should prohibit child-minders from smacking children in their charge and whether the law should ban tobacco advertising. The arguments for and against the involvement of the law in such areas revolve around the freedom of the individual on the one hand and of protection of the weak and vulnerable on the other. If the law is seen as too restrictive of the freedom of the individual it will lose respect and the result may be criminalisation of conduct considered morally acceptable whereas if it is seen to be too liberal it may lose its moral authority in failing to protect those in need.

Rules that are Laws

Law is a system of rules imposed by the State or those with authority which give rise to sanctions or penalties for breach.

The nature of law

Four things should be taken into account when considering the nature and characteristics of law. These are:

- its role in society and the purposes served;

- the reasons why law is obeyed;

- its relationship with morality; and

- its relationship with justice.

Theories explaining the nature and purpose of law fall into two groups: the 'positivist' and the 'natural law' schools of thought.

The 20th century saw a revival in the latter following 19th century decline in the face of the theories of John Austin and Jeremy Bentham. Modern proponents of the positivist school are Professor HLA Hart and Hans Kelsen.

The positivist concludes that law is concerned with what is and not with what ought to be. Law and morality are distinct and no matter how bad a law is it nevertheless remains law. The natural law school measures law against Divine or higher law and concludes either that a bad law is not law at all or morally it need not be obeyed.

The functions of law

Several theories are considered including Robert Summers' 'techniques of law' theory to which Professor Farrer made additions, the 'law jobs' theory of Karl Llewellyn and the sociological school of thought put forward by Roscoe Pound, Emile Durkheim, Max Weber and Karl Marx.

Law and morality

Morality is concerned with what is 'right' and 'wrong' and is closely related to religion and ethics. The essence of behaviour which is considered to be immoral is blameworthiness or transgression of a curb on behaviour rather than a failure to comply with a positive duty to act.

Two questions are pertinent when considering the relationship of law and morality, namely the extent to which one is shaped by the other and the extent to which one should shape the other.

| The relationship of law and morality | The overlap between law and morality can be represented by two partly intersecting circles. The main area of overlap is criminal law which imposes penalties on those found guilty of offences. |

The relationship of law and morality

The overlap between law and morality can be represented by two partly intersecting circles. The main area of overlap is criminal law which imposes penalties on those found guilty of offences.

Prosecution is in the name of the Crown and the terminology suggests wrongdoing and censure of anti-social conduct. Abortion and murder are mentioned as are suicide and euthanasia. *Airedale NHS Trust v Bland* (1993) held that a patient in a persistent vegetative state could have his life support treatment ended resulting in his death.

Life sentences for murder are also considered (*R v Secretary of State for the Home Department ex p Doody* (1993)).

Should law influence or merely reflect morality ?

The natural law school of thought emphasises the close relationship between law and morality. The ideas of Professor Fuller and Lord Devlin are mentioned.

Shaw v DPP (1961)

DPP v Withers (1974)

Knuller v DPP (1972)

R v Gibson (1991)

R v Brown (1992)

R v R (a Husband) (1991)

Re J (a Minor) (Medical Treatment) (1992)

Re J (a Minor) (Inherent Jurisdiction: Consent to Treatment) (1992)

Gillick v West Norfolk and Wisbech AHA (1985)

The Wolfenden Committee Report 1957 on Homosexual Offences and Prostitution

Proposed changes to the age of consent for homosexuals. Other issues with a moral dimension: test-tube babies for women over child-bearing age; sterilisation of mentally or physically handicapped; surrogate motherhood; the use of foetal tissue in embryo experimentation; defence of provocation for 'battered wives'; corporal punishment and a ban on tobacco advertising.

Chapter 12

Law and Justice

The concept of 'justice' is most often linked with that of law in that the former is an ideal which, in the minds of most people throughout time, should be the aim to be achieved by law. However, justice in the sense of fairness should, as a moral value, permeate all areas of social activity and it is ultimately for the law and legal system to enforce principles of fairness.

It must be noted, however, that in some societies and at different times law does not promote the principle of justice or fairness and may be used as an instrument of repression of a section or sections of society or as an instrument of terror against the general population. Moreover, particular laws may be seen by members of a society as unjust and the question may arise as to the moral imperative to obey such law.

In considering the English legal system, the words 'law' and 'justice' may often be used interchangeably. For example, with reference to the courts of justice, justice of the peace, the criminal and civil justice systems but this is not to say that law or the legal system and justice are identical or that justice is achieved. In relation to the criminal justice system this appears to be particularly true in the light of a considerable number of appeals to the Court of Appeal alleging miscarriages of justice and radio and television programmes which have publicised failings in the system whereby the guilty go free, either through non-detection or technicalities in the trial process or the innocent are wrongly convicted.

It might be argued that any criminal justice system must accept the former as the price to be paid for preventing the latter which by any standard of morality, ethics or fairness is never acceptable. The epitome of the aim of achieving justice in the criminal justice system is the statue of Justice on the Old Bailey in London holding outright the evenly balanced scales of justice.

It is to be noted that there are four components to be measured:

- The pre-trial process

  This is the process by which evidence is collected and a charge is made against an accused. This has been found seriously wanting and given our accusatorial system the trial process cannot be any better than the evidence which

12.1   What is justice?

is brought before the court. If this has been fabricated or obtained as a result of duress whether, physical or psychological, a conviction secured on the basis of such evidence may, many years after the trial, be found to be wrong.

The trial of the Guildford Four in which Donaldson LJ presided, was at the time described as scrupulously fair, but it was only much later, as a result of press and other pressure, that fabricated evidence was shown to have caused great injustice.

- The trial process

  This should be fair in its form by which a person is tried and guilt determined. We will consider later some of the fundamental principles which contribute to a fair trial such as the presumption of innocence, the right to jury trial and the right to silence which is under threat as a result of the Criminal Justice Bill presently before Parliament.

- The adequacy of mechanisms for discovering and rectifying miscarriages of justice

  This has also been found lacking amid calls for an independent review body to replace the role presently performed by the Court of Appeal. The Runciman Royal Commission reporting in July 1993 recommended the establishment of such a body but so far little progress has been made.

- Substantive legal rules

  The fourth component to be measured is substantive legal rules, whether criminal or civil, and the penalties which can be imposed for breach, governing a person's conduct. If such rules are considered by sufficient numbers of the population to be unjust this can only result in loss of respect for the law and those who enforce it. A recent announcement that the penalties for drugs abuse are to be increased have incensed some commentators who had understood that government policy was moving towards a more liberal approach to some drug offences. Such increase may well be seen by some as unjust in that it attempts to penalise behaviour which has come to be seen as acceptable. The imposition of harsher penalties may well have an adverse effect than that desired in that people will go to greater lengths not to be apprehended.

12.2   Theories of justice

As we have already mentioned, law and justice are closely associated but by no means identical. We need now to consider some of the theories which have been constructed to explain this concept and its relationship with law and other social phenomena. We have already stated that justice can be used as a measure of the quality or fairness of the processes of the legal system and of substantive legal rules. Another way of making this distinction is between formal or procedural justice on the one hand and substantial justice on the other. We will consider each in turn.

Formal or 'procedural' justice requires a legal system to provide rules, principles and machinery for due application of the law to all persons without fear or favour. It is a fundamental principle founded in morality that no-one should be above the law and those who administer the law should do without prejudice, bias or fear of recrimination from those with power. The independence and impartiality of the judiciary is essential and the main way in which the citizen is protected from dictatorial government. However, this says nothing of the substance of the rules which are to be administered and applied. They may be considered to be unjust, wrong or immoral.

12.2.1   Formal justice

The positivist looks to the process by which law is made. If this has been complied with, no matter the content of the rules, they are to be obeyed and applied. The natural lawyer on the other hand will question the content or substance of the law and, in very extreme situations may be willing to question the authority of the legal system itself, and if this is found wanting will either conclude that it is not law at all or that the citizen is not morally obliged to abide by it.

Formal justice depends on the notion of 'equality'. Lloyd in *The Concept of Law* says that 'like should be treated as like'. This necessitates that those who administer the law do so impartially without preference for the rich, the powerful, or members of an elite. As Professor Fuller noted, law should manifest certain characteristics. It should be of general effect so that everyone falling within the remit of a rule should be treated in the same way. Thus, a person convicted of murder should be subject to the required penalty regardless of whether he or she is black or white, male or female or old or young or of high or low rank. The rule may well define exceptions so that those, for example, who are insane or of tender years will not be not be subject to penalty. Generality allows people to plan their activities so as to comply with the law. It follows that the law should have prospective effect and only in cases where a statute expressly provides will English law allow it to have retrospective effect. The law should be clear in its effect, provide for the possibility of compliance and there should be some congruence between the official rule and its application in practice. Judges, when making decisions, should do so in accordance with recognised principles in the absence of binding precedent so as to ensure that their decisions are reasoned and impartial. Improper considerations and motives should play no part in the decision-making process. This comes from training and experience as well as knowledge and understanding of how the law has developed and appreciation of the purposes it serves.

When considering formal justice, two important doctrines are the 'rule of law' and 'natural justice'.

2.2.2 The rule of law	The rule of law forms one of the cornerstones of democratic States and in those with written constitutions it is often guaranteed. Government excess can be found by the courts not only to be illegal but unconstitutional since the constitution is treated as a form of higher law by which the actions of government and others are measured. No person is above the law and even government itself is subject to law and is required to conduct its activities in accordance with duly established legal rules rather than by way of arbitrary or discretionary means.

It is, however, a broad and rather elusive concept and one which does not sit easily in the UK with the doctrine of sovereignty of Parliament. The role of the courts is also much more limited in respect of government activities. Government may act by way of statutory or prerogative power and this affords the courts little, if any, means of permitting any challenge by an aggrieved citizen.

However, if delegated powers are used, the delegate, whether a government minister, local authority or public body, can be found to have abused or exceeded the powers granted and the court may declare such actions *ultra vires* and void.

A useful illustration is that of the case of *M v Home Office and Another* (1993) where the House of Lords affirmed the decision of the Court of Appeal in holding the Home Secretary in contempt of court for failing to comply with a court order for the immediate return to this country of an asylum seeker unlawfully deported to Zaïre pending his application to the court for judicial review of the decision to deport.

2.2.3 The doctrine of natural justice	The doctrine of natural justice is rather a misnomer in that there is no appeal to natural law or to Divine law but rather to the fundamental need for fairness in the judicial process. The doctrine has been extended to decision-makers acting not only in a judicial capacity but also to those acting quasi-judicially.

Such distinctions are not easy to define but the courts have, on the one hand, classified judicial and quasi-judicial decisions and, on the other, administrative decisions where the rules of natural justice have not been strictly applied. However, this distinction has lost much of its importance following the case of *Re HK (an infant)* (1967) where it was stated that decision-makers, no matter their capacity, must act fairly.

In *Bushell v Secretary of State for the Environment* (1981) Lord Diplock stated that:

> '... the only requirement ... as to the procedure to be followed at a local inquiry ... is that it must be fair to all those who have an interest in the decision that will follow it.'

In *Council of Civil Service Unions v Minister for the Civil Service* (1985) (the GCHQ case) Lord Roskill said that natural justice might now be laid to rest and be 'replaced ... by a duty to act fairly'. Lord Scarman spoke of 'the requirement of natural justice namely the duty to act fairly' and observed that this applies to purely administrative acts.

Some cases still speak of the 'rules of natural justice' as opposed to a general duty to act fairly and so it is not settled whether these are still separate. However, what is clear is that the courts are not concerned with the merits of a claim under Order 53 (unlike an appeal) and will not substitute its decision for that of the decision-maker. Usually cases are sent back to the decision-maker who will be required to make a new decision in accordance with the recommendations of the court as to the extent of its legal powers. Thus, the reference to a duty to act fairly relates to process and not to the merits of a decision.

There are two limbs to the rules of natural justice:

- *nemo judex in res sua* (no man should be a judge in his own cause); and

- *audi alteram partem* (both sides have a right to be heard).

We have an adversarial legal system in which it is for the prosecution in criminal cases, and for the plaintiff in civil cases, to prove its case. The judge is an independent and impartial 'arbiter' of law and fact (or of law in Crown Court trials where the jury is the arbiter of fact), who decides cases coming before the court on the basis of the evidence produced and his knowledge and understanding of the law as applied to the facts.

It follows that in judicial proceedings both sides should have a right to make representations to the court but it is recognised that a defendant, particularly in criminal trials, need not say anything in his or her own defence and that the burden of proof rests with the prosecution or plaintiff. The rules of natural justice ensure that fair play operates so that a party knows the case he or she has to answer and the judge has no interest in the outcome.

The rules of natural justice have been developed by the judges as part of the common law and where one or both have not been complied with the aggrieved person may seek judicial review under Order 53 of the Rules of the Supreme Court. The relief granted will be an order of *mandamus, certiorari* or prohibition as appropriate in the circumstances.

It must be noted that neither rule has been defined with great precision with the effect that many limitations exist on their scope. This is particularly true of the right to be heard where there is no absolute right to legal representation. A person should be given adequate prior notice of charges or allegations and a reasonable opportunity to put his or her case. The rules provide for minimum standards so as to ensure safeguards to protect the interests of those in respect of whom decisions are made.

The rule against bias ensures that the judge or decision-maker leaves aside his or her personal preferences or prejudices due to age, background, education or sex. It also militates against the espousal of fixed views as in *R v Bingham Justices ex p Jowitt* (1974) where a magistrate said that he always believed police witnesses in preference to members of the public.

Pecuniary and proprietary interests, personal knowledge and relationships with a party or witness are also included. In short, the decision-maker should consider whether his or her position is compromised to the extent that he or she should stand down.

Over the years the courts have extended the scope of the rules of natural justice and now apply a wide duty to act fairly. Decision-makers are obliged to observe all or some of the aspects of both rules according to the circumstances. However, there are situations where the rules do not apply, including where a statute excludes their operation, where matters are dealt with at a preliminary stage or where a presumption excludes the doctrine. In professional relationships the rules only apply where a person's rights are affected.

12.2.4 Legitimate expectation

We have already referred to the *GCHQ* case which involved a union ban issued by the head of the civil service by way of an Order in Council. The House of Lords held that the employees had a legitimate expectation to be consulted before such action was taken. It had become a well established practice for the government to consult civil servants before making significant changes to their terms and conditions. This regular practice gave rise to a legitimate expectation that it would continue unless notice was given of revocation. Legitimate expectation may arise out of a promise or a regular practice. It may be an expectation of being consulted or a right to a hearing or to make representations.

In *A-G of Hong Kong v Ng Tuen Shiu* (1983), Ng, an illegal immigrant to Hong Kong, became aware, after registering as an illegal immigrant of an undertaking from the British government, that repatriation would only be made following an interview and consideration of the merits of each case. Ng was deported without any opportunity of giving his reasons for remaining in Hong Kong. It was held that the undertaking gave rise to a legitimate expectation in Ng that his case would be considered on its merits. In *R v Secretary of State for the Home Department ex p Khan* (1985) K and his wife wished to adopt a child from Pakistan. K obtained from a Citizens' Advice Bureau a standard letter from the Secretary of State stating that he 'may exercise his discretion and exceptionally allow a child to be brought here for adoption' when satisfied on four specified matters. K's application was refused and it was shown that the Secretary of State took into account a matter not mentioned in his letter. The court held that any change in policy should have resulted in a hearing at which K could have made representations. The Secretary of State was under a duty to act fairly and was obliged to reconsider the matter on the basis of his letter, or if the new policy was to apply, K should have an opportunity of being heard.

R v Secretary of State for the Home Department ex p Ruddock (1987) contains *obiter* statements that a legitimate expectation arose from the publication of the government's policy on 'phone tapping' that it would remain unchanged. Any change in policy was to be published. This, as with the other cases, illustrates that legitimate expectation only concerns procedural requirements and not substantive ones. The government could change its policy for the future but if it did so it would need to publicise the change so as to ensure those affected by the change had due warning. In *O'Reilly v Mackman* (1982) a prisoner had a legitimate expectation of remission and he had *locus standi* under Order 53 of the Rules of the Supreme Court to challenge a decision depriving him of it. *R v The Lord Chancellor ex p The Law Society* (1993) is a recent case where the Law Society challenged regulations made by the Lord Chancellor under the Legal Aid Act 1988, and it was held that the Law Society had *locus standi* and a legitimate expectation of being consulted before changes were made in legal aid provision. In the result the regulations were found to be *intra vires*.

12.2.5   Substantial justice

Leaving procedural justice we will move on to consider substantial justice. This concerns the content of a rule and measures it against a 'higher' or more fundamental set of principles such as fairness, justice or morality. The natural law school would use as its measure principles of morality or Divine law whereas in a State with a written constitution this will be the yardstick against which ordinary law is measured. The constitution will contain those principles which are considered to be fundamental and worth preserving and there may, in addition, be a bill of rights guaranteeing the rights of the citizen against the state.

In the UK there is no written constitution or bill of rights and law which has constitutional significance takes no special form and is not entrenched. Although the UK is a signatory of the European Convention on Human Rights this has not been brought into domestic effect by legislation and so the courts are not able to give effect to its provisions. Occasionally, the courts are willing to decide a case in such a way as to comply with the provisions of the European Convention by developing the common law. An illustration of this is the case of *Derbyshire County Council v Times Newspapers Ltd & Others* (1993) where the House of Lords held that at common law a local authority had no right to sue in defamation since this would place an undesirable fetter on freedom of speech. The Court of Appeal in reaching the same conclusion had referred to Article 10 of the European Convention.

Impartial application of legal rules does not of itself ensure substantial justice. It is the content of the rules and the extent to which particular circumstances are taken into account when a decision is made that ensure that a just result is achieved.

12.2.6   Remedial justice

What criteria are used to assess whether a just result is achieved? This depends on one's view of right and wrong. A distinction can be drawn between the theory of remedial justice and that of distributive justice. The former is concerned with the remedy provided for breach of a legal rule. The ordinary person looks to the judge or the legislator to provide a remedy where a wrong is committed. The judge adopts the 'reasonable man' test, once described as that of 'the man on the Clapham omnibus', to decide what the ordinary person would expect of the law.

Use of the term 'remedy' implies resolution of a dispute as in civil law where the wrongdoer pays compensation to the victim so as to put him or her into the position that he or she would have been in if the wrong had not been committed. However, 'remedy' should have a wide meaning so as to include penalties imposed by criminal law on those found guilty of criminal offences.

It is in the area of sentencing that questions of justice most often arise and whether the penalty imposed matches the crime committed by the defendant. The aims of sentencing are most often said to be:

- punishment of the offender;

- deterrence of offender and of others who might be tempted to commit an offence; and

- the rehabilitation of the offender.

It is difficult to assess the relative weight of each of these in any one offence but a sense of justice suggests that there should be an element of proportionality so that an offender is not made a 'scape-goat' for others and that as between different offences a trivial offence is not treated more seriously than a less trivial one. However, determining the relation of one offence with others involves value judgments as does the relative seriousness of different instances of one type of offence.

This has been clearly illustrated in the debate which has ensued following the report of the Committee of Inquiry chaired by Lord Lane which recommended the abolition of the mandatory life sentence for murder. In its place the judge would be free to impose a penalty suitable according to the facts of each case and life would be reserved for the most serious types of murder. The report criticises the involvement of the Home Secretary in deciding the length of term to be served by those found guilty of murder and suggests that justice would be best served by a more open approach whereby decisions would be reached by a judge in open court. The House of Lords in *R v Secretary of State for the Home Department ex p Doody* (1993) decided that the Home Secretary was obliged to allow those serving mandatory life sentences an opportunity to make written representations as to the term to be served and to inform the prisoner of the judicial recommendations as to term. If the Home Secretary then decided to depart from such recommendations he was obliged to give his reasons for so doing.

Distributive justice is also referred to as 'social' justice and attempts to share out the 'good' and the 'bad' things amongst members of society as equally as possible. The 'good' things are, for example, wealth, power and freedom and the 'bad' are

12.2.7   Distributive justice

duties and burdens such as liability to pay taxes, to be subject to restrictions over one's property and limitations on freedom so as to permit a degree of freedom in others.

Social justice recognises that not all members of society have the same advantages, physically, socially or mentally and so there has to be a redistribution of resources so as to achieve fair shares for all. The criteria employed to arrive at an apportionment of 'goods' will often be subjective and depend on value judgments. Apportionment of benefits might be according to the same thing to all but this can lead to unfairness in the sense that each person has a different starting point and no account is taken of age, ability, intelligence, wealth and so on. Apportionment might be according to merit or worth or to need or to status or according to legal entitlement but, whichever criterion is used, subjective factors come into play. For example, how should a person's worth be determined and how should need be defined? This is properly the province of policy which Professor Dworkin concluded was the role of Parliament to determine and not for the courts.

The law is said to be a means to an end and for substantial justice to exist not only must the procedures by which the law is applied be seen to be fair but also the content of the rules, that is, the social ends to be achieved. The analysis of substantial justice brings us back to such questions as to the role of law in society and the relationship of law and morality.

12.2.8   Certainty and equality

In any discussion of justice two concepts are of particular importance namely certainty and equality.

• Certainty

Law needs to be certain in its scope and effect if people are to know how to order their affairs and to accord the law respect. However the advantage of certainty must not be over-emphasised particularly with regard to substantial justice where a patently unjust law, no matter how certain in its terms or effect, will remain one which offends against principles of morality or notions of a 'higher' law.

Certainty can also easily slide into rigidity with the effect that the law and legal system will fail to meet changing social needs. This was a major criticism of the common law and one which Equity attempted to remedy. Once equity itself applied the doctrine of precedent it too became more rigid and less able to adapt to meet changing needs. A balance has to be found between, on the one hand, certainty and, on the other, flexibility. Another aspect of certainty is that of law taking prospective effect rather than a retrospective effect. If law applies to future actions those affected will be able to arrange their affairs in such a way so as to comply. With law which has a retrospective effect actions which were legal when taken become, at a later date, illegal and this is seen as anomalous unless very special circumstances necessitate a law having retrospective effect.

- Equality

Equality has been described as the 'foundation of justice' and is expressed in such principles as everyone is equal before the law and all persons are subject to the law regardless of race, colour, creed or rank.

Allied with these principles is the notion that the courts and legal system should be available to all and that judges should be independent and impartial. Equality and justice, however, are not identical if equality is used only to mean that all people are to be treated alike for this fails to take account of differences in character, upbringing, status, education and so on.

Discrimination on the grounds of age, sex, colour and so on should not be tolerated but recognition of human differences must be retained if justice, in its widest sense of fairness, is to be achieved. Some consider that in the interests of justice some individuals or groups should benefit from positive discrimination so as to even out the disadvantages experienced by such individuals or groups in the past. Others would see this as unfair and that promotion or preferment should be achieved only on merit.

Given that individuals or groups may discriminate against others in subtle as well as overt ways the law has had to develop the notion of direct and indirect discrimination in an attempt to change attitudes and ensure fairer treatment of those who would otherwise stand little chance of success in employment, education, housing or other social activities.

It is to be noted, however, that English law takes a limited view of discrimination. Only discrimination on grounds of sex and race are prohibited whereas other legal systems outlaw discrimination on grounds of age, for example. The legal profession and system is itself accused of discriminating against women and those from the ethnic minorities with the result that much talent is lost to the legal profession and judiciary. Selection is often conducted secretly and rarely will reasons be given for non-appointment. This is seen to fall far short of acceptable standards of openness and accountability although recent announcements suggest that changes are to be made in the process of appointment of members of the judiciary.

12.2.9   Rawls' theory

We have now considered some ideas of justice and before moving on to consider failings in the criminal justice system, brief mention must be made of John Rawls' *A Theory of Justice*, published in 1971. Rawls analysed law on the basis that the rational person will pay for those things wanted badly enough. His theory rejects utilitarianism which was based on maximising happiness and constructs a social contract aimed at establishing principles of justice. Free and rational persons concerned to further their own interests adopt principles of justice which define the basis of their association. People in the Original Position (POP) are shrouded in 'a veil of ignorance' when debating principles of justice. They do not know their sex, class, religion or social position or whether they are weak, strong, clever or stupid, the state or period in history in which they exist. Unanimous agreement has to be reached on the general principles underlying their society and they are assisted only by elementary knowledge of science and human psychology. They are governed by rational self-interest so that the worst condition in society will be the least undesirable of all alternatives. On 'lifting the veil' any one of the POP could be at the bottom of the social hierarchy.

Rawls considers that there are two principles of justice, namely liberty and equality, and the POP select the former over the latter.

* Liberty – ensures an equal right to basic liberties.

* Equality – has two parts:

    (i)   the just savings principle, which ensures that social and economic inequalities are arranged so as to be for the greatest benefit of the least advantaged;

    (ii)   the second ensures equality of opportunity.

    POP prefer the first to the second.

Some of the main criticisms of this theory concern its artificiality and the assumptions underlying it. It leaves unexplained why the POP should select liberty before equality and why natural talents are to be treated as collective assets. It fails to take account of deserts whereas, traditionally, a vital element of the notion of justice is 'just deserts' or apportioning blame or rewarding hard work or compliance with accepted standards.

12.2.10   Miscarriages of justice

We now move on to consider the idea of miscarriages of justice. This could arise in the context of the criminal law where those who have committed a crime are acquitted or are not brought to trial or because the innocent are wrongly convicted.

It is generally accepted that the price of a fair criminal justice system will be the acquittal on a technicality of those who have committed criminal offences or because of a failure of evidence, whereas conviction of the innocent is never acceptable and, should it arise, speedy measures should be taken to rectify the injustice.

Justice also needs to be achieved in civil law where a plaintiff seeks redress for a wrong committed by the defendant. Both parties should have 'their day in court' and the plaintiff will seek compensation for the alleged wrong providing it is one recognised by the law as giving rise to liability.

Miscarriages may arise where the law fails to compensate a plaintiff as has been illustrated in the case brought against the Law Society by Peggy Wood which is to go to appeal to the House of Lords in 1994. Injustice may result where a weak or vulnerable party is deprived of access to the courts or other means of bringing a claim.

Returning to the question of miscarriages of justice in criminal law, some fundamental principles of our system are the presumption of innocence, the use of juries in trials in the Crown Court, the prosecution having the burden of proving the defendant guilty beyond all reasonable doubt, the right for a defendant to remain silent during interrogation and trial and the discretion in the judge to exclude illegally obtained evidence. The presumption of innocence is seen to be under threat given the provisions of the Criminal Justice Bill presently before Parliament, aimed at removing the right to silence by allowing adverse comment to be made by the trial judge as to the reasons for a defendant failing to reveal information to the police. The Runciman Commission report recommended retention of the right to silence but proposed limitations to be placed on the defendant's right to jury trial. This was set up in the wake of some notorious appeals to the Court of Appeal alleging miscarriages of justice including the Guildford Four case, the Maguire Seven, the Birmingham Six, the Tottenham Three, the Judith Ward and the Stefan Kiszko cases.

The most serious failing in these cases was the fabrication of evidence by the police and the false confessions obtained as a result of duress. It was suggested that these cases, all but the Tottenham Three, had all occurred before the coming into effect of the Police and Criminal Evidence Act 1984 and that this statute provided sufficient safeguards for the suspect during police questioning. However, much criticism has been made of the effectiveness of this Act and codes of practice made under it and in any event in the case of alleged terrorist offences (with which all but the Tottenham Three and Kiszko were concerned) the Prevention of Terrorism Act 1991 excludes many of the safeguards for the suspect provided by the 1984 Act. As was shown in the Guildford Four trial this had been conducted scrupulously fairly and the injustice resulted from fabricated evidence.

Michael Mansfield QC in his book *Presumed Guilty* argued that our accusatorial system should be replaced, up to the time of trial, with an inquisitorial system to ensure that the investigation of crime by the police was properly supervised by the judge thereby seeking the truth rather than merely securing a conviction. The trial itself should retain the accusatorial approach so that the burden of proving guilt would rest with the prosecution and the judge would not take an active role in the trial process. Above all, the fundamental principles of the presumption of innocence and the right to silence should operate to ensure a fair trial. He suggested that we should return to first principles to ensure fair trials and the attainment of justice. Failings will always occur but these should be rectified by an independent review body. In the result the right to silence is under threat from the provisions of the Criminal Justice Bill presently before Parliament and it will be some considerable time before an independent review body is established.

As we have seen, the principle at the heart of the criminal justice system must be the acquittal of the innocent and conviction of the guilty if justice is to be attained.

Law and Justice

Justice is an ideal towards which the law should aim. It is epitomised by the evenly balanced scales held by the statue of Justice on the Old Bailey.

There are four components:

- the pre-trial process;

- the trial process;

- the adequacy of mechanisms for discovering and rectifying miscarriages of justice;

- the fairness of the substantive legal rules and the penalties or remedies imposed for breach.

The two main theories of justice distinguish formal or procedural justice and substantial justice.

Formal justice is otherwise known as 'procedural' justice and requires rules, principles and machinery for the due application of law to all persons without fear or favour within the system. The two components are equality and generality.

The doctrine of the rule of law as illustrated in *M v Home Office and Another* (1993) ensures that no one is above the law (including the government).

The doctrine of natural justice ensures fairness in the judicial process. Other decisions may also be covered:

Re HK (an Infant) (1967)

Bushell v Secretary of State for the Environment (1980)

Council of Civil Service Unions v Minister for the Civil Service (1985)

There are two limbs to the doctrine – *nemo judex in res sua* (no man should be a judge in his own cause) and *audi alteram partem* (both sides have a right to be heard).

R v Bingham Justices ex p Jowitt (1974)

A-G of Hong Kong v Ng Tuen Shiu (1983)

R v Secretary of State for the Home Department ex p Khan (1985)

R v Secretary of State for the Home Department ex p Ruddock (1987)

O'Reilly v Mackman (1982)

R v the Lord Chancellor ex p the Law Society (1993)

Substantial justice	This measures the content of a rule against a 'higher' or more fundamental set of principles such as fairness, justice or morality. The distinction between remedial justice and distributive (or social) justice is mentioned and the case of *R v Secretary of State for the Home Department ex p Doody* (1993) is noted.
Certainty and equality	Certainty has to be balanced with flexibility to allow people to order their affairs and have respect for the law and for the law to change to meet changing needs. As a general rule, law should have prospective (not retrospective) effect.
	Equality ensures that everyone is equal before the law and all persons are subject to law regardless of race, colour, creed or rank. Equality should not mean that all people are to be treated alike regardless of differences in character, upbringing, education and so on.
	John Rawls in *A Theory of Justice* constructed a social contract with the aim of establishing social justice. Liberty and equality are the two principles of justice and the People in the Original Position (POP) would select the former over the latter.
Miscarriages of justice	In criminal law this may arise from wrongful acquittal, conviction or where an offender is not brought to trial. Miscarriages may also arise in civil law. Notable miscarriages of justice including the 'Guildford Four', the 'Maguire Seven' and the 'Birmingham Six' led to the Runciman Royal Commission Report on Criminal justice in 1993. Trials are invariably conducted fairly but miscarriages have resulted from fabricated evidence.

PART THREE

ASPECTS OF EUROPEAN LAW

Chapter 13

The European Community

By 1945, Western Europe was devastated as a result of the Second World War. The Nazi threat was replaced by Stalin's Soviet expansionism. As a response to the latter, the US did not withdraw from Europe but in 1947 set in motion the Marshall Plan. This involved massive US economic assistance for the rebuilding of Europe.

In 1949 military and political institutions were set up as a response to the Soviet threat.

The North Atlantic Treaty Organisation (NATO) consisting of the USA, Canada and most of the Western European States was set up to provide military co-operation. An attack on one Member State was to be regarded as an attack on all members of the alliance. Parallel to this, the Council of Europe was set up. This consisted of the majority of the Western European non-communist States and was widely regarded as an embryo US of Europe. Although it did achieve a degree of political co-operation, this never went as far as political integration. (The experience of the European Community would seem to show that economic integration is necessary for political integration to follow.)

The great achievement of the Council of Europe has been the European Convention on Human Rights and Fundamental Freedoms which came into effect on 3 September 1953. This convention, administered by the Commission and Court of Human Rights at Strasbourg, is binding on all Council of Europe members and has gone some way to eradicate deficiencies in the legal systems of Member States.

Today, many of the ex-communist States have joined the Council of Europe which is seen as a useful bridge to the European Community, whose members all belong to the Council.

Meanwhile, a series of steps in the economic field has taken place which has had much greater significance for political integration. The authors of these developments always had in mind the creation of a federal European State as a means of eradicating conflict in Europe, especially between France and Germany. Economic integration was seen as the means of achieving political integration – the latter was always implicit in treaties of an economic nature.

13.1 Background

In 1948 the Benelux Union had removed customs barriers between the Benelux States of Belgium, the Netherlands and Luxembourg. In 1950 the Schuman Plan planned the integration of the coal and steel industries of France and Germany and other participants. Coal and steel were seen as the engines of war. The removal of national control in this area was regarded as fundamental in reducing the possibility of armed conflict between States.

As a result of this plan the Treaty of Paris 1951 established the European Coal and Steel Community (ECSC) consisting of Belgium, the Netherlands, Luxembourg, France, Germany (then West Germany) and Italy. The production of coal and steel in these Member States was placed under the control of supra-national institutions ie High Authority (equivalent to the European Community Commission), Council of Ministers and Court of Justice. In 1957 the same Member States set up the European Atomic Energy Community by what is usually referred to as the EURATOM treaty. The aim of this treaty was similar to that of the ECSC Treaty – the integration of the production of atomic energy within Member States and its control by supra-national institutions, in this case a Commission, Council of Ministers, Assembly and Court of Justice.

However, the other 1957 treaty between the same six States was to be much more significant. This was the Treaty of Rome setting up the European Economic Community (EEC). The aims of this treaty were far more ambitious. Article 2 says:

'The Community shall have as its task, by establishing a common market and progressively approximating the economic policies of Member States, to promote throughout the Community a harmonious development of economic activities, a continuous and balanced expansion, an increase in stability, an accelerated raising of the standard of living and closer relations between the states belonging to it'. Again, this economic integration was placed under the supra-national control of a Commission, Council of Ministers, Assembly and Court of Justice. The Merger Treaty of 1965 merged the institutions of the three communities (ECSC, Euratom and EEC) so that they were all under the supra-national control of one Commission, one Council of Ministers, one Assembly and one Court of Justice.

Although the UK had the opportunity of joining the EEC (now usually referred to simply as the European Community or EC) at its inception, it was originally hostile to membership.

Factors involved in this were the supra-national character of the supervisory institutions of the EC, the fact that the UK had a 'special relationship' with the USA, and also the fact that the UK had important preferential trading links with Commonwealth and Empire countries. The UK as a trading nation had traditionally taken a global, rather than a regional, view of inter-State commerce. However, the gradual loss of world power status precipitated by the Suez crisis of 1956 and the shrinking of the Empire helped to force a change of attitude.

An initial response was the UK's involvement in the setting up of the European Free Trade Association (EFTA) in 1959. This originally comprised Austria, Denmark, Norway, Portugal, Sweden, Switzerland and the UK. Simply a free trade area, EFTA lacked the supra-national institutional character of the EC.

The success of the EC during a period of high economic growth finally led the British Government to apply for membership in 1961 under the leadership of Prime Minister Harold Macmillan.

This attempt failed as did the application in 1967 by Harold Wilson's government. In both cases the French government objected on the grounds of the UK's continuing strong links with the USA. However, the application by Edward Heath's government in 1970 finally succeeded and the UK, Denmark and Ireland all joined the EC on 1 January 1973. This was accomplished by the 1972 Treaty of Accession by which the three new Member States acceded to, or agreed to, the obligations in the original 1957 Treaty of Rome (EEC Treaty).

Some dissatisfaction in the UK with the terms of membership was resolved in the 1975 referendum which confirmed the UK's continuing participation in the EC.

The EC acquired a more southern dimension in the acquisition of Greece as a member on 1 January 1981 by the 1979 Treaty of Accession and also by the acquisition of Spain and Portugal on 1 January 1986 by the 1985 Treaty of Accession. In the short-term the EC was enlarged by the admission of Austria, Sweden and Finland. These States joined the Community on 1 January 1995, having signed the Treaty of Accession in June 1994. Other States which wish to join the Community, such as Turkey, Poland, Hungary and the Czech Republic, are likely to be members in the longer-term (ie when their social and economic conditions are more approximate to those of existing Member States).

It was always envisaged that the objectives of the 1957 EEC Treaty would have to be gradually implemented as they involved a radical change of States' practices. However, the 1973 oil crisis precipitated by the Yom Kippur war between Israel and Egypt meant that important and necessary changes were put off.

A better economic climate in the 1980's and the feeling that the EC would either have to implement its original objectives or stagnate led to the EC Commission's White Paper of 1985. This laid out those Treaty objectives which had so far not been achieved and also detailed the means for their achievement by 31 December 1992. This report led to the first major amendment of the 1957 Treaty and is known as the Single European Act 1986 (SEA) which came into effect on 1 January 1987 and which, *inter alia*, at last introduced a free internal market in goods and services. Having set the Community back onto its original course, the momentum for further change became irresistible. The result has been the 1992 Maastricht Treaty on European Union which, *inter alia*, has important provisions on economic and monetary union.

3.2 The nature of Community law	

Article 2 of the EEC Treaty states that the objectives in setting up a common market consist of:

- a harmonious development of economic activities;

- a continuous and balanced expansion;

- an increase in stability;

- an accelerated raising of the standard of living; and

- closer relations between the States belonging to it.

In order to achieve these objectives, the Treaty contains principles which collectively are known as the *four freedoms*:

- free movement of goods;

- free movement of people;

- free movement of services; and

- free movement of capital between Member States.

The Treaty has provisions backing up these freedoms, for example, aimed at the elimination of customs duties and aimed at State monopolies and subsidies and also ensuring that competition in the common market is not distorted.

The major exception to this concept of a European level playing field of competition has been the Common Agricultural Policy (CAP). Originally designed so that Europe should have a stock of food in times of emergency, a proportion of the EC's budget is paid as a subsidy to European farmers in order to produce food even though there might not be a market for this food.

The EEC Treaty follows the continental approach to law-making of laying down general objectives and setting up supra-national institutions to make the detailed laws which fulfil those general objectives. In this context, the obligations laid down on Member States by the following Articles of the Treaty are important. Article 5 says:

> 'Member States shall take all appropriate measures ... to ensure fulfilment of the obligations arising out of this Treaty or resulting from action taken by the institutions of the Community. They shall facilitate the achievement of the Community's tasks.'

Similarly, Article 6(1) says:

> 'Member States shall, in close co-operation with the institutions of the Community, co-ordinate their respective economic policies to the extent necessary to attain the objectives of this Treaty.'

Again, the approximation or harmonisation of Member States' law is dealt with by Article 100 and Article 100a where the Council is given the power to issue Directives for the harmonisation of laws in Member States which directly affect the functioning of the common market (Article 100) and the internal market (Article 100a), (added by SEA).

The EEC Treaty provisions (as amended) are usually referred to as the 'primary sources of Community law'. The detailed laws made by the supra-national institutions to fulfil treaty objectives are known as the 'secondary sources of Community law', Article 189 of the EEC Treaty explains the nature of these secondary rules. It states:

> 'In order to carry out their task the Council and the Commission shall, in accordance with the provisions of this Treaty, make regulations, issue directives, take decisions, make recommendations or deliver opinions. A regulation shall have general application. It shall be binding in its entirety and directly applicable in all Member States. A directive shall be binding as to the result to be achieved, upon each Member State to which it is addressed, but shall leave to the national authorities the choice of form and methods. A decision shall be binding in its entirety upon those to whom it is addressed. Recommendations and opinions shall have no binding force.'

Of the rules outlined in Article 189, only Regulations and Directives are strictly laws.

* As regards Regulations, they are said to have 'general application'. This means that they are issued at all members of the Community. They enforce a policy common to all states eg agriculture. Thus, a restriction on milk quotas throughout the Community would be dealt with by means of a regulation. They are also said to be

'directly applicable'. From a legal point of view this is very important since it means that regulations have legal force in all Member States as soon as they are made – no enactment measures are required by the individual States.

- Directives are far more numerous. They are the means by which Member States' laws are harmonised for the proper functioning of the Community.

A benchmark Community standard is agreed on. Directives are then issued to any number of States from one to 15 which are required to raise their legal standards to that benchmark standard. Thus, on several occasions, directives have been issued solely to the UK where it has been out of step with its Community partners.

On the other hand, directives that regulate the internal market are generally issued to all 15 Member States. Also, States are allowed a certain amount of time in which to give legal force to directives. In some cases, this can be up to five years. They are not, therefore, directly applicable. Member States can also choose the method of incorporation of a directive into national law according to their constitutions.

- Decisions are binding on States, companies and individuals. Arguably, they are more administrative in character but they do have legal consequences. For example, if a company asked for an exemption from competition policy and it received an adverse decision, then acting contrary to that decision would result in legal action against the company.

- Recommendations and opinions are often given and sought. Although not legally binding, they do have persuasive authority if they are relied on in a legal action.

It should be noted that Article 189 uses the phrase 'in accordance with the provisions of this Treaty'. Therefore, the secondary rules are not unlimited in their law-making scope. However, Article 8(a) (added by SEA) introduced the internal market which 'shall comprise an area without internal frontiers in which the free movement of goods, persons, services and capital is ensured in accordance with the provisions of this Treaty'. As a result of this provision and other SEA amendments, there has been a great increase in Community legislative activity in areas other than those relating purely to the original Treaty-based policies. For example, increased protection for employees under Health and Safety Directives has recently been introduced. The EC Commission's view has been that the increased rigours of competition should be offset by increased social protection for employees. This has not always been the view of the British Government.

Article 4 of the EEC Treaty names four institutions which deal with the operation of Community affairs. These are the Council of Ministers, the Commission, the European Parliament (formerly Assembly) and the European Court of Justice. Article 4 says, 'Each institution shall act within the limits of the powers conferred upon it by this Treaty.'

13.3 Community institutions

The composition and powers of the Council can be found in Article 145 to 154 of the EEC Treaty (as subsequently amended).

13.3.1 The Council of Ministers

The Council is composed of representatives of each of the Member States, normally members of the government of each Member State. General Council meetings are attended by the ministers of foreign affairs whilst Specialist Council meetings are attended by ministers responsible for the appropriate area, eg ministers of agriculture, financial affairs, etc.

13.3.2 Composition

The ministers, as delegates of their governments, act on the basis of instructions received from their governments. Thus, although the ministers try to further the interest of the Community, they also try and make sure that the national interests that they represent are not unduly jeopardised by achieving Community objectives. The Presidency of the Council passes to each Member State in turn for a period of six months.

- Legislative

  Under the EEC Treaty it is the Council whose task it is to 'ensure that the objectives in this treaty are attained' (Article 145). In this context, it is the major law-making institution of the Community (not the Parliament), utilising the power conferred by Article 189 of the EEC Treaty. However, this power is balanced by the fact that in most cases the Council can only act on the basis of a proposal from the Commission and under the judicial control of the Court of Justice. Council legislation is, therefore, undertaken on the basis of a draft placed before it by the Commission. If the Council wishes to amend the draft proposal it may only do so by acting unanimously.

13.3.3 Functions and powers

- Procedural

  The meetings of the Council are in private, although attended by the president of the Commission and those members of the Commission who are responsible for the item under discussion. The President conducts the proceedings, putting issues to the vote and signing the agreed measures.

  Article 148 of the EEC Treaty says, 'Save as otherwise provided in this Treaty, the Council shall act by a majority of its members.' However, since the passing of the Single European Act there has been an extension of the system of qualified majority voting. Most of the Council's legislative powers have now to be exercised by this method, for which a weighted voting system is used.

Under this system each Member State is given a number of votes according to size. A total of 65 votes is required for the Council to adopt a measure. The system means that the large States cannot, between them, force through a measure – they need the co-operation of some of the smaller States.

Member States	Votes
France	10
Germany	10
Italy	10
UK	10
Spain	8
Belgium	5
Greece	5
Netherlands	5
Portugal	5
Denmark	3
Ireland	3
Luxembourg	2
Sweden	4
Austria	4
Finland	3

Thus, at present, 25 votes are sufficient to block a measure.

- Economic

Under Article 145 of the EEC Treaty, the Council must 'ensure co-ordination of the general economic policies of the Member States.' The same Article requires that it delegates to the Commission the power of implementation of the decisions taken by the Council.

- Additional

The Committee of Permanent Representatives of Member States (COREPER) was set up by the Merger Treaty. It consists of representatives of Member States with ambassadorial rank. Its main task is to achieve continuity of the Council's work.

As a permanent body it monitors Community activities on a day-to-day basis, whilst the Council only meets for a few days at a time. Whilst the Council is not bound to accept COREPER's recommendations, in general once this body has reached agreement the Council tends to accept them and transform them into legally binding acts.

The European Council was set up by the Single European Act. The practice had evolved of regular summit meetings being held between Heads of State and Government. These tended to deal with broad political questions, eg the EC's policy on the Palestinian question. As this type of activity was not contemplated by the EEC Treaty, the SEA merely institutionalised and recognised this practice by establishing such meetings as those of the European Council – quite a distinct body from the Council of Ministers.

The composition and powers of the Commission can be found in Articles 155-163 of the EEC Treaty (as subsequently amended).

13.3.4 The Commission

- The Commissioners

  In the present Community of 15 there are 20 Commissioners: two from the UK, France, Germany, Italy and Spain and one from Belgium, Denmark, Greece, Ireland, Luxembourg, The Netherlands, Portugal, Sweden, Austria and Finland.

  13.3.5 Composition and organisation

  They are appointed by their national governments for renewable periods of four years. However, they are obliged to act in the interests of the Community and not in the interests of their own States. The Commission also has a President and six Vice-Presidents who hold office for renewable periods of two years. Commissioners may resign or be compulsorily retired if they fail to fulfil the conditions required for the performance of their duties or are guilty of serious misconduct.

- Organisation of the Commission

  Unlike the Council, which meets at various locations, the Commission is permanently located in Brussels. It is a collegiate body, acting collectively by a majority vote at regular weekly meetings. Its rules of procedure lay down that the quorum consists of nine members and that at least nine votes in support of a measure will produce a conclusion to the matter.

  Each Commissioner is allocated special areas of policy. He is assisted by a cabinet (department staff), generally of the same nationality as the Commissioner. This is headed by a chef de cabinet who can attend Commission meetings in place of the Commissioner.

In addition, there are 22 Directorates-General (D-G) to assist the Commissioners. Each D-G is headed by a Director-General who is responsible to the Commissioner whose area of policy includes that D-G. Thus, there is a permanent EC civil service at Brussels consisting of over 14,000 members.

3.3.6   Functions and powers

- Legislative

  Under Article 189 of the EEC Treaty, the Commission can make regulations, issue directives and take decisions.

  However, this has to be in accordance with the provisions of this Treaty. Most of the Commission's legislative activity takes place within the sphere of Community competition and anti-dumping policy.

- Executive

  The Commission is often referred to as the 'Guardian of the Treaties'. Under Article 155 of the EEC Treaty, it is stated:

  'In order to ensure the proper functioning and development of the common market, the Commission shall:- ensure that the provisions of this Treaty and the measures taken by the institutions pursuant thereto are applied.'

  Thus, the Commission has the power to initiate inquiries into alleged infringements of EC law by Member States, corporations or individuals and to take appropriate measures, eg under Article 169 of the EEC Treaty, the Commission can bring an action against a Member State before the Court of Justice because of non-compliance with a Treaty obligation.

  Also, under Articles 145 and 155 of the EEC Treaty, powers are conferred by the Council on the Commission to ensure the enforcement of general rules which the Council lays down. This delegated executive function has been utilised a great deal by the Commission in the implementation of the common agricultural policy.

- Policy Initiator

  Article 155 of the EEC Treaty states that the Commission shall 'formulate recommendations or deliver opinions on matters dealt with in this Treaty'. Neither recommendations or opinions are legally binding in EC law. However, as they are made to ensure the proper functioning and development of the common market, they are highly persuasive in character and in practice are not disregarded.

  Article 155 of the EEC Treaty also states that the Commission shall:

'... have its own power of decision and participate in shaping of measures taken by the Council and by the European Parliament in the manner provided for in this Treaty'.

This is one of the most significant roles of the Commission because in most instances the Council may only pass Community legislation when it is based on a proposal from the Commission. The Commission formulates its proposals for submission to the Council only after lengthy deliberation involving consultation with interested parties and representatives from the Member States.

The composition and powers of the European Parliament can be found in Articles 137-144 of the EEC Treaty (as subsequently amended).

13.3.7	The European Parliament

Article 137 of the EEC Treaty states:

13.3.8	Background

'The European Parliament, which shall consist of representatives of the peoples of the States brought together in the Community, shall exercise the advisory and supervisory powers which are conferred upon it by this Treaty.'

The establishment of this body, originally referred to as the 'Assembly', reflected the desire of many in the Community to develop towards closer political union. It was also seen as a means of exercising some degree of democratic control over the Commission and the Council. For example, Article 144 of the EEC Treaty gave the Assembly the power to force the Commission to resign by a motion of censure if carried by a two-thirds majority of the votes cast.

However, the Assembly lacked authority because it was comprised of nominees of the Member States (originally 142 members, 198 following the accession of the UK, Ireland and Denmark). Also, at most, the Council of Ministers only had to consult the Assembly when making laws. Its limited role in the legislative process has always been at the heart of the debate concerning how to make the European Institutions more susceptible to democratic control.

A series of steps increased the status and power of the Assembly. First of all, on 30 March 1962 the European Assembly decided to describe itself as the European Parliament. In 1975 new budgetary powers were acquired for the Parliament. In 1976 the Council approved direct elections to the Parliament which took place between 7-10 June 1979. The first meeting of this directly elected Parliament of 410 members took place on 17 July 1979. The number increased to 518 following the accession of Greece, Spain and Portugal. The second direct elections took place between 14-17 June 1984, and the third between 15-18 June 1989. The fourth direct elections took place between 9-12 June 1994. Of equal significance, the entry into force of the Single European Act in 1987 allocated increased legislative powers to the Parliament. It also gave Treaty status to the title 'European Parliament'.

13.3.9   Composition

There are currently 626 members (MEPs) who are directly elected for a term of five years. All Member States, apart from the UK, use various systems of proportional representation to elect their members. Proportional representation is also used in Northern Ireland. The remainder of the UK uses the traditional 'first past the post' system of voting. Members sit in multinational political groupings.

The Parliament holds its plenary sessions in Strasbourg but has offices and staff in both Brussels and Luxembourg. From 1994 there was an increase from 518 to 567 MEPs, reflecting demographic changes within the Community, principally the re-unification of Germany. The number increased to 626 MEPs as from 1 January 1995.

Member States' members:

	Previously	From the 1994 Elections	From 1 January 1995
UK	81	87	
Germany	81	99	
Italy	81	87	
France	81	87	
Spain	60	64	
Netherlands	25	31	
Belgium	24	25	
Greece	24	25	
Portugal	24	25	
Denmark	16	16	
Ireland	15	15	
Luxembourg	6	6	
Sweden			22
Austria			21
Finland			16

The Parliament's advisory and supervisory functions take effect in the following areas:

- Budgetary control

  The Parliament participates with the Council of Ministers in preparing and adopting the Community budget. In this respect, it can approve the draft budget within 45 days, adopt amendments or modifications or reject the budget. However, in the last resort the Parliament only has real control over 'non obligatory' expenditure eg allocation of regional funds. It can certainly influence 'obligatory' expenditure (the agriculture budget) but ultimately has to give effect to what is a legal obligation under the Common Agricultural Policy.

- Political control

  The Parliament monitors the work of the Commission and the Council and, as we have seen, can adopt a motion of censure if it disapproves of the Commission's activities. As the only democratically elected body in the Community, the Parliament's resolutions in this field (passed by absolute majority) have great persuasive authority. In effect, the Parliament operates vis-à-vis the Commission and the Council as a giant pressure group on behalf of the European electorate.

- Legislative powers

  The Parliament's role in the legislative process was largely consultative. Commission proposals were sent by the Council to the Parliament for its opinion. Although persuasive, the Parliament's role was very limited. The extension of the Parliament's powers in the legislative process at the expense of the Council of Ministers has been argued for by those who wish to see a transfer of power from national governments to elected representatives of the peoples of Europe.

  The Single European Act introduced an important extension to the Parliament's legislative powers – the Co-operation Procedure involving the Commission, Council and the Parliament. Whilst allowing the Parliament to exercise greater influence over the legislative process, this influence, however, was limited.

  The co-operation procedure only extended to Community legislation regulating the following areas: the elimination of discrimination on the grounds of nationality, the freedom of movement for workers, the right of establishment (the right to set up a business), the freedom to provide services, and harmonisation measures relating to the establishment and functioning of the internal market.

- The co-operation procedure

The process still depends on the Commission formulating a proposal which is submitted to the Council which in turn obtains the opinion of the Parliament. The Council of Ministers is then required to reach a 'common position' a consensus on the basic elements by qualified majority voting. The Parliament is then informed of the 'common position' and within three months may approve the Council decision, amend it or reject it. If the Parliament has rejected the proposal, the Council has to agree unanimously on the 'common position' in order to proceed to a second reading. The Commission, within a period of one month, re-examines the proposal in the light of amendments suggested by the Parliament and sends back the re-examined proposal to the Council. Within three months the Council can either adopt the re-examined Commission proposal by qualified majority or adopt Parliament's amendments not approved by the Commission by unanimous voting or otherwise amend the Commission proposal, again by unanimous voting.

The legislative process within the European Community

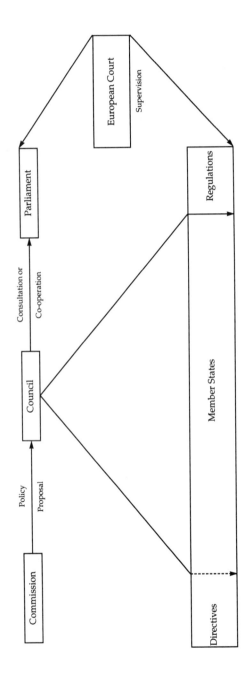

Commission → Policy Proposal → Council → Consultation or Co-operation → Parliament

European Court — Supervision

Member States

Regulations

Directives

Article 164 of the EEC Treaty says 'The Court of Justice shall ensure that in the interpretation and application of this Treaty the law is observed'. The Court sits in Luxembourg.

13.3.11   The European Court of Justice

Articles 165-168 of the EEC Treaty (as amended) deal with the composition of the Court.

13.3.12   Composition and organisation

- Judges

  The Court is composed of 16 judges unanimously elected by the governments of the Member States. Article 167 of the EEC Treaty provides that they 'shall be chosen from persons whose independence is beyond doubt and who possess the qualifications required for appointment to the highest judicial offices in their respective countries or are jurisconsults of recognised competence'. The Court, therefore, consists of a mixture of practising and academic lawyers. The judges are appointed for renewable periods of six years. Each Member State has a judge of its nationality sitting on the Court with the thirteenth held in rotation.

- Presidents

  The President of the Court holds office for a three-year renewable term. He is appointed by the judges from among their own number in a secret ballot by an absolute majority. There are also four Presidents presiding over the Chambers of the Court. If the matter is a staff case or if the nature of the case does not require a plenary session, then a Chamber of three or five judges will be formed to adjudicate the matter. Presidents of Chambers hold office for a one year renewable term and are selected in the same way as the President of the Court.

- Advocates-General

  Article 166 of the EEC Treaty states 'The Court of Justice shall be assisted by six Advocates-General'. Again, Article 167 of the EEC Treaty says that they 'shall be chosen from persons whose independence is beyond doubt and who possess the qualifications required for appointment to the highest judicial offices in their respective countries or who are jurisconsults of recognised competence'. They are appointed for renewable periods of six years. Article 166 of the EEC Treaty states:

  'It shall be the duty of the Advocate-General, acting with complete impartiality and independence, to make, in open court, reasoned submissions on cases brought before the Court of Justice, in order to assist the Court in the performance of the task assigned to it in Article 164'.

There is no precise equivalent in the UK legal system to the office of Advocate-General. It is similar to the Commissaire du Gouvernement at the French Conseil d'Etat. Acting as the independent conscience of Community law the advocate-general will propose a solution to the case which is before the Court in the context of the case law of the Court. The Advocate-General's submissions are not binding on the Court, although in the majority of cases the Court tends to agree with them. The more detailed evaluation of the Advocate-General is also usually published with the briefer Court judgment. By examining the Advocate-General's submissions, one is thereby able to gain a valuable insight into the development of Community law.

- The registrar

  The administration of the Court is under the control of the Registrar and his staff. The Registrar holds office for a renewable period of six years having been elected by the judges by majority vote after consultation with the Advocates-General.

- A plenary session of the Court consists of a quorum of seven judges. If a case is brought by a Member State or a Community institution then the Court must sit in a plenary session. The same applies to preliminary rulings where the chambers do not have the required jurisdiction.

- The Court has drawn up a set of Rules of Procedure which determine the practice and procedure of the Court.

- Stages in Court Proceedings

  There are three stages: a written stage, a preparatory enquiry stage and an oral stage.

  The *written stage* consists of the pleadings of the plaintiff, ie the legal nature of the claim against the defendant. The defendant will receive notification of the application and has one month in which to submit a statement of defence to the Court. The plaintiff may submit a written reply to the defence and the defendant may then make a final rejoinder. Once the written stage commences, the President of the Court appoints one of the judges as juge-rapporteur in order to prepare a report of the facts of the case and the legal arguments which will be submitted for consideration by the Court. At the end of the written stage the juge-rapporteur examines the pleadings and decides whether or not the case requires the preparatory enquiry stage or whether it can proceed directly to the oral stage.

  At the *preparatory enquiry stage*, if the Court agrees that this is necessary, then the parties and witnesses will appear to be

13.3.13   Procedure

examined by the Court or chamber. In other words, the continental inquisitorial approach is adopted here, an attempt to arrive at the truth by the Court, rather than the English accusatorial approach which relies principally on what the parties decide to submit. The Court will inspect documentary evidence and also hear expert testimony.

The juge-rapporteur submits his report to the Court immediately before the commencement of the *oral stage*. Here, the legal representatives of the parties put forward their legal arguments. Counsel can be questioned by the Court or by the Advocate-General. This stage is closed by the Advocate-General putting forward his submissions.

• Judgment

The Court arrives, following continental practice, at a single judgment. Dissenting opinions are not disclosed. The Court normally agrees with the conclusions of the Advocate-General. However, it has the freedom to disagree with them should it so decide.

The Court's judgments have binding force from the date of their delivery. They are published, along with the conclusions of the Advocate-General, in each of the official languages of the Community, ie Danish, Dutch, English, French, German, Greek, Italian, Portuguese and Spanish.

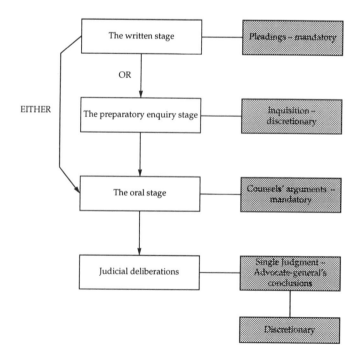

- Enforcement of judgments against:

  Member States – Article 171 of the EEC Treaty merely states: 'If the Court of Justice finds that a Member State has failed to fulfil an obligation under this Treaty, the State shall be required to take the necessary measures to comply with the judgment of the Court of Justice';

  Community institutions – under Article 173 of the EEC Treaty the Court can uphold or render void Community secondary legislation;

  Corporations or individuals – fines can be imposed which are enforceable eg for a breach of Community competition policy.

- Actions against Member States

  Under Article 169 of the EEC Treaty the EC Commission can bring an action against a Member State. Article 169 states:

  'If the Commission considers that a Member State has failed to fulfil an obligation under this Treaty, it shall deliver a reasoned opinion on the matter after giving the State concerned the opportunity to submit its observations. If the State concerned does not comply with the opinion within the period laid down by the Commission, the latter may bring the matter before the Court of Justice.'

  Under Article 170 of the EEC Treaty a Member State can bring an action against another Member State. Article 170 states:

  'A Member State which considers that another Member State has failed to fulfil an obligation under this Treaty may bring the matter before the Court of Justice'.

- Judicial review

  Articles 173 and 175 of the EEC Treaty – the EEC Treaty imposes a framework of legality around the actions of the EC Commission and Council. If these bodies exceed their powers then an action can be brought against them under Article 173. Also, if those bodies fail to act where they have a duty to act then an action can be brought against them under Article 175.

  Article 173(1) states:

  'The Court of Justice shall review the legality of the acts of the Council and the Commission other than recommendations or opinions. It shall for this purpose have jurisdiction in actions brought by a Member State, the Council or the Commission on grounds of lack of competence, infringement of an essential procedural

13.3.14   Jurisdiction

requirement, infringement of this Treaty or of any rule of law relating to its application, or misuse of powers.'

Note – what can be challenged? Regulations, Directives or Decisions. Who can challenge? A Member State, the Council or the Commission, not a corporation or an individual. What are the grounds for challenge? Lack of competence – this means that the body does not have the legal power to make the secondary legislation. It is thus equivalent to the English doctrine of substantive *ultra vires*.

Infringement of an essential procedural requirement means that a legally required procedure has not been complied with in the formulation of the secondary legislation and is equivalent to the English doctrine of procedural *ultra vires*.

Infringement of this Treaty or of any rule relating to its application provides a very broad ground for challenge and encompasses a breach of general principles of law recognised by Member States, eg breach of the rules of natural justice (see above, in General Principles of English Law).

Misuse of powers has no precise English equivalent and this ground for challenge is rarely successful. However, it embraces the concept of abuse of discretionary powers.

What about Individuals and Corporations? Paragraph 2 of Article 173 provides them only with the power to challenge decisions which are addressed to them.

- What about the European Parliament?

  This was not expressly mentioned in para 1 of Article 173 as having the right to challenge. However, in 1990 the European Court of Justice decided that the Parliament should have this right where the action concerned the nature of the powers of the Parliament.

- What is the result of a successful action?

  Article 174 of the EEC Treaty states 'If the action is well founded, the Court of Justice shall declare the act concerned to be void.'

  Article 175(1) states:

  'Should the Council or the Commission, in infringement of this Treaty, fail to act, the Member States and the other institutions of the Community may bring an action before the Court of Justice to have the infringement established.'

Note – less widely used than Article 173, this action is broadly similar to that of mandamus in English law. Unlike Article 173, the Parliament is included because of the use of the term 'other institutions'.

Article 175(2) gives the institution concerned two months to react to a call to act. The action can only take place if nothing happens during this time period.

Unlike Article 173, corporations and individuals are given similar powers of challenge under Article 175(3).

- Community law and national law – Article 177 of the EEC Treaty

This is an extremely important provision. Here the European Court pronounces on the conformity of national law with Community law. Several case examples can be found later in the text, especially in the sections on Supremacy of Community law and The Principle of Direct Effect. It is worth noting, however, at this stage that this is the Treaty provision by which the European Court has effectively developed Community law into a federal system of law for the benefit of all citizens of the Community.

Article 177 states:

'The Court of Justice shall have jurisdiction to give preliminary rulings concerning:

(a) the interpretation of this Treaty;

(b) the validity and interpretation of acts of the institutions of the Community;

(c) the interpretation of the statutes of bodies established by an act of the Council, where those statutes so provide.

Where such a question is raised before any court or tribunal of a Member State, that court or tribunal may, if it considers that a decision on the question is necessary to enable it to give judgment, request the Court of Justice to give a ruling thereon.

Where any such question is raised in a case pending before a court or tribunal of a Member State, against whose decisions there is no judicial remedy under national law, that court or tribunal shall bring the matter before the Court of Justice.'

Preliminary rulings occur where the national court does not feel that it has the expertise to rule on whether its own State's laws comply with Community law. Domestic court proceedings are suspended and the case is sent to Luxembourg to be examined by the European Court. The preliminary ruling of that court will then be sent back to the national court to guide it in its decision.

The European Court will accept requests for preliminary rulings from any courts, however lowly in a State's hierarchy of courts. However, different Member States have different policies as to which courts can submit requests. In the UK, for example, the domestic appeals procedure must normally be exhausted before a request for a preliminary ruling is sent to Luxembourg.

Discretionary and mandatory reference – para 2 of Article 177 deals with the discretion of the Member States' courts to request a preliminary ruling. This is indicated by the use of the word 'may' in para 2 of Article 177. Most requests for preliminary rulings arise under this part of Article 177. By contrast, para 3 of Article 177 deals with the right of a plaintiff, once the domestic appeals system has been exhausted, to have the case referred to Luxembourg, ie mandatory reference. Exhaustion of appeals is indicated by the phrase 'no judicial remedy' and the mandatory nature of the reference is indicated by the word 'shall' in para 3 of Article 177.

Limitations on reference – the extent of mandatory reference was considered by the European Court in the *Cilfit* case. It stated:

'... the third paragraph of Article 177 of the EEC Treaty is to be interpreted as meaning that a court or tribunal against whose decisions there is no judicial remedy under national law is required, where a question of Community law is raised before it, to comply with its obligation to bring the matter before the Court of Justice, unless it has established that the question is irrelevant or that the Community provision in question has already been interpreted by the Court or that the correct application of Community law is so obvious as to have no scope for any reasonable doubt.'

Thus, even where the appeals procedure has been exhausted, a court is entitled to refuse to refer on the ground that the answer is clear. This is an application of the continental legal doctrine of Acte Clair.

Precedent – the European Court answers specific questions concerning the interpretation of Community law that are referred to it by the national court. It is left to the national courts to comply with the ruling in the context of the domestic situation. Thus, although the European Court is not supposed to rule on the compatibility of national law with Community law, the effect of its ruling might well be to achieve that result.

The Court, following continental practice, is not bound by its previous decisions. There is no rigid system of stare decisis. Also, the ruling is addressed to the courts of one particular Member State. However, the Court, in practice, often refers to its previous decisions where a well-developed doctrine like 'direct effect' is under consideration. In general, however, the Court has great flexibility to alter and develop its policies.

- Other areas of jurisdiction

  Compensation for damage – Article 178 of the EEC Treaty provides 'The Court of Justice shall have jurisdiction in disputes relating to the compensation for damage provided for in the second paragraph of Article 215'. This covers the vicarious liability of the Community in tort for the wrongful acts of its servants.

  Staff Disputes – Article 179 of the EEC Treaty provides 'The Court of Justice shall have jurisdiction in any dispute between the Community and its servants within the limits and under the conditions laid down in the Staff Regulations or under the Conditions of Employment'.

  Arbitration Clauses – Article 181 of the EEC Treaty provides 'The Court of Justice shall have jurisdiction to give judgment pursuant to any arbitration clause contained in a contract concluded by or on behalf of the Community, whether that contract be governed by public or private law'.

Article 168a of the EEC Treaty (added by the Single European Act) provided the legal basis for the establishment of a Court of First Instance sitting in Luxembourg. This Court was set up in response to the increasing workload of the European Court of Justice. It became operational in September 1989.

13.3.15   The Court of First Instance

- Judges

  The Court has 15 judges. Article 168(a)(3) of the EEC Treaty provides:

  'The members of that court shall be chosen from persons whose independence is beyond doubt and who possess the ability required for appointment to judicial office, they shall be appointed by common accord of the governments of the Member States for a term of six years. The membership shall be partially renewed every three years. Retiring members shall be eligible for re-appointment.'

  The judges elect a President from their number for a renewable period of three years. The function of Advocate-General is performed by members of the court.

13.3.16   Composition and organisation

- Procedure

  Article 168(a)(4) of the EEC Treaty enabled the Court to establish its own rules of procedure. Also, the Court may appoint its own registrar. Although the Court can sit in plenary session, should the case merit this, in general, the Court sits in chambers of three or five judges.

- Jurisdiction

  Judicial review actions under Article 173 now go to this Court as do Article 175 actions involving a failure to implement competition law. Actions for compensation for damage under Article 178 also lie within the jurisdiction of the Court of First Instance, as do actions involving staff disputes under Article 179.

  Article 168(a)(1) of the EEC Treaty provides that there is a right of appeal to the European Court of Justice 'on points of law only'. Article 168(a)(1), referring to the Court of First Instance, also states:

  'That court shall not be competent to hear and determine ... questions referred for a preliminary ruling under Article 177.'

  Thus, questions involving the conformity of national law with Community law are reserved for the European Court of Justice.

The European Community

The post-Second World War historical background to the setting up of European Institutions. A comparison between the objectives in setting up the Council of Europe, EFTA and the ECSC, Euratom and EEC. The enlargement of the Community by Treaties of Accession. Amendments to the EEC Treaty by the Single European Act and the Maastricht Treaty on European Union.

Background

The objectives in setting up a common market as laid down in Article 2 of the EEC Treaty. The principles of free movement to achieve those objectives. The obligations laid down in Articles 5 and 6 of the EEC Treaty. Harmonisation of Member States' laws under Article 100 and Article 189 – the differences between 'directly applicable' regulations and directives. The nature of decisions, recommendations and opinions.

The nature of Community law

- The Council of Ministers

  The composition of the Council, Member States' representatives acting as delegates of their governments. The legislative powers of the Council under Article 189 in relation to Article 145. The extension of qualified majority voting by the Single European Act and the nature of the weighted voting system. The economic functions under Article 145 and the work of COREPER. The different functions of the European Council.

Community institutions

- The Commission

  Composition of the Commission: 20 Commissioners, a President and 6 vice-presidents. The bureaucratic organisation of the Commission. The legislative powers of the Commission under Article 189. The executive functions under Article 155 and the power to take actions against Member States under Article 169. The role of the Commission as a policy initiator under Article 155.

- The European Parliament

  Powers given by Article 137 and 144 of the EEC Treaty. Direct elections. Composition – increase in numbers from 1994 elections. Control over non-obligatory expenditure. The motion of censure as a form of political control. The Single European Act and the Co-operation Procedure – legislation covered and the steps involved.

- The European Court of Justice

  Function of the Court: Article 164

  Nature of judges: Article 167

  The President of the Court and Presidents of Chambers of the Court. Role of Advocates-General: Article 166

  Nature of Advocates-General: Article 167

  Function of Registrar. The written, preparatory enquiry and oral stages of procedure. The nature and enforcement of judgments. Jurisdiction in actions against Member States: Articles 169 and 170 of the EEC Treaty

  The different objectives of judicial review under Articles 173 and 175 of the EEC Treaty.

  Article 177 – the difference between discretionary and mandatory reference. Limitations on reference and attitude towards precedent.

  Cilfit Case

- The Court of First Instance

  Article 168(a) as the basis for the Court. The nature of the judges: Article 168(a)(3). Rules of procedure and Article 168(a)(4). Jurisdiction of the Court and appeal from it under Article 168(a)(1).

Chapter 14

The UK and the European Community

The UK's acceptance of Treaty obligations required an unconditional incorporation of not only the primary but also of the secondary rules of Community law into UK law.

14.1 Incorporation of Community law

Article 5 of the EEC Treaty reminds the Member States that they must:

'... take all appropriate measures, whether general or particular, to ensure fulfilment of the obligations arising out of this Treaty or resulting from action taken by the institutions of the Community. They shall facilitate the achievement of the Community's tasks. They shall abstain from any measure which could jeopardise the attainment of the objectives of this Treaty.' (Article 6(1) of the EEC Treaty.)

Also, the Member States must 'in close co-operation with the institutions of the Community, co-ordinate their respective economic policies to the extent necessary to attain the objectives of this Treaty'.

Since Community policies are enforced through the processes of law, the Member States must modify their laws in order to remove the legal constraints to the effective operation of the Community.

Thus, the accumulated volume of Community law was necessarily incorporated into UK law at the time of the accession of the UK to the EEC. It was not legally possible for the UK, or any other new Member State, to be a party to the EEC Treaty purely in international law. The accumulated provisions of the Treaty required that the UK incorporate Community law into its domestic legal system.

The duty to incorporate Community law was met with the passing of the European Communities Act 1972 which came into effect on 1 January 1973. (The word 'Communities' was used because by the Treaty of Accession, the UK acceded to the three European Communities: the EEC, the ECSC and Euratom.)

The UK adopts a dualist approach to treaties, ie the provisions of a treaty do not automatically have the force of law in the UK.

14.1.1 Incorporation of the EEC Treaty into the law of the UK

Statutory incorporation is necessary in order to enable the provisions of a treaty to be enforced in UK Courts.

This principle applies also to the EEC Treaty, that the accession of the UK to that Treaty did not give it the force of law within the UK. Legislation was necessary to achieve that result and the absence of such legislation would mean that the Community Treaty would not fall within the jurisdiction of the Courts of the UK.

Thus, one of the aims of the European Communities Act 1972 was to give the force of law to those provisions of the Treaty which are intended to be incorporated into Member States' legal systems.

Section 2(1) says that all rights, powers, liabilities, obligations and restrictions created by or arising under the Treaties and all such remedies and procedures provided by or under the Treaties are without further enactment to be given legal effect in the UK. They shall be recognised and available in law. The expression 'enforceable Community right' shall be read as referring to one which the subsection applies.

4.1.2   Incorporation of Community secondary legislation into UK law

- Directly applicable regulations

  Under Article 189 of the EEC Treaty, Regulations are binding on the UK as soon as they are made – they are 'directly applicable'. However, statutory incorporation was also required here. The wording of s 2(1) of the European Communities Act 1972 is broad enough to cover Regulations. Section 2(1), therefore, incorporated regulations into domestic UK law, both those made before and after 1 January 1973.

- Directives (not directly applicable)

  Under Article 189 of the EEC Treaty the choice of the means of their implementation is left to the individual Member States. Thus, Directives are incorporated according to the constitutional procedures of each Member State. In the case of the UK, statutes are sometimes used, eg the Sex Discrimination Act 1986 incorporated the Equal Treatment Directive into UK law. However, most Directives are incorporated by means of delegated or subordinate legislation as provided by the European Communities Act.

  Section 2(2) confers extensive authority upon Her Majesty in Council and upon ministers and government departments to make subordinate legislation in order to incorporate Directives into domestic UK law.

- Incorporation of the Single European Act into UK law

  During the early 1980s, the Member States began to realise that the completion of the single market was necessary to enable the Community to compete successfully with the world's other trading blocs. In 1985, the European Commission published its White Paper listing 300 measures which it considered the Council would need to reach agreement on in order to reach this objective.

In 1986, the White Paper was followed by the agreement of the Member States to the Single European Act (SEA) which was one of the most important amendments to the Treaty of Rome since its conclusion in 1957. In order to comply with its obligations under the Single European Act, the UK had to incorporate its provisions into UK domestic law. This it did with the passing of the European Communities (Amendment) Act 1986 which came into effect on 1 January 1987.

The main provisions and objectives of the Single European Act were:

- to establish a new decision making procedure – the 'co-operation procedure' – involving the Council, the European Parliament and the Commission of the European Communities and strengthen the role of the European Parliament in the legislative process of the European Community;

- to give the Council the power to create a Court of First Instance, attached to the European Court of Justice;

- to complete the Internal Market by 31 December 1992;

- for qualified majority voting by the Council to apply in an increased number of areas concerning the Internal Market;

- to extend the European Community's competence to cover co-operation in economic and monetary policy, social policy, economic and social cohesion, research and technological development and the environment;

- to extend European co-operation by EC Member States in the sphere of foreign policy.

Many of the provisions of the SEA are strengthened and developed by the Maastricht Treaty which is being incorporated into UK Law by the European Communities (Amendment) Act 1993.

- The question of supremacy and the 1972 Act

  It has been repeatedly laid down by the European Court of Justice that the Treaties have established a new and distinct system of law, the rules of which are superior to the rules of the domestic laws of Member States. Thus, the 1967 White Paper dealing with the UK's entry into the European Community said that Parliament will have to refrain from passing fresh legislation inconsistent with Community law. This was a recognition of the existing case law of the European Court of Justice.

The orthodox doctrine is that statutes designed to implement treaty provisions are not different from other statutes and may be expressly or impliedly amended or repealed by subsequent inconsistent statutes. If this doctrine were to be applied to Community law, however, the European Court of Justice would not look favourably on any legislation that was contrary to Community law. In fact, the 1972 Act avoids any outright statement of the supremacy of Community law. It was probably thought unnecessary in view of the practice of the European Court of Justice.

However, s 2(4) provides that 'any enactment passed or to be passed, shall be construed and have effect subject to the foregoing provisions of this section'. This means that Parliament should beware of passing legislation that is contrary to Community law. Also, s 3(1) provides that:

'... for the purposes of all legal proceedings any question as to the meaning or effect of any of the Treaties, or as to the validity, meaning or effect of any Community instrument, shall be treated as a question of law (and, if not referred to the European Court, be for determination as such in accordance with the principles laid down by and any relevant decision of the European Court).'

Thus, the Courts of the UK have to defer to the European Court of Justice in matters of Community law, the court which has created the doctrine of Supremacy of Community law. Therefore, the various provisions of the European Communities Act 1972 collectively guarantee the effectiveness of Supremacy of Community law within the UK constitution.

Thus, in *Esso Petroleum Co Ltd v Kingswood Motors Ltd* (1974) Bridge J observed that where Community law is in conflict with our domestic law the effect of the ECA 1972 is to require that Community law shall prevail.

Also, in *Aero Zipp Fasteners v YKK Fasteners* (1973) Graham J said that the ECA 1972 enacted that relevant Common Market law should be applied in this country and should, where there is a conflict, override English law.

- Attitude of the European Court of Justice

  The Court of Justice has repeatedly ruled that it considers the relationship between national law and Community law to be a significant one. Community law must be of direct use to Community citizens within their national legal systems and in the case of a conflict arising then

Community law must take priority over national law irrespective of the date when the latter legislation was adopted.

This doctrine of supremacy of Community law was elaborated gradually by the European Court in the course of its interpretation of the Treaties.

The stage was set in the *Van Gend en Loos* case (1963). The case arose out of the imposition by the Netherlands Government of new import duties, which, it was argued, were in contravention of Article 12 of the EEC Treaty.

Article 12 says that:

'Member States shall refrain from introducing between themselves any new customs duties on imports or exports or any charges having equivalent effect, and from increasing those which they already apply in their trade with each other.'

The plaintiff was a company affected by an increase from 3% to 8% in import duties on certain plastics despite the provisions of Article 12 of the Treaty. It paid the higher import duties and then brought an action in the Dutch Court for the return of the increased import duties. The Dutch Court referred the case to the European Court for a preliminary ruling under Article 177 of the EEC Treaty. The European Court declared that Community law was applicable not only to the Member States in the form of international law but also to the citizens of the Member States in the form of a federal law.

Thus, the obligation under Article 12 was owed to the Dutch people, companies and anybody else adversely affected by the breach of Article 12. The latter provision prevailed over the contrary Dutch legislation. Therefore, the Dutch government repaid the money wrongfully taken as customs duties.

The case of *Flaminio Costa v Enel* (1964) can be regarded as the cornerstone of the doctrine of supremacy. The European Court went much further. An Italian small claims court asked for a ruling whether or not the Italian law, which nationalised the electricity industry after the entry into force of the EEC Treaty was compatible with Articles 37, 53, 93 and 102 of the Treaty. The plaintiff had argued that Italian shareholders in the private electricity companies had received a lower level of compensation than applied in other EC states.

In its preliminary ruling, the European Court said that unlike ordinary treaties, the EEC Treaty has created its own legal system which, on the entry into force of the treaty, became an integral part of the legal systems of the Member States and which they are bound to apply.

The precedence of Community law is confirmed by Article 189 whereby a regulation 'shall be binding' and 'directly applicable in all Member States'. This provision would be quite meaningless if a State could unilaterally nullify its effects by means of a legislative measure which could prevail over Community law. The European Court went on to say that the transfer by the States from their domestic legal systems to the Community legal system of the rights and obligations arising under the Treaty carries with it a permanent limitation of their sovereign rights, against which a subsequent unilateral act incompatible with the concept of the Community cannot prevail.

In the *Simmenthal* case (1979), an Italian law of 1970 imposed a charge for the inspection of beef and veal imported from France into Italy. The case was concerned whether the 1970 charge was in breach of Article 30 of the EEC Treaty:

'Quantitative restrictions on imports and all measures having equivalent effect shall, without prejudice to the following provisions, be prohibited between Member States.'

An action in Italy against the Exchequer for repayment of veterinary charges succeeded. However, the Italian Government objected and the case was brought before the European Court under Article 177.

The question was, what was the scope of Article 30? Was it so wide that it prohibits veterinary charges at the frontier? In answering 'yes' to this, the European Court said:

(a) The Treaty Provision (Article 30), by the very fact of entry into force, not only repealed any conflicting provisions of existing domestic law but also

(b) Prevents the valid enactment of any new domestic legislation to the extent to which such legislation is incompatible with Community provisions.

Thus, a duty lay on the national courts to refrain from applying subsequent conflicting legislation. A national court which is called upon to apply provisions of Community law is under a duty to give full effect to those provisions.

Further, a national court should not have to await the repeal of inconsistent legislation before giving effect to Community.

Therefore, by the time of the *Simmenthal* decision, the European Court of Justice had moved gradually from saying that Community law prevailed over conflicting national law to a position where it stated that such conflicting law was effectively void and of no legal effect.

At last, in *R v Secretary of State for Transport ex p Factortame Ltd* (1990) the opportunity came to test UK legislation against the *Simmenthal* approach. In this case the plaintiffs were companies which owned and operated fishing vessels. Although the ships were registered as British under the Merchant Shipping Act 1894, and the plaintiff companies were incorporated under UK law, the majority of the shareholders and directors were Spanish. It was felt by the UK government that the use of a British 'flag of convenience' by Spanish ships was a means of access to British fishing quotas. Part II of the Merchant Shipping Act 1988 sought to deal with this situation. Section 14 of the Act provided that a vessel could only be registered in the UK if its owner were a British citizen resident in the UK or a company incorporated in the UK and having its principal place of business in the UK with at least 75% of its shareholders who were British citizens resident in the UK. The plaintiffs' vessels did not qualify for registration under the 1988 Act and, therefore, were deprived of the right to fish.

They challenged the 1988 Act as being contrary to Article 52 of the EEC Treaty on the grounds that the UK statute discriminated against the right of establishment, ie the freedom to set up a business.

The question was referred by the House of Lords to the European Court of Justice under Article 177. In agreeing that the 1988 Act did contravene Article 52 of the EEC Treaty, the European Court said that the statute should be disapplied to the extent that it contravened Community law. The House of Lords subsequently issued injunctions against the UK government to prevent the application of the offending provisions of the 1988 Act against the plaintiff companies.

Factortame is a landmark decision because, historically, the UK courts have not been able to challenge the validity of legislation due to the doctrine of sovereignty of Parliament. Now, when it comes to legislation which is contrary to Community law, it seems that they have little choice but to do so.

The concept of 'direct effect' in Community law is the principle that individuals and companies can bring actions against Member States for violation of Community law, ie it is not simply a system of International law actionable only by Member States.	**14.1.3** **The European Court of Justice and the principle of 'direct effect'**
It will be recalled that the three major sources of Community law consist of Treaty Provisions, Regulations and Directives.	**14.1.4** **Treaty provisions**

As regards Treaty provisions, it was decided very early on in the *Van Gend an Loos case* (1962) that these were capable of being of direct effect. The Treaty provision in question here was Article 12 of the Treaty of Rome by which Member States had undertaken to refrain from introducing between themselves any new customs duties on imports and from increasing those that they already applied in their trade with each other. Van Gend an Loos imported chemical products into the Netherlands. A Dutch law of 1959 increased the import duty on ureaformaldehyde from 3% to 8% despite the obligation under Article 12 of the EEC Treaty. Van Gend brought an action before the Tarifcommissie, Amsterdam, on the basis of objection to paying the extra 5% duty. The Dutch Court referred the matter under Article 177 of the EEC Treaty for a preliminary ruling as to whether, *inter alia*, Article 12 of the EEC Treaty could produce direct effects in the legal relationship between Member States and their subjects.

Answering in the affirmative, the European Court said:

'Independently of the legislation of Member States, Community law therefore not only imposes legislation on individuals but is also intended to confer upon them rights which become part of their legal heritage ... The wording of Article 12 contains a clear and unconditional prohibition which is not a positive but a negative obligation. The very nature of this prohibition makes it ideally adapted to produce direct effects in the legal relationship between Member States and their subjects.'

As a result of the landmark decision in *Van Gend en Loos* we now take it for granted that Treaty provisions are capable of being directly effective in favour of individuals and corporations as against Member States.

14.1.5   Secondary legislation

Article 189 of the EEC Treaty states:

'In order to carry out their task the Council and the Commission shall, in accordance with the provisions of this Treaty, make regulations, issue directives ... A regulation shall have general application. It shall be binding in its entirety and directly applicable in all Member States. A directive shall be binding, as to the result to be achieved, upon each Member State to which it is addressed, but shall leave to the national authorities the choice of form and methods.'

In *Yvonne van Dyn v Home Office* (1974) the European Court of Justice said 'by virtue of the provisions of Article 189 regulations are directly applicable and, consequently, may by their very nature have direct effects'. Member States had readily accepted that regulations could produce direct effect because they were directly applicable and became part of the law of all Member States as soon as they were made. Some Member States, including the UK, resisted the idea that directives could produce direct effect. It was argued that as they were issued to Member States then, therefore, they could not confer rights on individuals until specifically incorporated into national law.

However, in *MH Marshall v Southampton and South-West Hampshire Area Health Authority (Teaching)* (1984) the European Court of Justice stated:

> ' It is necessary to recall that, according to a long line of decisions of the Court ... whenever the provisions of a directive appear, as far as their subject-matter is concerned, to be unconditional and sufficiently precise those provisions may be relied upon by an individual against the State where the State fails to implement the directive in national law by the end of the period prescribed or where it fails to implement the directive correctly.'

In this case Miss Marshall was employed by the health authority as a dietician. The policy of the authority was to retire male employees at 65 and female employees at 60. Compensation was claimed for unlawful sex discrimination, utilising the EEC Equal Treatment Directive 76/207 which had not been fully implemented into UK law. Article 5(1) of Directive 76/207 prohibits any discrimination on grounds of sex with regard to working conditions, including the conditions governing dismissal. The case was referred to the European Court of Justice who considered that the dismissal violated Article 5(1) of Directive 76/207 which was sufficiently precise and unconditional to be relied on before a national court and that Article 5(1) may be relied upon as against a State authority acting in its capacity as employer.

In the *Marshall* case the European Court made it clear that unincorporated directives can only be utilised against the State or a body for which the State is responsible. Thus, such unincorporated directives are said to have vertical direct effect.

The European Court confirmed that such unincorporated directives cannot be utilised against individuals or bodies for which the State is not responsible, ie they cannot have horizontal direct effect.

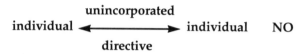

In this situation the specific incorporation of the directive into national law would have to be awaited.

The issue of private organisations which were formerly the concern of the State has also given rise to the argument as to whether they are still the State's responsibility vis-à-vis unincorporated directives (vertical effect). In *Foster and others v British Gas* (1991) the House of Lords applied the ruling of the European Court of Justice. In this case the appellants were women who were employed by the British Gas Corp (BGC). British Gas plc, the respondent, was now responsible for the liabilities of BGC. The latter had a policy of retiring male employees at the age of 65 and female employees at the age of 60. Lord Templeman referred to the European Court's ruling of 1990:

'On the basis of those considerations, the court has held in a series of cases that unconditional and sufficiently precise provisions of a directive could be relied on against organisations or bodies which were subject to the authority or control of the State or had special powers beyond those which result from the normal rules applicable to relations between individuals ... The answer to the question referred by the House of Lords must therefore be that Article 5(1) of Directive 76/207 may be relied on in a claim for damages against a body, whatever its legal form, which has been made responsible, pursuant to a measure adopted by the State, for providing a public service under the control of the State and which has for that purpose special powers beyond those which result from the normal rules applicable in relations between individuals.'

Lord Templeman examined the provisions of the Gas Act 1972 which established BGC as a body corporate. He concluded:

'... it seems to me that the 1972 Act created a body, the BGC, which provided a public service, the supply of gas, to citizens of the State generally under the control of the State, which could dictate its policies and retain its surplus revenue; the BGC was equipped with a special monopoly power which was created and could only have been created by the legislature. The BGC is therefore a body against which the relevant provisions of the equal treatment directive may be enforced.'

However, the principles laid down by the European Court of Justice and as applied by the House of Lords in *Foster v*

British Gas produced a different effect when applied in *Doughty v Rolls-Royce plc* (1992).

Acting under statutory authority, the government formed Rolls-Royce in 1971 as a private limited company in which all the shares were held by nominees of the Crown. Rolls-Royce's shares have always been held on behalf of the Crown. In this case Mrs Doughty claimed that her compulsory retirement at the age of 60 on 28 February 1986 by her former employers Rolls-Royce plc was unlawful sexual discrimination contrary to Article 5(1) of the EEC Directive 76/207 – the 'Equal Treatment Directive'.

In the Court of Appeal, Mustill LJ went on to examine whether the three criteria established in *Foster* were satisfied by the respondent. Regarding the first, he was unable to see how it could be said that the respondent 'was made responsible pursuant to a measure adopted by the State for providing a public service'. His reasoning was that Rolls-Royce was a commercial undertaking which as part of its business traded with the State on terms which were negotiated at arm's length. As to the second criterion, Mustill LJ was prepared to accept that whatever 'service' Rolls-Royce provided was at the material time 'under the control of the State'. However, regarding the third criterion, he could find no evidence that the respondent possessed any 'special powers' of the type enjoyed by the British Gas Corporation. Therefore, as the appellant did not fulfil the requirement of the *Foster* ruling, her appeal was dismissed.

14.1.6   The 'Francovitch' principle

To summarise, therefore, it had been well-established that a clear, precise, unconditional directive which the State had failed to fully implement into its domestic law by the due date could be invoked against a body for which the State was responsible, subject to the *Foster* criteria – the doctrine of vertical effect.

However, soon after the *Doughty* appeal was heard the European Court of Justice gave judgment in *Francovitch v Italian Republic* and *Bonifaci v Italian Republic* (1992). This has opened up the whole concept of direct effect by allowing the possibility of an action in damages by an individual against the State for failure to implement a directive by the due date even though the individual is affected by the actions of a purely private party. This is getting close to a doctrine of horizontal effect.

In these joined cases, the directive under consideration was EEC Directive 80/987 on the protection of employees in the event of the employer's insolvency. In *Commission v Italy* the

European Court held that the Italian Government had failed to implement the directive into its national law by 21 October 1983 as required.

Generally, Directive 80/987 defines the rights of employees to obtain guarantees of payment of their outstanding claims relating to pay in the event of the insolvency of their employer. Mrs Bonifaci and Mr Francovitch were both owed arrears of pay by their former private employers and sought to enforce Directive 80/987 against the Italian State. The Italian courts referred the cases to the European Court of Justice for a preliminary ruling.

The Court held that Directive 80/987 was not capable of producing direct effect against the Italian State. As regards the identity of the institutions liable under the guarantee the provisions of the directive were insufficiently precise and unconditional. Therefore, in the absence of implementing provisions, the directive could not be enforced against the State in proceedings before the national courts. However, the Court then examined the second matter referred to it – is a Member State under an obligation to make good the damage suffered by individuals arising out of the failure to implement Directive 80/987?

In its revolutionary judgment, the European Court replied that, yes, it was for the national court to ensure, within the context of national law on liability, the right of employees to obtain compensation for the damage they have suffered by reason of the State's failure to implement the directive. However, the Court laid down conditions for the operation of State liability in this type of situation where a directive is not implemented into national law as required by Article 189(3) of the EEC Treaty. In order to give rise to liability for damages:

- the result required by the directive includes the conferring of rights for the benefit of individuals;

- the content of these rights may be determined by reference to the provisions of the directive;

- there must exist a causal link between the breach of the obligation of the State and the damage suffered by the person affected.

These conditions were fulfilled in the present cases.

Direct effect after Francovich

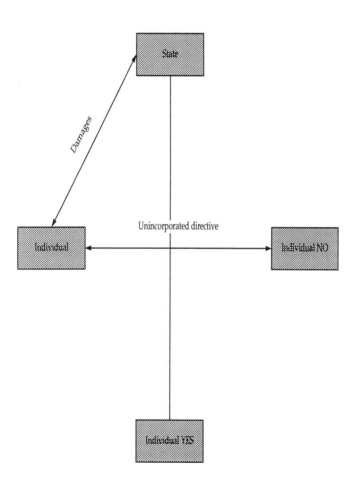

14.1.7	Maastricht: the Treaty on European Union

With the successful passage of the European Communities (Amendment) Act 1993 through Parliament the UK ratified the Maastricht Treaty. The final obstacle to the implementation of the Treaty disappeared with its acceptance by the German Constitutional Court on 12 October 1993, paving the way for German ratification, the final one. Accordingly, the Treaty came into effect on 1 November 1993.

The Treaty is a large, complex instrument which says, in Article A:

'... marks a new stage in the process of creating an ever closer union among the peoples of Europe, in which decisions are taken as closely as possible to the citizen.'

Article B sets out the objectives of the Union which include the promotion of economic and social progress, the disappearance of internal frontiers, the establishment of economic and monetary union and the implementation of a common foreign policy including an eventual common defence policy.

Much of the Treaty consists of a series of amendments to the original EEC Treaty. They consist of about half of the text of Maastricht. Thus, many areas of activity are strictly within the ambit of the European Community whilst new areas are covered by the European Union.

14.1.8	New Community objectives

Article G of Maastricht states that the Treaty establishing the European Economic Community shall be amended so that the term 'European Economic Community' shall be replaced by the term 'European Community'. This provision reflects what has tended to happen in practice. Also, a new Article 2 of the EC Treaty states that the objectives in setting up a common market and an economic and monetary union consists of:

- a harmonious and balanced development of economic activities;

- sustainable and non-inflationary growth respecting the environment;

- a high degree of convergence of economic performance;

- a high level of employment and of social protection;

- the raising of the standard of living and quality of life; and

- economic and social cohesion and solidarity among Member States.

A new Article 3 of the EC Treaty sets out a timetable for, *inter alia*:

- the elimination of customs duties between Member States;

- the operation of an internal market characterised by the abolition of obstacles to the free movement of goods, persons, services and capital; and

- the approximation of the laws of Member States to the extent required for the functioning of the common market.

Concern at the intrusion of Community law into national law is reflected by a new Article 3b which says:

14.1.9   The principle of 'subsidiarity'

'The Community shall act within the limit of the powers conferred upon it by this Treaty and of the objectives assigned to it therein. In areas which do not fall within its exclusive competence, the Community shall take action, in accordance with the principle of subsidiarity, only if and in so far as the objectives of the proposed action cannot be sufficiently achieved by the Member States and can therefore ... be better achieved by the Community.'

It remains to be seen how far this principle will extend in practice. The European Court of Justice has recognised it – in recent case law concerning the UK the laws on Sunday trading have been held to be within the exclusive competence of the State.

A new concept is introduced here. Articles 8 to 8e of the EC Treaty deal with 'Citizenship of the Union'. Article 8 states that 'Every person holding the nationality of a Member State shall be a citizen of the Union'. Article 8 also provides that citizens of the Union shall enjoy the rights conferred by the Treaty, including:

14.1.10   European citizenship

- the right to move and reside freely within the territory of the Member States;

- the right to vote and to stand as a candidate at municipal elections in the Member State in which he or she resides, regardless of nationality;

- the right to vote and to stand as a candidate in elections to the European Parliament in the Member State in which he or she resides, regardless of nationality;

- the right to diplomatic protection by any Member State in a situation where the national State is not represented;

- the right to petition the European Parliament and to apply to the Ombudsman.

This is the most controversial and potentially most important aspect of Maastricht. It is mainly dealt with by Articles 102 to 109m. New institutions are provided for which have an important bearing on Community law.

14.1.11   Economic and monetary union

- A single economy

  The scene is set by Article 3a which mentions the 'irrevocable fixing of exchange rates leading to the introduction of a single currency, the ECU, and the definition and conduct of a single monetary policy and exchange rate policy the primary objective of both of which shall be to maintain price stability'.

  Article 103 says 'Member States shall regard their economic policies as a matter of common concern and shall co-ordinate them with the Council'. This Article goes on to say that the 'Council of Ministers, acting by a qualified majority, can adopt recommendations setting out broad guidelines for the economic policies of the Member States and of the Community'.

  Article 104(c) provides that 'Member States shall avoid excessive governmental deficits'. This provision also provides that the Council of Ministers, acting by a qualified majority on a recommendation from the Commission, has the power to decide whether an excessive deficit exists. If so, the Council can require the State concerned to make a deposit with the Community until the excessive deficit has been corrected or to fine the State.

- Monetary policy

  Article 105 deals with the tasks of the European System of Central Banks (ECB) which shall be composed of the European Central Bank (ECB) and of the national central banks. These tasks shall be: to define and implement the monetary policy of the Community; to conduct foreign exchange operations; to hold and manage the official foreign reserves of the Member States and to promote the smooth operation of payment systems.

  Article 105(a) says that the ECB shall have the exclusive right to authorise the issue of bank notes within the Community. Article 108(a) has important ramifications for Community law-making. It says:

  'In order to carry out the tasks entrusted to the ESCB, the ECB shall, in accordance with the provisions of this Treaty ... make regulations ... take decisions ... make recommendations and deliver opinions.'

  Article 109(a) says that the Governing Council of the ECB shall consist of the members of the Executive Board of the ECB and the Governors of the national central banks. Only nationals of Member States can be members of the Executive Board which will consist of a President, Vice-President and four other members appointed for a non-renewable term of eight years.

- Transitional provisions

  Transitional provisions provide for a gradual changeover to Economic and monetary union. Article 109(e) provides that the second stage for achieving economic and monetary union will begin on 1 January 1994.

  On that date a European Monetary Institute (EMI) was established (in Frankfurt) to smooth the path towards a single currency by (Article 109f), *inter alia*, strengthening the co-ordination of monetary policies of the Member States and facilitating the use of the ECU and overseeing its development.

  Article 109(j) provides that a meeting of Heads of State or Government will take place no later than 31 December 1996. By a qualified majority this meeting will decide whether a majority of the Member States fulfil the conditions for the adoption of a single currency and decide a date for the beginning of the third stage of economic and monetary union if appropriate. If by the end of 1997 the date for the beginning of the third stage has not been set, the third stage will start on 1 January 1999, the European Council having confirmed which States fulfil the conditions for the adoption of a single currency.

  Article 109(k) provides that Member States which do not fulfil the conditions for the adoption of a single currency will be called 'Member States with a derogation'. Such a Member State and its national central bank will be excluded from rights and obligations within the ESCB, and the State's voting rights within the Council on related matters will be suspended.

- The third stage

  Article 109(l) provides that as soon as the date for the entry into force of the third stage of economic and monetary union has been decided upon then the governments of the Member States without a derogation will appoint the Executive Board of the ECB. As soon as this happens, the ESCB and the ECB will be established and their powers exercised from the first day of the third stage. As soon as the ECB is established it shall take over the tasks of the EMI which shall go into liquidation.

  Article 109(l) provides that:

  'At the starting date of the third stage, the Council shall ... adopt the conversion rates at which their currencies shall be irrevocably fixed and at which irrevocably fixed rate the ECU shall be substituted for these currencies, and the ECU shall become a currency in its own right'.

The Third Stage of EMU will limit states' sovereignty tremendously. The conduct of economic policy in many important areas will have to be carried out within a more integrated European framework. For this reason, in one of the protocols to the Maastricht Treaty, the UK is stated not to be obliged to move to the third stage of EMU without a separate decision to do so by its government and Parliament.

4.1.12   Institutional changes

- The European Parliament

The emphasis in Maastricht is to increase the powers of the European Parliament in order to increase the democratic accountability of the European Community. This is recognised in a new Article 189 of the EC Treaty, where the first paragraph is altered to 'In order to carry out their task and in accordance with the provisions of the Treaty, the European Parliament acting jointly with the Council, the Council and the Commission shall make regulations and issue directives, take decisions, make recommendations or deliver opinions'.

This amendment to Article 189 is due to the Parliament's new powers of co-decision with the Council of Ministers provided by Article 189b. This effectively allows the Parliament to reject certain proposals for legislation by an overall majority eg in the field of single market legislation and health and safety. The procedure is similar to the existing 'co-operation procedure', in that the Parliament may approve the common position of the Council or propose amendments.

However, the new element is that the Parliament, by an absolute majority of its members, may reject the common position. In this case, or if the Council does not approve the amendments, then the matter must be referred to a Conciliation Committee, composed of equal members of the Council and Parliament. The Commission is required to take part in the proceedings with a view to reconciling the positions of the Council and Parliament. If a joint text is approved then the Council and Parliament may jointly adopt it. However, if they cannot agree on a common proposal the Parliament may reject the text by an absolute majority of its members.

The 'co-operation procedure' is now contained in Article 189c of the EC Treaty. Many new areas of legislation, eg environmental protection laws made under Article 130r are brought within the qualified majority voting/co-operation procedure for the first time.

The Parliament's increased authority is recognised by the new Article 137 of the EC Treaty where 'shall exercise the advisory and supervisory powers which are conferred upon it by this Treaty' is altered to 'shall exercise the powers conferred upon it by this Treaty'.

In legislative areas covered by the 'co-decision' and 'co-operation' procedures of Article 189b and Article 189c then Article 138b of the EC Treaty provides that 'The European Parliament may, acting by a majority of its members, request the Commission to submit any appropriate proposal on matters on which it considers that a Community act is required for the purpose of implementing this Treaty'. This is an important provision which places the Parliament close to being an initiator of policy.

Article 138(c) gives the Parliament the power to investigate by means of a Committee of Inquiry, 'alleged contraventions or maladministration in the implementation of Community law'. Article 138(d) allows any citizen of the Union residing in a Member State or company registered in a Member State to petition the Parliament 'on a matter which comes within the Community's fields of activity and which affects him, her or it directly'. Article 138(e) gives the Parliament the power to appoint an Ombudsman to receive complaints 'concerning instances of maladministration in the activities of the Community institutions or bodies, with the exception of the Court of Justice and the Court of First Instance acting in their judicial role'.

- The Commission

    Article 158 says that 'The President and the other members of the Commission ... shall be subject as a body to a vote of approval by the European Parliament'. This procedure will take effect from 7 January 1995. Also, from that date Article 158 provides that members of the Commission shall be appointed for renewable periods of five years.

- The Council

    Article 146 of the EC Treaty defines the Council:

    'The Council shall consist of a representative of each Member State at ministerial level, authorised to commit the government of that Member State'.

    This new Article also outlines the order of the six month presidency of the Council:

    '– for a first cycle of six years: Belgium, Denmark, Germany, Greece, Spain, France, Ireland, Italy, Luxembourg, Netherlands, Portugal, UK;

– for the following cycle of six years: Denmark, Belgium, Greece, Germany, France, Spain, Italy, Ireland, Netherlands, Luxembourg, UK, Portugal.'

• The Court of Justice

The Court's powers are considerably extended against Member States. A new Article 171 of the EC Treaty says 'If the Court of Justice finds that the Member State concerned has not complied with its judgment it may impose a lump sum or penalty payment on it'. This fine will only be imposed if the Commission feels that the Member State has failed to comply with the Court's judgment within the time-limit laid down by the Commission. If so, then the Commission can go to the Court and request the payment that it considers appropriate in the circumstances.

With regard to judicial review, a new Article 173 of the EC Treaty takes account of the Court's case law and also of new institutions and powers created by the Maastricht Treaty. Paragraph 1 now reads:

'The Court of Justice shall review the legality of acts adopted jointly by the European Parliament and the Council, of acts of the Council, of the Commission and of the ECB, other than recommendations and opinions, and of acts of the European Parliament intended to produce legal effects vis-à-vis third parties ... The Court shall have jurisdiction under the same conditions, in actions brought by the European Parliament and by the ECB for the purpose of protecting their prerogatives.'

For the same reasons, a new Article 175 of the EC Treaty has been created whose para 1 now reads 'Should the European Parliament, the Council or the Commission, in infringement of this Treaty, fail to act, the Member States and the other institutions of the Community may bring an action before the Court of Justice to have the infringement established'. A new para 4 reads:

'The Court of Justice shall have jurisdiction, under the same conditions, in actions or proceedings brought by the ECB in the areas falling within the latter's field of competence and in actions or proceedings brought against the latter.'

Concerning Preliminary Rulings, a new Article 177 of the EC Treaty takes account of changes elsewhere in the Maastricht Treaty. The provision is essentially the same except that Article 177(b) now reads 'the validity and interpretation of acts of the institutions of the Community and of the ECB'.

- The Court of Auditors

  A new Article 4 of the EC Treaty adds this ancillary Community institution to the list of institutions which deal with the operation of Community affairs. Its purpose is outlined in Article 188c which states:

  'The Court of Auditors shall examine the accounts of all revenue and expenditure of the Community. It shall also examine the accounts of all revenue and expenditure of all bodies set up by the Community in so far as the relevant constituent instrument does not preclude such examination. The Court of Auditors shall provide the European Parliament with a statement of assurance as to the reliability of and the legality and regularity of the underlying transactions ... It shall assist the European Parliament and the Council in exercising powers of control over the implementation of the budget.'

  The addition of this body to Article 4 is a recognition of the need for sound financial control over the increasingly complex affairs of the Community and the need to eradicate fraud.

- A common foreign and security policy

  This is a controversial section and it remains to be seen how it will develop. Article J says 'A common foreign and security policy is hereby established'. Article J1 says 'The Union and its Member States shall define and implement a common foreign and security policy ... covering all areas of foreign and security policy'.

- Co-operation in the fields of justice and home affairs

  Article K1 recognises that many areas are of common interest, eg asylum policy, immigration policy, combatting drug addiction and police co-operation in combatting terrorism and drug trafficking and other serious crime.

  Article K3 allows for the possibility of qualified majority voting on these issues in the Council of Ministers '... in so far as the objectives of the Union can be attained better by joint action than by the Member States acting individually on account of the scale or effects of the action envisaged'.

- Conclusion

  Despite the fact that the UK has opted out of the agreement on social policy, the so-called 'Social Chapter', which is contained in a separate protocol, the content of the Maastricht Treaty lays the framework for a federal European Union. How it develops in practice is a matter of conjecture. However, the momentum for serious change has been set in place and further treaty revisions are due in

1996. The various changes, especially institutional and EMU proposals, will have far-reaching effects on the sovereignty of the UK Parliament.

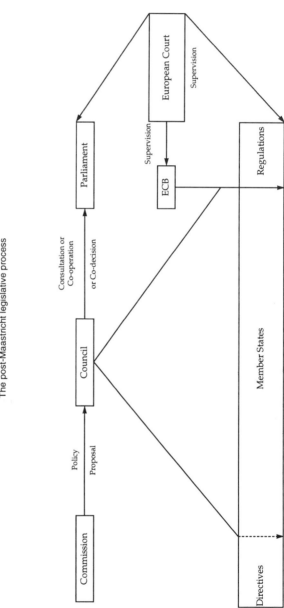

The post-Maastricht legislative process

The UK and the European Community

Articles 5 and 6(1) of the EEC Treaty and the obligation to incorporate Community law into national law. The dualist UK constitution. Section 2(1) of the European Communities Act 1972 and the incorporation of Treaty obligations and regulations. Section 2(2) of the Act and incorporation of directives. The provisions of the Single European Act and incorporation by the European Communities (Amendment) Act 1986. Maastricht and the European Communities (Amendment) Act 1993. The question of supremacy and ss 2(4) and 3(1) of the 1972 Act. The statements of UK judges:

Esso Petroleum v Kingswood Motors Ltd (1974)

Aero Zipp Fasteners v YKK Fasteners (1973)

Incorporation of Community law

The doctrine of supremacy of Community law as elaborated by the Court in its interpretation of the Treaties. Community law must be of direct use to the Community citizen. The Court's gradual movement from saying that Community law prevails in case of conflict with national law to stating that offending national law is void:

Van Gend en Loos case (1963)

Flaminio Costa v Enel (1964)

Simmenthal case (1979)

R v Secretary of State for Transport, ex p Factortame Ltd (1990)

Attitude of the European Court of Justice

Meaning of 'Direct Effect' – using Community law against Member States

    The Court's elaboration of the principle in interpretation of the Treaty provisions provided the measure was clear and unconditional in nature. Regulations are also capable of producing direct effect. The extension by the Court of the principle to unincorporated directives provided that the time-limit for incorporation had expired and the measure was unconditional and precise. The Court's limitation of this to vertical direct effect. The Court's elaboration of the principles for the operation of vertical direct effect. The non-operation of a principle of horizontal direct effect. The Court's willingness to allow an action against the State where the directive does not have vertical direct effect:

The European Court of Justice and the principle of direct effect

Van Gend en Loos Case (1962)

Yvonne van Dyn v Home Office (1974)

MH Marshall v Southampton and South-West Hampshire Area Health Authority (Teaching) (1984)

Foster and others v British Gas (1991)

Doughty v Rolls-Royce plc (1992)

Francovitch v Italian Republic (1992)

Maastricht: The Treaty on European Union

The European Communities (Amendment) Act 1993 and entry into effect of the Treaty with the Union's objectives set out in Article B(TEU). New Community objectives set out in Articles G(TEU) and 2(EC). The principle of subsidiarity as set out in Article 3(b) (EC). The concept of European citizenship as set down in Articles 8 to 8e (EC). The scene set for a single economy by Article 3a (EC) and the detailed provisions on economic and monetary union as detailed by Articles 102 to 109m (EC). Of particular importance is Article 105 (EC) which deals with the tasks of the ESCB and Article 108(a) (EC) which gives the ECB law-making powers. The transitional provisions for EMU are outlined in Article 109(e) (EC) and the third stage in Article 109(1) (EC). The power of co-decision given to the European Parliament is outlined in Article 189b (EC) and recognised in a new Article 189 (EC). The Parliament's authority is strengthened in Articles 137, 138b, 138c, 138d and 138e (EC). Membership of the Commission is subject to Parliament's approval (Article 158 (EC)). The Court of Justice is given new powers against Member States in a new Article 171 (EC) Articles 173, 175 and 177 are amended to take account of institutional developments. Article J(TEU) provides for a common foreign and security policy and Article K(TEU) for increased co-operation in the fields of justice and home affairs with the possibility of qualified-majority voting in this area.

PART FOUR
ASPECTS OF CONSTITUTIONAL LAW

Chapter 15

Nature and Characteristics of the UK Constitution

A *constitution* is the fundamental law of a State, usually in the form of a written legally binding document which sets out the rights and duties of citizens and the State and which regulates the three arms of government – legislature, executive and judiciary.

The UK has no written constitution (ie no one document or series of documents setting out fundamental law). Instead our constitution is to be found in the ordinary sources of law including statutes, case law, custom and European Community law.

In addition, constitutional rules are to be found in conventions (ie unwritten rules by which those subject to them feel obliged to be bound). Conventions are not exclusive to systems with unwritten constitutions but may well have a part to play in systems with written constitutions also.

The UK is one of the few states to have an unwritten constitution, as do Israel and New Zealand.

Constitutional law defines the three types of governmental powers (legislative, executive and judicial) and the relationship between each of them and their relationship with the citizen. *Administrative law* deals with the controls over power, in particular the power of the executive, by the courts. Other controls are described as administrative controls including the Parliamentary Commissioner for Administration.

The main characteristics of the UK constitution will be considered including its unitary nature, that it is unwritten, flexible, is based on the legislative supremacy of Parliament and has a constitutional or limited monarchy. In addition it is noted that no strict separation exists between the legislative, executive and judicial powers.

The UK is a union of England and Wales, Scotland and Northern Ireland governed centrally by the Westminster Parliament. Northern Ireland and Scotland each have their own legal systems and England and Wales form a legal entity.

The question of devolution of legislative power to Scotland and Wales arose in 1979 but was answered in the negative by means of a referendum in each country. Another question

15.1   Introduction

15.2   Characteristics of the UK constitution

15.2.1   Unitary

concerning the Union is the relationship of the UK, in particular Northern Ireland and the Irish Republic in the light of the Anglo-Irish Agreement entered into in 1985.

Unions can be compared with federations as in the USA where legislative functions are exercised centrally by Congress and regionally by State legislatures. Confederations such as Switzerland are formed by alliances between independent regions.

Thus, legislative and other power can reside at the centre or be devolved to the parts. This question is very much in point when considering the position of the UK as a member of the European Community, and in particular following the passage of the European Communities (Amendment) Act 1993 through Parliament providing for the ratification of the Treaty of European Union. It is too early to say how far along the road to full European Union we have moved but legal and political sovereignty has moved from the UK to European institutions and this was a process recognised from the start of membership.

15.2.2   Unwritten

As already mentioned, the UK has no one document or series of documents setting out a fundamental law against which the legality of actions by organs of government can be measured.

Written constitutions tend to be entered into following revolution or colonial occupation. The UK might well have set up a written constitution following the Glorious Revolution of 1688 but the Bill of Rights of 1689 merely attempted to settle the feud between Crown and Parliament and establish Parliament as the supreme law maker. It did not attempt to create a fundamental law of State and citizen. What is more, it takes the form of an ordinary statute which like any other can be repealed at any time. This applies to all our constitutional law – it can altered at any time by Parliament.

15.2.3   Flexible

The notion of flexible constitutions is closely linked with the earlier one of unwritten constitutions but written constitutions may be flexible in that they are easily changed or contain no entrenched provisions as to the method by which changes can be made. The legal theory of the UK constitution is that the Queen in Parliament can change any law at any time. The reality is somewhat different in that political restraints may apply and in any event UK membership of the EC restricts the doctrine of Parliamentary supremacy.

15.2.4   Supremacy of
            Parliament

The Supremacy of Parliament doctrine arose out of the 17th century conflict between Crown and Parliament, and provides that Parliament can legislate on any matter and the courts cannot review the legality of legislation. The courts are merely the interpreters of legislation and have no role as a 'constitutional' court able to strike down legislation as unconstitutional and void (*Pickin v BRB* (1974)).

However, the power of interpretation can be a wide one and under the European influence the UK courts are taking a broader approach to statutory interpretation than in the past. Ultimately, Parliament must decide on matters of policy and how the law should change but, nevertheless, the courts have residual power to make law.

A court asked to interpret a statute must look at the intention of Parliament as expressed by the words of the Act. If that Act expressly or impliedly conflicts with an earlier Act the court is obliged to apply the later Act. This can be put in another way, namely that Parliament is not bound by its predecessors but can enact law afresh, and the courts are obliged to apply the later law.

Two issues are of major importance:

- UK membership of the EC; and

- whether supremacy applies both to content and 'manner and form' of legislation.

So far as EC membership is concerned, the UK signed the Treaty of Accession in 1972 and this was given effect to by the European Communities Act 1972. Of particular importance is s 2(1)(2) and (4). The constitutional position is that the Royal Prerogative was used to sign the Treaty and in order to give effect to it and all other EC law in domestic law, Parliament passed the 1972 Act which could then be applied by the courts.

The 1972 Act was amended in 1986 to give effect to the Single European Act and now further amended by the European Communities (Amendment) Act 1993. Strict legal theory would allow the repeal of these statutes although political reality would deny this. In any event the question of direct repeal has never come before the courts, but in cases of implied conflict the courts have construed statutory provisions in such a way as to avoid conflict with EC law. The nearest we have come to a direct conflict is *R v S of S for Transport ex p Factortame* (1990).

In *R v Secretary of State for Foreign Commonwealth Affairs ex parte Rees Mogg* (1994) Lord Rees-Mogg, former Editor of *The Times* newspaper, asked the Queen's Bench Division Divisional Court for judicial review under Order 53 of the Supreme Court Rules. The case raised the interesting question whether the exercise of the Royal Prerogative had been given effect to fully by Parliament. If it had not, the question arose as to whether the courts could strike the statute down. The answer depended on the second issue mentioned above.

Traditionally, the courts have not questioned the process by which Bills have become law. All that a court enquires into is whether it has passed all its stages and received the royal assent. The formula recited at the start of all Acts confirms this. By Article 9 of the Bill of Rights, proceedings in Parliament cannot be impeached or questioned in any court or other place outside Parliament.

Parliament is not only not bound by its predecessors as to content but also as to manner and form and the courts have no means of challenging the legality of changes. The challenge to the European Communities (Amendment) Act thereby failed.

In this context the Parliament Acts 1911 and 1949 deserve mention. The first limited the power of the House of Lords to delay legislation introduced in the House of Commons to three sessions or up to two years following the second reading in the Commons. The result of using this Act would be that a bill that had passed all stages in the Commons but which on reaching the Lords was amended could become law on receiving royal assent once the time limit had been met. The 1949 Act itself purported to further limit the power of delay, from three to two sessions and from two years to one and passed into law by the 1911 Act procedure.

Learned writers, including O Hood Phillips, suggest that the 1949 Act is not an Act at all, not having been passed by Queen, Commons and Lords. Only the War Crimes Act 1991 has been passed under the 1949 Act procedure and no challenge in the courts has ever been made as to the legality of the 1949 Act. The reason given for the 1949 Act not being valid is that it concerned a constitutional change and such changes can only be effected in the time honoured way.

It is not suggested that the 1993 Act had not passed into law in the time honoured way – Queen, Commons and Lords – since in the event both Houses of Parliament have voted in favour of the Bill but the question was whether the Act gave effect to the Treaty of European Union. The court held that it had.

5.2.5   Separation of powers

Taken to the extreme, the separation of powers would prevent any government taking place. However, some separation of the legislative, executive and judicial powers is warranted. Indeed, the independence of the judiciary from the other two branches of government is essential. This doctrine, as stated by the 18th Century jurist Montesquieu, required separation of persons, the absence of control or interference by one organ with the exercise of another's functions and one organ not exercising the functions of another.

This doctrine is given formal recognition in most written constitutions, for example, in the USA constitution the President has executive power, the Supreme Court the judicial power, capable of questioning the legality of State and federal laws, and Congress made up of Senate and House of Representatives having legislative powers.

The UK constitution neither formally or otherwise recognises such a doctrine. The epitome of the reverse is the office of Lord Chancellor who fulfils roles in all three areas as Speaker of the House of Lords, head of the judiciary and an executive role with a seat in the Cabinet. The position has shown signs of strain since Lord McKay has been in post, in particular, given the challenges by the Law Society under Order 53 RSC of the cuts in legal aid funding brought into effect by statutory instrument.

Although this is the most important area of overlap there are others, including the royal assent to bills (by convention not refused); the administration of justice in the name of the Crown; the House of Lords both as a legislative chamber and the highest appeal court (by convention only the Law Lords make judicial decisions).

15.2.6   The rule of law

The rule of law is an elusive concept but one which is often invoked by lawyers and politicians in support of the notion that no-one should be above the law and that decisions should be reached in accordance with law. Coke's doctrine stated that Crown and government are subject to law and in his time the ultimate source of 'good' law was God.

In modern times the doctrine has been taken to mean that the executive power should act in accordance with law and not arbitrarily or by discretion. However, this doctrine does not sit easily with that of Sovereignty of Parliament in that a strong government would be able to pass whatever laws it wished subject, of course, to practical limitations and those now applicable as a result of EC membership. At the extreme, the spirit of the doctrine of the rule of law can be lost in that law could be used as an instrument of oppression.

Dicey in *The Law of the Constitution* noted three aspects:

- all men and women are subject to the law;

- all are equal before the law; and

- constitutional rules are judge-made.

Much criticism has been levelled against Dicey's analysis, notably that the last point bears little relationship to the others and does not truly reflect reality and that the second point fails to recognise that the law confers wide powers on, for example, the police and other officials.

This notion has been confirmed in the historic House of Lords' judgment on 27 July 1993 in *M v Home Office and Another* where the court affirmed the decision of the Court of Appeal in finding the former Home Secretary Kenneth Baker in contempt of court for failing to comply with a court order not to deport a foreign national pending the outcome of judicial review proceedings. The House of Lords stated that the Crown and government ministers are subject to law.

5.2.7	Constitutional conventions

Unlike custom, conventions are not law and so their breach does not give rise to legal action. They are, nevertheless, rules which are treated as binding by those affected by them. Breach may cause a constitutional crisis and may result in change in the rules or resignation or censure of the offending party.

Conventions develop over time and help to 'oil the wheels' of the constitution. They not only assist the workings of unwritten constitutions but may be found in written constitutions where otherwise the rules would have to change by a formal procedure.

Conventions are not mere habits or practices, but are ways of behaving which have stood the test of time but which given changing circumstances may change or cease to have effect.

Some examples are the royal assent to bills, individual and collective ministerial responsibility, the so-called 'Salisbury' convention whereby the House of Lords does not delay or refuse to pass a bill approved by the House of Commons except where the bill involves a significant constitutional or national issue, the powers of the Queen to decide whether to dissolve Parliament at the request of the Prime Minister or to take alternative action.

The use of conventions come into their own when things do not go to plan as so easily could have happened during the course of the European Communities (Amendment) Act 1993 – could the House of Lords have delayed the Bill pending the outcome of a referendum? Would the Queen have had to agree to the request for dissolution of Parliament if the vote of confidence called by the Prime Minister on 23 July 1993 had not been successful?

5.2.8	Judicial independence

The independence of the judiciary from interference by the executive is a fundamental principle of the UK constitution.

Written constitutions usually guarantee this principle and elevate the judiciary so that the judges can question the legality not only of executive action but also legislation.

With increasing frequency we are seeing our judges questioning executive actions by way of the judicial review procedure and more recently by way of holding a government minister liable for contempt of court. However, judicial review does not empower the courts to challenge the merits of a decision but only to ensure that the correct process has been used or that there has not been an abuse or excess of power.

A fundamental change in the role of the judiciary would have to come about to permit the judges to challenge the merits of executive action and even more fundamental changes in the constitution would be needed if judges were to be able to question the validity of legislation.

By the s 11 Supreme Court Act 1981 all High Court and Court of Appeal judges (other than the Lord Chancellor) hold their offices during good behaviour subject to a power of removal by the Monarch on an address by both Houses of Parliament.

By the s 6 Appellate Jurisdiction Act 1876, Lords of Appeal in Ordinary (the Law Lords) hold office during good behaviour subject to a power of removal on the address of both Houses of Parliament introduced in the House of Commons.

Thus, an office holder can be removed where he or she has misbehaved in respect of the office or other cause and thereby has forfeited the confidence of the both Houses.

In addition, the Crown could remove a judge without an address of both Houses where official misconduct or neglect of official duties is proved and probably where convicted of a serious offence.

The Judicial Pensions and Retirement Act 1993, to come into effect on a day to be appointed by the Secretary of State, provides for a retirement age of 70. At present, the retirement age for Law Lords and judges of the Supreme Court is 75 and, for Circuit judges, 72. It is likely that this change will be phased in and in any event will not apply to existing judges.

Judges' salaries are charged on the Consolidated Fund and so are not reviewed by the House of Commons annually. Salaries may be increased by Order in Council.

Circuit judges may be removed by the Lord Chancellor for incapacity or misbehaviour under s 17(4) Courts Act 1971 and by s 21(6) of that Act a Recorder may be removed for incapacity or misbehaviour or failure to comply with the terms of appointment.

Magistrates may be removed by the Lord Chancellor if he thinks fit but convention dictates that this can only be for good cause. The Justices of the Peace Act 1979 provides for the keeping of a Supplemental List of justices no longer entitled to exercise judicial functions. This may be due to age or infirmity or for neglect of duty. When a JP reaches the age of 70 his name must be placed on the list.

5.3 Governmental powers

Traditionally, governmental powers are divided into legislation, executive and judicial powers and, as has already been mentioned there is no strict separation between them. Each will be considered in turn, together with the main overlaps, in particular the office of Lord Chancellor who performs roles in all three areas.

5.3.1 The legislature

The legislature is made up of House of Lords (the Upper Chamber), the House of Commons and the Queen who, by convention, does not refuse royal assent.

The House of Commons has some 651 members elected by universal adult suffrage in one of the Parliamentary constituencies by way of the 'first past the post' system. The Representation of the People Acts disqualify persons under 21, peers of the realm, Church of England clergy and bankrupts, for example, from sitting as an MP. A number of MPs have been put at risk of losing their seats should they be made bankrupt following the Lloyd's financial losses.

The House of Commons has two main functions – passing legislation and control of the executive. The doctrine of Parliamentary Supremacy and the procedure for the passage of bills has already been noted.

Control of the executive takes different forms, principally by way of financial control. The executive demands money to carry out its policies and the House of Commons grants it (known as 'supply') and provides 'ways and means' (taxation and public money) to meet these demands.

The Queen's Speech at the start of a new Parliamentary year sets out the government's proposed legislative programme and public expenditure proposals. Public expenditure is scrutinised by the House of Commons (the House of Lords can only consent).

The expenditure is granted by way of annual Appropriation Acts for the financial year. The Opposition has 20 days for debate on the government's financial estimates and matters of policy and pending the passing of the Appropriation Acts continuity is ensured by way of the Consolidated Fund Acts.

The Speaker acts as an impartial arbiter who keeps order in the proceedings of the House and ensures that its rules of procedure (standing orders) are complied with. The Speaker may certify a bill to be a Money Bill' under the Parliament Act 1911 and has a casting vote.

The House of Commons jealously guards its powers of financial control over government (no taxation without representation (*A-G v Wilts United Dairies* (1922); *Bowles v Bank of England* (1913)).

Other means of control are by way of debates, question time, the Select Committees who scrutinise the work of government departments and have power to call for 'persons, papers and records'.

Select Committees must not be confused with Standing Committees whose main role is the scrutiny of bills at the committee stage.

The House of Commons (and to a lesser extent the House of Lords) under Article 9 of the Bill of Rights 1688 and as the High Court of Parliament also claims various rights and privileges so as to assert its freedom from the courts, the executive and others. At the start of a new Parliament the Speaker in an ancient ceremony claims freedom of speech, freedom from arrest, freedom from molestation, freedom to regulate proceedings, the right to punish for contempt and to regulate its own composition.

'Contempt' is a broad concept and can be invoked not only against outsiders who offend the rules of the House but also its members whether they be MPs or ministers.

Conduct both inside and outside the House may be censured and the Select Committees on Parliamentary Privilege and Procedure and on Members' Interests regulate conduct of members.

The House of Lords is made up of Lords Temporal and Spiritual. The former comprise some 750 hereditary peers and peeresses, 300 life peers and peeresses created by the Life Peerages Act 1958 and the Lords of Appeal in Ordinary.

The latter are the Archbishops of Canterbury and York, Bishops of London, Durham and Winchester and 21 senior Bishops of the Church of England.

Despite many critics who have advocated its abolition or reform and the curbs on its powers by the Parliament Acts 1911 and 1949, the House of Lords as an unelected chamber, continues to act as a check on government and initiate bills that would stand little chance of being promoted in the House of Commons.

Some of the most recent proposals for reform were contained in Tony Benn's Commonwealth of Britain Bill which would abolish the House of Lords and replace it with an elected second chamber.

15.4   The executive

The executive is a broad term the meaning of which is determined by context. It can refer to the Crown, the PM, Cabinet, civil servants and government departments.

The Crown and those acting as servants or agents of the Crown, derive power both from statute and the Royal Prerogative which is the residue of discretionary powers at any time in the hands of the Crown.

The political prerogative powers concern both domestic and foreign affairs. We have mentioned examples of the former in particular the power of the Queen, at the request of the Prime Minister, to dissolve Parliament. Another example is that exercised in the name of the Queen by the Home Secretary namely the prerogative of mercy. Use of this power is illustrated in the case of *R v Home Secretary ex p Bentley* (1993) below.

So far as foreign affairs are concerned the prerogative powers are most clearly shown by the process by which treaties are entered into. The Crown signs a treaty and commits the UK to the obligations of the treaty in International law. So far as domestic law is concerned it is usual for effect to be given to the treaty by way of legislation. The European Communities Act 1972 and its later amendments gave effect in domestic law to the obligations entered into on the accession of the UK to membership of the European Community.

The extent to which the courts can question the exercise of the royal prerogative was clearly shown in *CCSU v Minister for Civil Service* (1985) (the *GCHQ* Case) where the head of the civil service banned unions at the Cheltenham HQ without consultation despite a legitimate expectation on the part of the workforce. Providing the issues were justiciable the court by a majority of three to two said *obiter* that the prerogative was subject to judicial review. On the facts a plea of national security by the government which was accepted by the court prevented it going further.

A more recent case concerning review of the direct exercise of the prerogative is the case of *R v Home Secretary ex p Bentley* (1993). In the *GCHQ* case it should be remembered that the case concerned an instruction given in the exercise of a delegated power (by way of Order in Council) under the prerogative.

In July 1993 the former Editor of *The Times* newspaper, Lord Rees-Mogg, sought to challenge, by way of judicial review, the provisions of the European Communities

(Amendment) Act 1993 giving effect to the Treaty of European Union. In the result although leave was granted the application was refused and no appeal was heard. The court concluded that the issues involving the exercise of the royal prerogative in entering into treaties and the passing of legislation was outside its remit.

Another notable treaty signed by the UK is the European Convention on Human Rights, which has not been given domestic legal effect. Numerous judicial statements state that it is not part of UK law but that domestic courts should have regard to its provisions where domestic law is not settled. One such statement was made by Lord Fraser in *A-G v BBC* (1981). Reference to the Convention might then assist a judge in deciding what the domestic law on a particular matter is.

In the case of *Derbyshire CC v Times Newspapers Ltd* (1993), concerning the question whether a local authority had a right to claim damages for defamation, the House of Lords decided that there was no such right known to the common law and that it was not necessary to refer to Article 10 of the Convention.

15.5   The judiciary

The courts are unable to question the legality of legislation but the Queen's Bench Division Divisional Court has a supervisory jurisdiction over inferior courts and tribunals and can declare delegated legislation *ultra vires*. Order 53 RSC also permits decisions by public bodies to be reviewed on the basis that the powers by which such decisions have been made have been abused or exceeded.

A fundamental issue concerning the constitutional position of the judiciary is that of independence from the other arms of government in particular the executive. It is a well espoused principle that our judges are not only independent but also impartial in the way in which they reach decisions. One means of testing this would be by way of the doctrine of separation of powers but we have seen that this doctrine is not well developed in particular with regard to the position and role of the Lord Chancellor.

We have already mentioned the Supreme Court Act 1981 and the Appellate Jurisdiction Act 1876 concerning removal of superior judges and the charge on the Consolidated Fund for salaries. Judges are also immune from suit for things said during the course of a trial and, by ss 108 and 109 of the Courts and Legal Services Act 1990, this has been extended to include magistrates. Full immunity from civil action applies for matters within their jurisdiction and also to matters outside their jurisdiction providing they act in good faith.

The Contempt of Court Act 1981 regulating interference with the course of justice and failure to comply with orders of the court, as shown in *M v Home Office and Another* (1993), is also important in maintaining the independence and authority of the courts.

Those who flout the authority of the court may be found to be in contempt and liable to imprisonment of up to two years. The recent case involving a father taking his son out of the jurisdiction of the court against the order of the court who on his return was sentenced to 18 months' imprisonment is a good illustration.

- Order 53 Rules of the Supreme Court and s 31 of the Supreme Court Act 1981

This is properly the subject of administrative law whereby the court reviews the exercise of public powers.

Unlike on an appeal where the court can impose its own decision, judicial review allows the court only to question the process by which a decision was reached. The court does not question the 'merits' (ie the substance) of the decision but must be satisfied that the decision was reached in accordance with prescribed procedure, or the rules of natural justice or that the decision maker had power to make the decision.

Given that the UK has no written constitution and that the doctrine of the sovereignty of Parliament still applies in matters not governed by the European Community the judges cannot question the validity of legislation. However, they may review the way in which statutory (and in limited circumstances the prerogative powers) are exercised by, for example, Ministers of the Crown and local authorities. The case of *R v Panel on Take-Overs and Mergers ex p Datafin plc* (1987) established that judicial review may also be available against private bodies exercising public powers.

The principles by which the judges have asserted their power of review are founded in the common law and the cases in which the citizen has successfully challenged public decision-making demonstrate the creativity of the courts in curbing excess or abuse of power.

Where the words of a statute are clear and unambiguous the doctrine of the sovereignty of Parliament prevents the courts from doing other than giving effect to the words used. Where the words used are open to interpretation the courts may, and it may be argued, should interpret the words used to give effect to accepted common standards and in accordance with the expectations of citizens.

Constitutional theory provides for no formal separation of powers and given the doctrines of Parliamentary Sovereignty and the Rule of Law, the executive owes responsibility for the exercise of its power to Parliament.

The reality suggests that Parliament is often not an effective check on the workings of the executive and so it is vital that the courts exercise powers of review, albeit that this will be impossible where statutory provisions are clear and unambiguous. This limitation has resulted in calls for fundamental constitutional change by way of a written constitution and Bill of Rights.

An applicant for judicial review must apply for leave (permission) to a High Court judge. This is granted at the judge's discretion provided the applicant has an 'arguable' case, can show *locus standi* (a relevant interest in the outcome) and that the case is not misconceived, otherwise frivolous or vexatious.

Proceedings must be brought promptly and this usually means within three months from the date on which grounds arose. Extensions are at the judge's discretion. If leave is granted the application for judicial review is made to the Queen's Bench Division Divisional Court. If refused, the applicant may appeal to a High Court Judge or to the Court of Appeal. Even if an applicant is successful in obtaining leave to bring a claim this does not mean that the court will, on hearing the case, grant the remedy asked for. This is illustrated in the recent applications by the Law Society to challenge decisions by the Lord Chancellor to amend the legal aid rules. Leave was granted but the court refused the relief sought (*R v the Lord Chancellor ex p The Law Society* (1993)).

The remedies available are the prerogative orders of *certiorari* (to quash an *ultra vires* decision or one made in breach of the rules of natural justice or where there is an error of law); prohibition (an interim order prohibiting the taking of proposed action where *ultra vires* or breaches of natural justice are alleged) and *mandamus* (an order enforcing public duties).

In addition, a declaration (an order stating the legal position where *ultra vires* and breaches of natural justice alleged) or an injunction (a discretionary remedy which is not available where an alternative statutory remedy is available) may be granted.

A major shortcoming is the inability of the court to award damages against public bodies. This can only be done where the aggrieved party can rely on a private law right in contract or tort.

The ancient and now rarely used writ of habeas corpus is still available against public bodies (and others) who unlawfully detain a person. The court can call the captor before it to account for the detention.

The House of Lords' decision in *R v Independent Television Commission ex p TSW Broadcasting Ltd* (1992) which concerned an application for the renewal of a broadcasting licence by TSW for the South West region illustrates when an application for judicial review will be successful. Parliament had not provided an appeal procedure from the decisions of the Commission and Lord Templeman stated that 'the courts were not to invent an appeal machinery'. The court endorsed the statement of principle in the cases of *Council of Civil Service Unions v Minister for the Civil Service* (1984) (the *GCHQ* case) and *Associated Provincial Picture Houses Ltd v Wednesbury Corporation* (1947) that judicial review was only available where it was shown that there had been 'illegality, irrationality or procedural impropriety'. Proof merely of a mistake on the part of the decision-maker was insufficient and it was not for the court to substitute its view of the case for that of the decision-maker.

Lord Diplock in the *GCHQ* case stated that 'illegality, irrationality or procedural impropriety' were the well recognised grounds for judicial review. He queried whether a fourth ground had been developed, namely 'proportionality'.

This concept derives from Continental legal systems and ensures a reasonable relationship between the end to be achieved and the means used to achieve it. Sir John Donaldson in *R v Secretary of State for the Home Department ex p Brind* (1990) doubted that this was a separate ground and suggested that it was part of 'Wednesbury unreasonableness' or as it has in recent years been called, 'irrationality'.

An inherent danger of the court adopting the principle of 'proportionality' is that it will attempt to test the merits of a case with the result that it would substitute its decision for that of the public body.

Brief mention must be made of each of these three grounds: illegality may be proved, for example, where the decision-maker has purported to exercise a power he does not have or where he has misdirected himself in law or he has used a power for an improper purpose or where he has failed to take into account all relevant considerations.

The *Wednesbury* case concerned a condition attached to the grant of a cinema licence preventing those under 15 from being admitted on Sundays. This was held to be lawful but Lord Greene's statement of principle has been often quoted and included four propositions: the decision-maker should consider all relevant matters, disregard all irrelevant matters, when exercising a discretion properly direct himself in law and act reasonably.

Procedural impropriety may take one of three forms. The first two are often referred to as the rules of natural justice (or in a purely administrative context, procedural fairness) namely the rule against bias and the right to a fair hearing.

The third is of much more recent origin and is referred to as a 'legitimate expectation'. The scope of this principle has not yet been settled and it is unclear from the case law whether it is merely a means of ensuring a fair procedure or goes further and ensures that a particular decision will be reached. The danger with the second proposition is that the court would be exercising an appeal function rather than one of review.

In the *GCHQ* case the trade union would have had a legitimate expectation of being consulted about the proposed ban if it had not been for the defence of national security. This was a legitimate expectation of being consulted which had arisen from previous conduct.

In the case of *R v Secretary of State for Home Department ex p Khan* (1985) an order of *certiorari* was granted against the Home Secretary quashing his refusal of an entry certificate for a Pakistani child who Khan wished to adopt. Khan had relied on a Home Office standard form letter setting out the criteria to be satisfied for an adoption to be successful. The Home Secretary applied other criteria without first giving Khan a hearing so as to put forward reasons why the adoption should go ahead. If the Home Secretary was to resile from the undertaking in the letter he was obliged to allow Khan an opportunity to make representations.

The case of *A-G of Hong Kong v Ng Tuen Shiu* (1983) held that where the government announced a policy of repatriation and stated that each case would be considered on its merits it could not order the removal of Ng without first giving him a hearing so as to allow him to put forward any grounds which might have allowed him to stay.

Thus, where a public body makes a promise, or a statement or gives an undertaking or acts in accordance with a regular procedure this may give rise to a legitimate expectation in those affected that decisions will be made in accordance with the statement or practice or that changes will be notified and those affected will have an opportunity of making representations.

A recent illustration of an application for judicial review is the case of *R v Home Secretary ex p Bentley* (1993) where the applicant sought judicial review of the Home Secretary's refusal to recommend a posthumous free pardon for her brother. He did so on the basis that it had been long established policy of successive Home Secretaries only to grant a free pardon where the person in question was both morally and technically innocent of the crime. The Home Secretary had concluded that there was no evidence in this case for such a conclusion. The Queen's Bench Division Divisional Court of the High Court made no formal order but invited the Home Secretary to reconsider the matter and to exercise the prerogative by the grant of a conditional pardon in recognition that an injustice had occurred.

The court was not willing to question the established policy of Home Secretaries in setting the criteria for exercise of the prerogative but considered that there had been an error of law by the Home Secretary in failing to consider whether to grant a conditional pardon where clearly imposition of the death penalty had been wrong.

Another recent case which illustrates the use and scope of judicial review is that of *R v Secretary of State for the Home Department ex p Doody & Others* (1993) in which the respondents to the appeal to the House of Lords, who had each been sentenced to mandatory life sentences for murder, sought review of the Home Secretary's refusal to supply information as to how the dates fixed for the first review of their cases had been arrived at. It was held that such prisoners were entitled to submit representations in writing to the Home Secretary before he decided the first review date and that prisoners should be informed of the judicial view as to the period to be served. Where the Home Secretary decided to depart from the judicial view (and the court held that this was possible) he was obliged to give reasons to the prisoner for so doing.

Dicta in the case illustrates the relationship between the judiciary and the Home Secretary, both in respect of sentencing policy and judicial review of administrative decisions. Three points are of particular note:

- It was stressed that sentencing was regulated by a statutory scheme which vested power in the Home Secretary to decide release dates in such cases. The Home Secretary was able to delegate these powers and in the exercise of his discretion he took into account the judicial view but was not required to do more. The judges did not have a role as advisers or otherwise and the Home Secretary was free to depart from the judicial view provided he gave his reasons for so doing.

- As stated by Lord Mustill, the present law did not recognise any general duty to give reasons in administrative decisions although it was clear that in appropriate circumstances such a duty would be implied.

- it was not for the courts in a judicial review case to attempt to make fundamental changes in the relationship between the State and a prisoner. Although procedural differences existed between mandatory and discretionary life sentences any change in policy was for Parliament.

15.6   Administrative controls of power

An aggrieved citizen may decide not to resort to court action against a public body or such action may be inappropriate. An alternative is to have recourse to the Parliamentary Commissioner for Administration or the Local Government Commissioner or the National Health Service Commissioner, depending on whether the complaint relates to maladministration at central, local or health service level.

By the Parliamentary Commissioner Act 1967 the PCA or Ombudsman investigates acts or omissions by public bodies specified in Schedule 2 of the Act provided the conditions in ss 4 and 5 are met. These provide, *inter alia*, that the allegation must be one of maladministration and a written complaint must be made to an MP within 12 months of knowledge of the complaint. Reference must be made by the MP with the consent of the complainant to the PCA and no alternative remedy would be available before a court or tribunal, or that it is unreasonable to resort to such remedy.

Schedule 3 excludes investigation of health service matters, foreign relations and armed forces matters for example.

The Ombudsman has the powers of a High Court Judge and can call for documents (except Cabinet papers) and has full powers over conduct of the investigation which is held in private. Two major shortcomings must be noted: the Act does not define 'maladministration' but this has been taken to include such things as delay, bias, incompetence, neglect and inattention; no formal system of remedies exist merely the report and recommendations made by the PCA.

The PCA reports annually to Parliament and where maladministration is found a special report is prepared. From time to time general reports are submitted.

Another means open to the aggrieved citizen is to seek redress by way of a tribunal. The work of tribunals is supervised by the Council on Tribunals under the Tribunals and Inquiries Act 1992. The Franks Committee Report 1957 recommended the setting up of a review body to monitor the constitution and workings of administrative tribunals. It is an advisory body and does not handle complaints from individuals. It submits annual reports to Parliament.

Nature and Characteristics of the UK Constitution

A constitution is the fundamental law of a State, usually in written form, setting out the rights and duties of citizens and the State and regulating legislative, executive and judicial arms of government.

Introduction

The UK has no written constitution and instead this is to be found in the ordinary sources of law and, in addition, conventions.

Constitutional law defines governmental power in its three branches of legislative, executive and judicial and the inter-relationship one with another. Administrative law is concerned with controls of such power, in particular, judicial control of executive power.

Constitutional and administrative law

- Unitary

- Unwritten

- Flexible

- Supremacy of Parliament

  This deserves special mention following the European Communities (Amendment) Act 1993 and the *Factortame* and *Francovitch* cases and the changing attitude of the UK courts to the validity of legislation which conflicts with European Community law.

- Separation of powers

Characteristics of the UK constitution

- The rule of law

- Constitutional conventions

- Judicial independence

- The legislature

  The powers, functions and composition of the House of Commons and House of Lords are considered as is the control over the executive exerted by Parliament, in particular, the House of Commons. Reform of the House of Lords mentioned.

Governmental powers

- The executive

  Broadly defined to include the Crown, the Prime Minister, Cabinet, civil servants and government departments.

Executive power derives from statute or the royal prerogative. The powers of the Crown are exercised for and on behalf of the Monarch by ministers with only very limited power personally in the hands of the Monarch.

- The judiciary

  Independence, impartiality and immunity from suit (*M v Home Office and Another* (1993)).

Supreme Court Act 1981

Appellate Jurisdiction Act 1876

Courts and Legal Services Act 1990 ss 108 and 109

Contempt of Court Act 1981

Judicial control of power	Judicial review: Order 53 Rules of the Supreme Court and s 31 Supreme Court Act 1981. Distinction between judicial review (concerned with process of public law decision-making) and appeals (concerned with the merits of an action). Remedies: prerogative orders of *mandamus*, *certiorari* and prohibition; injunction, declaration and damages.

R v Panel on Take-Overs and Mergers ex p Datafin (1987)

R v Independent Television Commission ex p TSW Broadcasting Ltd (1992)

R v Secretary of State for the Home Department ex p Brind (1990)

R v Secretary of State for the Home Department ex p Khan (1985)

A-G of Hong Kong v Ng Tuen Shiu (1983)

R v Home Secretary ex p Bentley (1993)

R v Secretary of State for the Home Department ex p Doody & Others (1993)

Administrative control of power	The Parliamentary Commissioner for Administration (Ombudsman): Parliamentary Commissioner Act 1967

Local Government Commissioners

National Health Service Commissioner

Their powers and functions regulating maladministration in public service decision-making. Remedies and the question of whether damages ought to be available on proof of maladministration.

The recommendations of the Franks Committee Report 1957.

Tribunals and the role of the Council on Tribunals under the Tribunals and Inquiries Act 1992 .

Index